THE ROUTLEDGE ATLAS OF AMERICAN HISTORY

' … especially clear and helpful … well laid out and useful for quick reference.'

The Economist

' … full of good ideas and is brought right up to date.'

Oxford Mail

This new edition of *The Routledge Atlas of American History* presents a series of 156 clear and detailed maps, accompanied by informative captions, facts and figures, updated with additional maps and text to include the 2004 presidential election and recent events in Iraq. The complete history of the United States is unrolled through vivid representations of all the significant landmarks, including:

- **Politics** – from the struggle against slavery and the battle for black voting rights to the present day
- **Military events** – from the War of Independence, the Civil War and America's participation in two world wars to the conflicts in Korea, Vietnam and the Gulf, up to the events of 9/11, the war in Iraq and its aftermath
- **Social history** – including the fate of the American Indians, the growth of female emancipation, and recent population movements and immigration
- **Transport** – from nineteenth-century railroads and canals to the growth of air travel and recent ventures into space
- **Economics** – from early farming and industry to urbanisation and the ecological struggles of the present day

Sir Martin Gilbert is a leading historian of the modern world. An Honorary Fellow of Merton College, Oxford – of which he was a Fellow for thirty years – he is the official biographer of Winston Churchill and the author of seventy-five books, among them *Churchill: A Life*, *First World War*, *Second World War*, *The Holocaust: The Jewish Tragedy*, and *Israel: A History*. Details of his books can be found on his website at www.martingilbert.com

BOOKS BY MARTIN GILBERT

The Routledge Atlas of American History
The Routledge Atlas of the Arab–Israeli Conflict
The Routledge Atlas of British History
The Routledge Atlas of the First World War
The Routledge Atlas of the Holocaust
The Routledge Atlas of Jewish History
The Routledge Atlas of Russian History

Recent History Atlas, 1860–1960
The European Powers, 1900–1945
History of the Twentieth Century (in three
    volumes and in a single volume)
First World War
Second World War
The Appeasers (with Richard Gott)
The Roots of Appeasement
D-Day
Churchill, A Photographic Portrait
In Search of Churchill
Churchill and America
Sir Horace Rumbold, Portrait of a Diplomat
The Jews of Hope, The Plight of Soviet Jewry Today

Jerusalem Illustrated History Atlas
Jerusalem, Rebirth of a City
Exile and Return, The Struggle for Jewish
    Statehood
The Holocaust, The Jewish Tragedy
The Righteous: The Unsung Heroes of the
    Holocaust
Letters to Auntie Fori: The 5000-Year History
    of the Jewish People and their Faith
From the Ends of the Earth: The Jews in the
    Twentieth Century
Auschwitz and the Allies
Scharansky, Hero of our Time
Children's Illustrated Bible Atlas

THE CHURCHILL BIOGRAPHY

Volume I. Youth, 1874–1900 *by Randolph S. Churchill*
    Volume I. Companion (in two parts)
Volume II. Young Statesman, 1900–1914 *by Randolph S. Churchill*
    Volume II. Companion (in three parts)
Volume III. 1914–1916 *by Martin Gilbert*
    Volume III. Companion (in two parts)
Volume IV. 1917–1922 *by Martin Gilbert*
    Volume IV. Companion (in three parts)
Volume V. 1922–1939 *by Martin Gilbert*
    Volume V. Companion 'The Exchequer Years' 1922–1929
    Volume V. Companion 'The Wilderness Years' 1929–1935
    Volume V. Companion 'The Coming of War' 1936–1939
Volume VI. 1939–1941, 'Finest Hour' *by Martin Gilbert*
    The Churchill War Papers: Volume I 'At the Admiralty'
    The Churchill War Papers: Volume II 'New Surrender', May–December
    The Churchill War Papers: Volume III '1941, The Ever-Widening War'
Volume VII. 1941–1945, 'Road to Victory' *by Martin Gilbert*
Volume VIII. 1945–1965, 'Never Despair' *by Martin Gilbert*

Churchill – A Life *by Martin Gilbert*

Editions of documents
Britain and Germany Between the Wars
Plough My Own Furrow, The Life of Lord Allen of Hurtwood
Servant of India, Diaries of the Viceroy's Private Secretary, 1905–1910

THE ROUTLEDGE ATLAS OF
AMERICAN HISTORY

5th Edition

Martin Gilbert

Routledge
Taylor & Francis Group

LONDON AND NEW YORK

First published 1968 as *The Atlas of American History*
by Weidenfeld & Nicolson

Revised edition published 1985
by J.M. Dent Ltd.
Third edition published 1993

Reprinted 1995
by Routledge
2 Park Square, Milton Park, Abingdon, Oxfordshire, OX14 4RN

Simultaneously published in the USA and Canada
by Routledge
29 West 35th Street, New York, NY 10001

Fourth edition first published 2003
Reprinted 2003, 2004

Fifth edition published 2006

Routledge is an imprint of the Taylor & Francis Group

© 1968, 1985, 1993, 2003, 2006 Martin Gilbert

Typeset in Janson Text by Bookcraft Ltd, Stroud, Gloucestershire
Printed and bound in Great Britain by TJ International Ltd, Padstow, Cornwall

British Library Cataloguing in Publication Data
A catalogue record for this book is available from the British Library

Library of Congress Cataloging in Publication Data
A catalog record for this book has been requested

ISBN10: 0-415-35902-3   ISBN13: 9-78-0-415-35902-3 (hbk)
ISBN10: 0-415-35903-1   ISBN13: 9-78-0-415-35903-0 (pbk)

Preface

The idea for this atlas came to me while I was teaching at the University of South Carolina in 1965. Its aim is to provide a short but informative visual guide to American history. I have tried to make use of maps in the widest possible way, designing each one individually, and seeking to transform statistics and facts into something easily seen and grasped. My material has been obtained from a wide range of historical works, encyclopaedias, and newspaper and government reports.

More than twenty-five years have passed since the first publication of this atlas. It was a period marked first by the intensification and then by the ending of the Vietnam war, with more than 55,000 American dead. It was also a period marked by a substantial increase in the population of the United States, and continued immigration. This same period has seen the development of outer space as a region of defence policy. New maps cover these recent developments.

Since the revised edition was published in 1985, the pattern of events has led me to draw twenty-six new maps to cover, among recent developments, the continuing growth of immigration, new ethnic and population changes, and the military and humanitarian actions of the United States overseas, culminating in the Gulf War (1991), aid to Somalia (1992), and air drops to Bosnia (1993). New domestic maps show the natural and accidental disasters of the past two decades, the continuing high death rate from motor accidents (more than a million dead in twenty years), murder (a quarter of a million dead in a single decade), and the new scourge of AIDS (170,000 deaths in a decade).

The United States has also been the pioneer in exploring the solar system and in defence preparedness in space, for both of which I have drawn a special map. United States' arms sales, and economic help to poorer countries, as well as the ending of the Cold War confrontation, also required new maps, as did pollution. The continuing United States' presence in the Pacific, and her defence preparedness at home and abroad, are also mapped.

I have been helped considerably in the task of updating this atlas by Abe Eisenstat and Kay Thomson. Many individuals and institutions have provided extra material for the maps. I am particularly grateful to Martin Adams, Bureau of Political-Military Affairs, State Department, Washington DC; James T. Hackett, Member of the President's General Advisory Committee on Arms Control; Louan Hall, National Highway Traffic Safety Administration; Michael Hoeffer, Statistics Division, Immigration and Naturalisation Services; John Richter, Agency for International Development, State Department; and Joshua Gilbert for help on the space map.

For the first and second edition of this atlas, my draft maps were turned into clear and striking artwork by Arthur Banks and Terry Bicknell. For this new edition, I am grateful to the cartographic skills of Tim Aspden. At my publishers, J.M. Dent, David Swarbrick has made it possible to realise my ambition to re-issue all of my historical atlases updated. It is my hope that they will be of interest and service to teachers, students, and the general reader for whom the past is not a forbidden planet, but an integral part of today's world.

MARTIN GILBERT
Merton College, Oxford

14 June 1993

Note to the Fourth Edition

For this fourth edition, I have prepared eleven new maps, which bring the story of the United States into the twenty-first century. As with the previous edition, this could not have been done without the cartographic expertise of Tim Aspden. I am also grateful to the Librarian at the United States Embassy, London, for access to reference material.

Martin Gilbert
Merton College, Oxford

12 July 2002

Note to the Fifth Edition

The seven new maps in this edition bring the story up to the re-election of President George W. Bush in November 2004, and the continuing conflict in Iraq following the overthrow of Saddam Hussein.

I have tried in this atlas, within the span of 156 maps, to give a visual account of American history from the earliest settlements of Native Americans to the conflicts and achievements of the post-1945 era.

Once more, I have been fortunate in the cartographic skills of Tim Aspden, who has turned my rough drafts and statistical material into clear and informative maps.

In the thirty-seven years since the first edition was published, I have added almost fifty new maps. I would welcome now, as I welcomed in 1968, any amendments to the existing maps, or suggestions or material for new maps.

Martin Gilbert
Merton College, Oxford

11 March 2005

Maps

Early Years

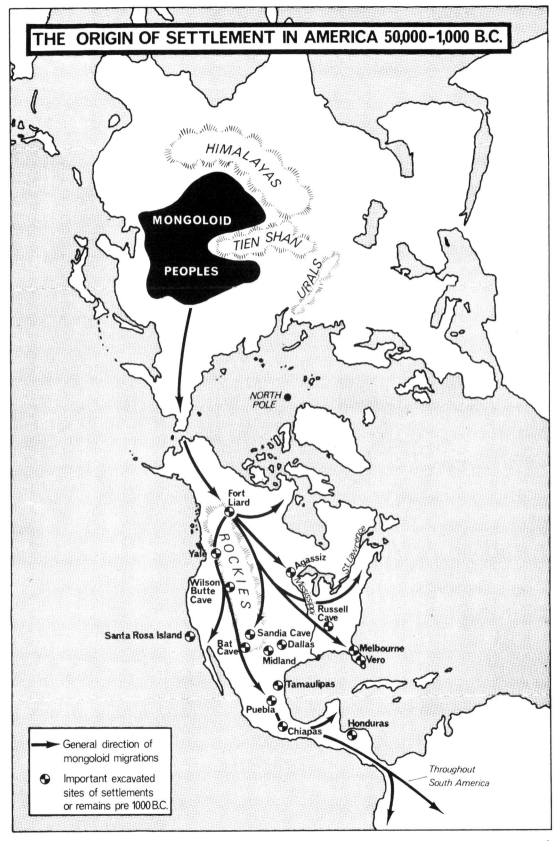

THE ORIGIN OF SETTLEMENT IN AMERICA 50,000–1,000 B.C.

HIMALAYAS

MONGOLOID

TIEN SHAN

PEOPLES

URALS

NORTH POLE

Fort Liard

Yale

ROCKIES

Agassiz

St. Lawrence

Mississippi

Wilson Butte Cave

Russell Cave

Santa Rosa Island

Bat Cave

Sandia Cave

Dallas

Midland

Melbourne

Vero

Tamaulipas

Puebla

Chiapas

Honduras

General direction of mongoloid migrations

Important excavated sites of settlements or remains pre 1000 B.C.

Throughout South America

1

THE INDIAN TRIBES OF NORTH AMERICA BEFORE 1492

Eskimo
Koyukon
Ingalik
Tanaina
Aleut
Kutchin
Han
Tanana
Nabesna
Tuchone
Ahtena
Kaska
Tahltan
Tlingit

Hare
Bear Lake
Dogrib
Yellowknife
Slave
Sekani
Beaver

Eskimo

Tsimshian
Bella Coola
Haida
Bella Bella
Kwakiutl
Nootka
Salish
Makah Puyallup
Nisqually
Chehalis
Chinook
Cowlitz
Tillamook
Yakima
Klikitat
Molala
Kalapuya
Coos
Umpqua
Takelma
Karok
Yurok
Wiyot
Shasta
Hupa
Yana
Mattole
Maidu
Yuki
Pomo
Wintun
Miwok
Costanoan
Yokuts
Salinan
Chumash

Chipewyan

Carrier
Chilcotin
Shuswap
Lillooet
Thompson
Okanagan
Sanpoil
Colville
Spokane
Palouse
Walla Walla
Klamath
Modoc
Chomawi
Tsugewi
Kawaiisu
Mono
Panamint

Kaigani
Piegan
Kutenai
Kalispel
Coeur D'Alene
Flathead
Crow
Nez Perce
Bannock
Shoshoni
Paviotso
Washo
N. Paiute
S. Paiute
Navaho
Pueblo

Sarsi
Siksika (Blackfoot)
Cree

Ojibwa (Chippewa)
Ottawa
Plains Cree
Assiniboin

Atsina
Hidatsa
Arikara
Teton
Yankton
Dakota
Pawnee
N.Cheyenne
Arapaho
S.Cheyenne
Jicarilla Apache
Kiowa
Kiowa Apache
Mescalero Apache

Mandan

Menomini
Sauk
Dakota
Ponca
Iowa
Omaha
Oto
Kansas
Osage
Missouri

Tobacco
Neutral
Winnebago

Naskapi Montagnais
Micmac
Malecite
Passamaquoddy
Penobscot
Abnaki
Huron

Beothuk

Pennacook

Mahican
Mohawk
Nipmuc Oneida
Massachuset
Wampanoag
Narraganset
Pequot
Mohegan
Wappinger
Onondaga
Cayuga
Seneca
Delaware
Nanticoke
Powhatan
Chickahominy
Mattapony
Tutelo
Pamlico
Nottoway
Tuscarora
Catawba

Erie
Potawatomie
Kickapoo
Miami
Wea
Peoria
Pamunkey
Piankashaw
Illinois
Quapaw
Shawnee
Cherokee
Yuchi
Chickasaw

Susquehanna

Ute
Gosiute
Kavasupai
Chemehuevi
Walapai
W.Apache
Lipan Apache

Hopi
Zuni

Comanche Wichita
Kichai
Waco
Tonkawa

Tawakoni Choctaw Creek
Caddo Natchez
Tunica

Mohave
Serrano
Yavapai
Cahuilla
Yuma
Pima
Maricopa
Papago

Cochimi
Seri

Opata
Concho
Tarahumara
Cahita
Acaxee
Huichol

Karankawa

Coahuiltec
Tamaulipec

Atakapa
Chitimacha
Biloxi
Mobile
Apalachee

Yamasee
Guale
Timucua
Hichiti

Seminole
Calusa

Taino

Ciboney

Walcur
Pericu
Yaqui
Toltec
Tarascan
Otomi

Huastec
Totonac
Tlaxcalan
Aztec
Mixtec

Yucatan Maya

Zapotec
Lacandon
Maya
Quiche
Maya

Mosquito

Chontal

There were approximately one million Indians
north of Mexico in 1492

0   600
Miles

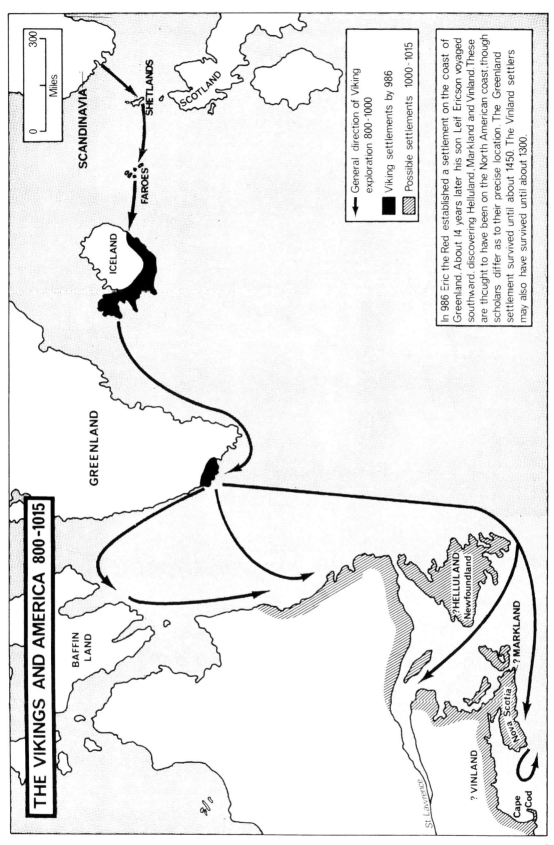

THE VIKINGS AND AMERICA 800-1015

300
0
Miles

SCANDINAVIA

SHETLANDS

SCOTLAND

FAROES'

ICELAND

GREENLAND

BAFFIN LAND

St. Lawrence

?HELLULAND
Newfoundland

? MARKLAND

? VINLAND

Nova Scotia

Cape Cod

General direction of Viking exploration 800-1000

Viking settlements by 986

Possible settlements 1000-1015

In 986 Eric the Red established a settlement on the coast of Greenland. About 14 years later his son Leif Ericson voyaged southward, discovering Helluland, Markland and Vinland. These are thought to have been on the North American coast, though scholars differ as to their precise location. The Greenland settlement survived until about 1450. The Vinland settlers may also have survived until about 1300.

3

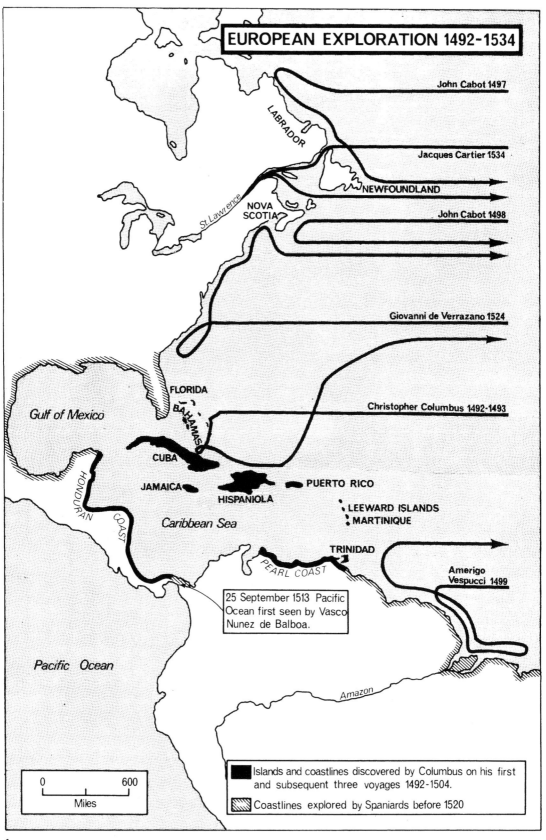

EUROPEAN EXPLORATION 1492-1534

John Cabot 1497

LABRADOR

Jacques Cartier 1534

NEWFOUNDLAND

NOVA SCOTIA

St.Lawrence

John Cabot 1498

Giovanni de Verrazano 1524

FLORIDA

BAHAMAS

Gulf of Mexico

Christopher Columbus 1492-1493

CUBA

JAMAICA

HISPANIOLA

PUERTO RICO

LEEWARD ISLANDS

MARTINIQUE

HONDURAN COAST

Caribbean Sea

TRINIDAD

PEARL COAST

Amerigo Vespucci 1499

25 September 1513 Pacific Ocean first seen by Vasco Nunez de Balboa.

Pacific Ocean

Amazon

0   600
Miles

■ Islands and coastlines discovered by Columbus on his first and subsequent three voyages 1492-1504.

▨ Coastlines explored by Spaniards before 1520

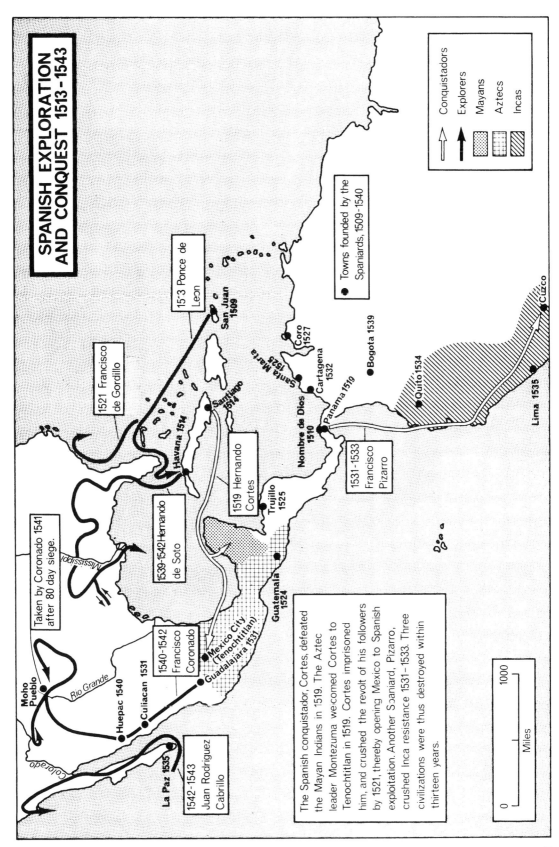

SPANISH EXPLORATION AND CONQUEST 1513-1543

Conquistadors
Explorers
Mayans
Aztecs
Incas

Towns founded by the Spaniards, 1509-1540

15'3 Ponce de Leon

1521 Francisco de Gordillo

San Juan 1509

Coro 1527

Santa Marta 1525

Cartagena 1532

Bogota 1539

Panama 1519

Quito 1534

Cuzco

Havana 1514

Santiago 1514

1519 Hernando Cortes

Trujillo 1525

Nombre de Dios 1510

1531-1533 Francisco Pizarro

Lima 1535

1541 Taken by Coronado 1541 after 80 day siege.

Mississippi

1539-1542 Hernando de Soto

Guatemala 1524

Moho Pueblo 1540

Rio Grande

Huepac 1540

Culiacan 1531

1540-1542 Francisco Coronado

Mexico City (Tenochtitlan) 1531

Guadalajara 1531

Colorado

La Paz 1535

1542-1543 Juan Rodriguez Cabrillo

The Spanish conquistador, Cortes, defeated the Mayan Indians in 1519. The Aztec leader Montezuma welcomed Cortes to Tenochtitlan in 1519. Cortes imprisoned him, and crushed the revolt of his followers by 1521, thereby opening Mexico to Spanish exploitation. Another Spaniard, Pizarro, crushed Inca resistance 1531-1533. Three civilizations were thus destroyed within thirteen years.

0   Miles   1000

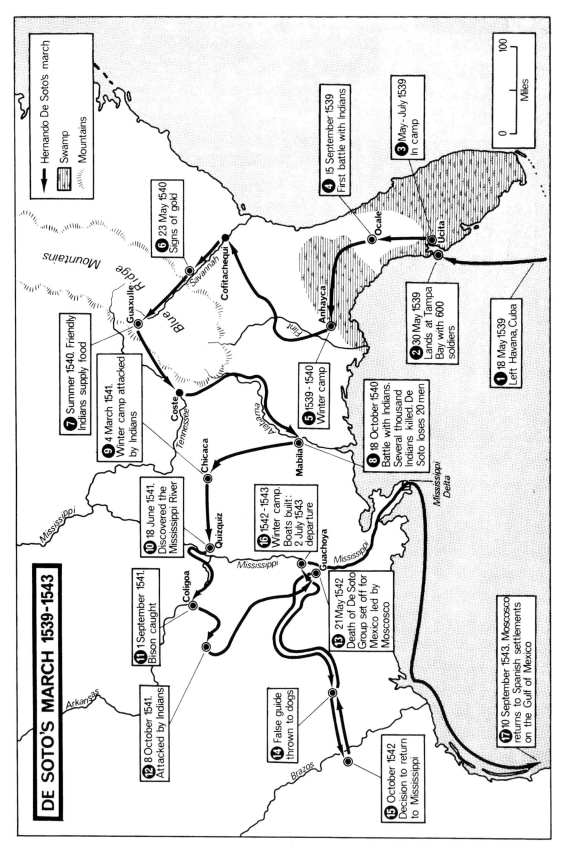

DE SOTO'S MARCH 1539-1543

1 18 May 1539 Left Havana, Cuba

2 30 May 1539 Lands at Tampa Bay with 600 soldiers

3 May – July 1539 In camp

4 15 September 1539 First battle with Indians

5 1539 - 1540 Winter camp

6 23 May 1540 Signs of gold

7 Summer 1540. Friendly Indians supply food

8 18 October 1540 Battle with Indians. Several thousand Indians killed. De Soto loses 20 men

9 4 March 1541. Winter camp attacked by Indians

10 18 June 1541. Discovered the Mississippi River

11 1 September 1541. Bison caught

12 8 October 1541. Attacked by Indians

13 21 May 1542 Death of De Soto Group set off for Mexico led by Moscosco

14 False guide thrown to dogs

15 October 1542 Decision to return to Mississippi

16 1542 - 1543 Winter camp. Boats built: 2 July 1543 departure

17 10 September 1543 Moscosco returns to Spanish settlements on the Gulf of Mexico

Hernando De Soto's march
Swamp
Mountains

0 100
Miles

Mountains

Blue Ridge

Mountains

Savannah

Cofitachequi

Guaxulle

Coste

Tennessee

Chicaca

Quizquiz

Coligoa

Mississippi

Arkansas

Brazos

Mississippi

Mississippi

Guachoya

Mabila

Alabama

Flint

Anhayca

Ocale

Ucita

Mississippi Delta

6

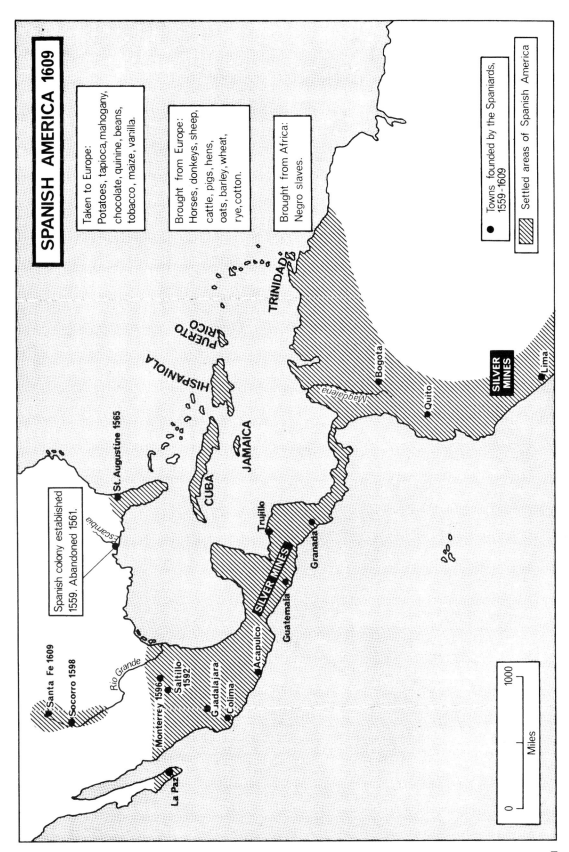

SPANISH AMERICA 1609

Taken to Europe:
Potatoes, tapioca, mahogany, chocolate, quinine, beans, tobacco, maize, vanilla.

Brought from Europe:
Horses, donkeys, sheep, cattle, pigs, hens, oats, barley, wheat, rye, cotton.

Brought from Africa:
Negro slaves.

● Towns founded by the Spaniards, 1559-1609

▨ Settled areas of Spanish America

Spanish colony established 1559. Abandoned 1561.

Santa Fe 1609
Socorro 1598
Monterrey 1596
Saltillo 1592
Guadalajara
Colima
La Paz
Rio Grande
Escambia
St. Augustine 1565
Acapulco
SILVER MINES
Guatemala
Granada
Trujillo
CUBA
JAMAICA
HISPANIOLA
PUERTO RICO
TRINIDAD
Bogota
Magdalena
Quito
SILVER MINES
Lima

Miles
0   1000

7

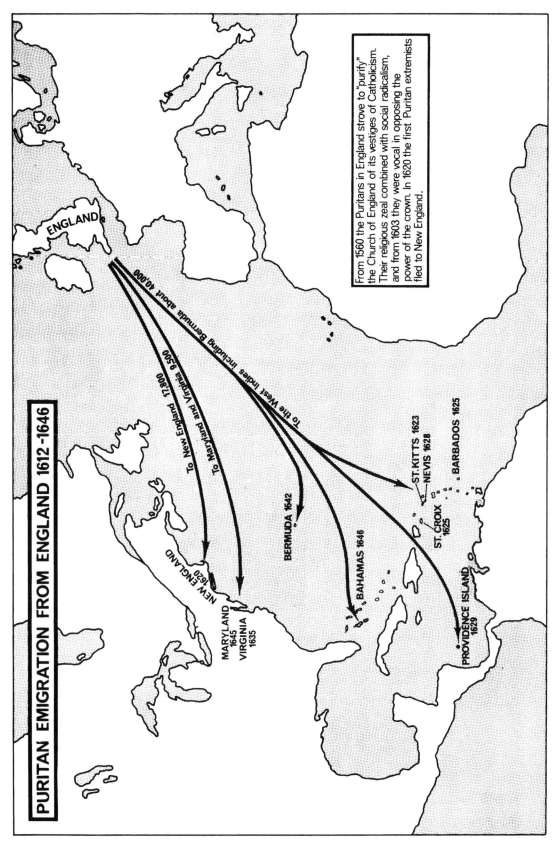

PURITAN EMIGRATION FROM ENGLAND 1612-1646

ENGLAND

From 1560 the Puritans in England strove to "purify" the Church of England of its vestiges of Catholicism. Their religious zeal combined with social radicalism, and from 1603 they were vocal in opposing the power of the crown. In 1620 the first Puritan extremists fled to New England.

To the West Indies including Bermuda about 40,000

To Maryland and Virginia 9,500

To New England 17,800

NEW ENGLAND 1620

MARYLAND 1645
VIRGINIA 1635

BERMUDA 1642

BAHAMAS 1646

ST.KITTS 1623
NEVIS 1628
BARBADOS 1625

ST.CROIX 1625

PROVIDENCE ISLAND 1629

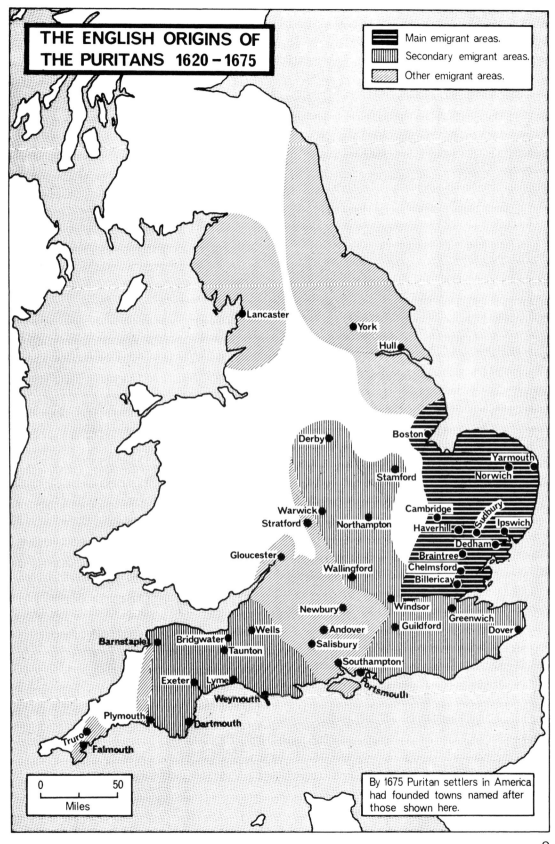

THE ENGLISH ORIGINS OF
THE PURITANS 1620 – 1675

Main emigrant areas.
Secondary emigrant areas.
Other emigrant areas.

Lancaster

York

Hull

Derby

Boston

Yarmouth
Norwich

Stamford

Cambridge
Warwick
Stratford
Northampton
Haverhill
Sudbury
Ipswich
Dedham

Gloucester

Braintree
Chelmsford
Billericay

Wallingford

Newbury
Windsor
Greenwich
Andover
Guildford
Dover

Barnstaple
Bridgwater
Wells
Salisbury

Taunton
Southampton

Exeter
Lyme
Portsmouth

Weymouth

Plymouth
Truro
Dartmouth
Falmouth

0   50
Miles

By 1675 Puritan settlers in America
had founded towns named after
those shown here.

9

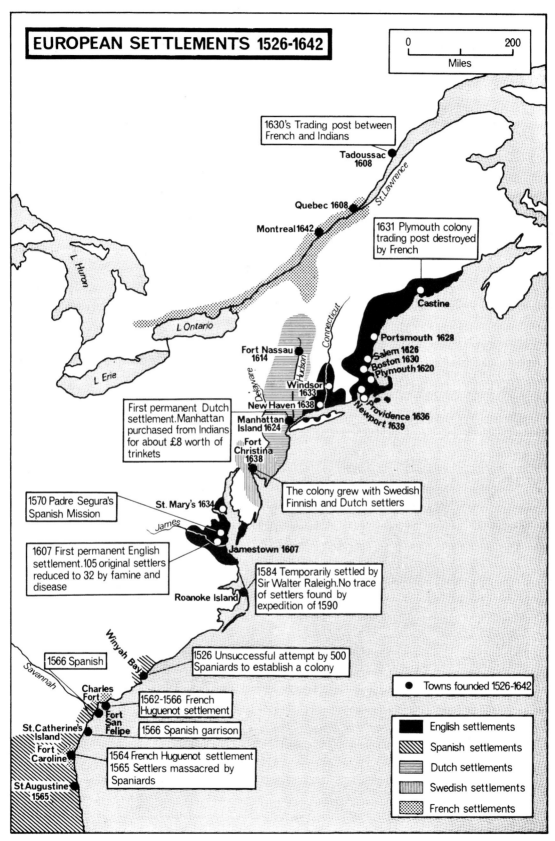

EUROPEAN SETTLEMENTS 1526-1642

0   200
Miles

1630's Trading post between French and Indians

Tadoussac 1608

Quebec 1608

Montreal 1642

1631 Plymouth colony trading post destroyed by French

L. Huron

L. Ontario

L. Erie

Castine

Portsmouth 1628

Salem 1626
Boston 1630
Plymouth 1620

Fort Nassau 1614

Windsor 1633
New Haven 1638

Providence 1636
Newport 1639

First permanent Dutch settlement. Manhattan purchased from Indians for about £8 worth of trinkets

Manhattan Island 1624

Fort Christina 1638

1570 Padre Segura's Spanish Mission

St. Mary's 1634

James

The colony grew with Swedish Finnish and Dutch settlers

1607 First permanent English settlement. 105 original settlers reduced to 32 by famine and disease

Jamestown 1607

1584 Temporarily settled by Sir Walter Raleigh. No trace of settlers found by expedition of 1590

Roanoke Island

Winyah Bay

1566 Spanish

Savannah

1526 Unsuccessful attempt by 500 Spaniards to establish a colony

Charles Fort

1562-1566 French Huguenot settlement

Fort San Felipe

1566 Spanish garrison

St. Catherine's Island

Fort Caroline

1564 French Huguenot settlement 1565 Settlers massacred by Spaniards

St. Augustine 1565

● Towns founded 1526-1642

◼ English settlements
▨ Spanish settlements
▤ Dutch settlements
▥ Swedish settlements
▒ French settlements

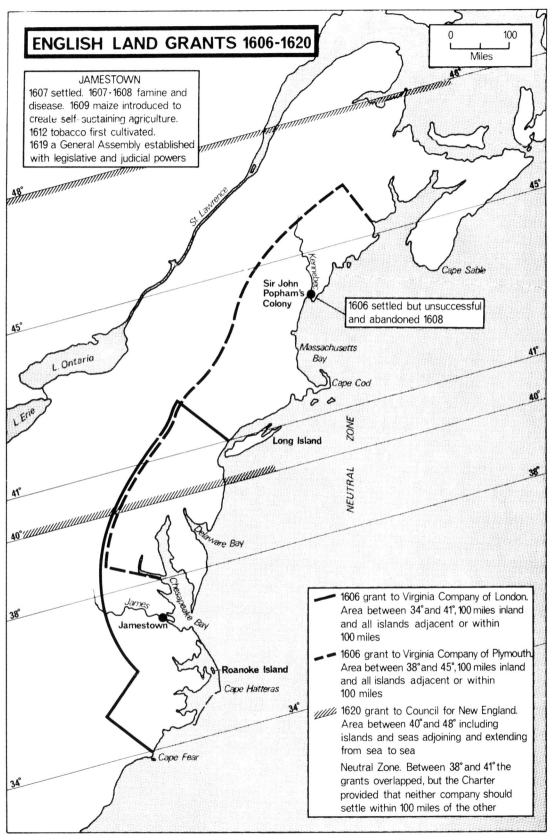

ENGLISH LAND GRANTS 1606-1620

0   100
Miles

JAMESTOWN
1607 settled. 1607-1608 famine and
disease. 1609 maize introduced to
create self-sustaining agriculture.
1612 tobacco first cultivated.
1619 a General Assembly established
with legislative and judicial powers

48°

45°

45°

41°

40°

41°

40°

38°

38°

34°

34°

St Lawrence

Kennebec

L. Ontario

L. Erie

Cape Sable

Sir John
Popham's
Colony

1606 settled but unsuccessful
and abandoned 1608

Massachusetts
Bay

Cape Cod

Long Island

NEUTRAL ZONE

Delaware Bay

Chesapeake Bay

James

Jamestown

Roanoke Island

Cape Hatteras

Cape Fear

—— 1606 grant to Virginia Company of London.
Area between 34° and 41°, 100 miles inland
and all islands adjacent or within
100 miles

– – – 1606 grant to Virginia Company of Plymouth.
Area between 38° and 45°, 100 miles inland
and all islands adjacent or within
100 miles

///// 1620 grant to Council for New England.
Area between 40° and 48° including
islands and seas adjoining and extending
from sea to sea

Neutral Zone. Between 38° and 41° the
grants overlapped, but the Charter
provided that neither company should
settle within 100 miles of the other

11

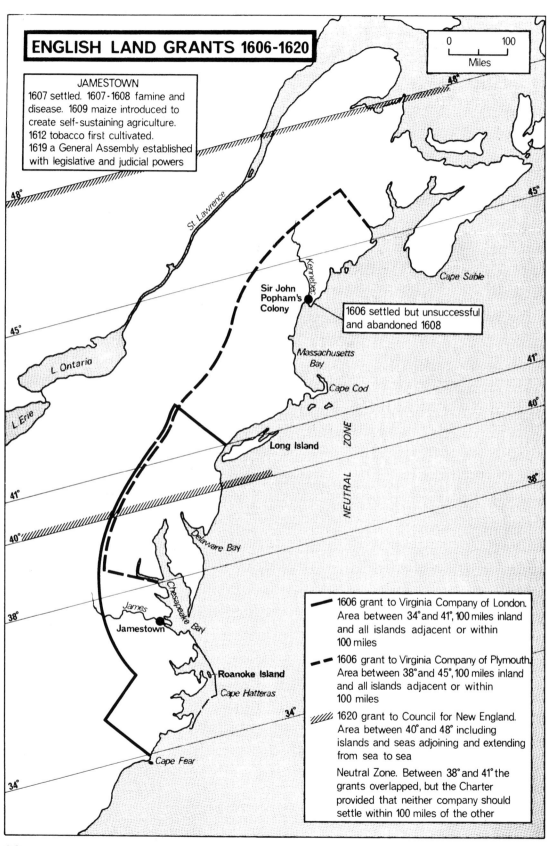

ENGLISH LAND GRANTS 1606-1620

JAMESTOWN
1607 settled. 1607-1608 famine and disease. 1609 maize introduced to create self-sustaining agriculture. 1612 tobacco first cultivated. 1619 a General Assembly established with legislative and judicial powers

0   100
Miles

Sir John Popham's Colony

1606 settled but unsuccessful and abandoned 1608

St Lawrence

Kennebec

Cape Sable

L. Ontario

Massachusetts Bay

Cape Cod

L. Erie

Long Island

NEUTRAL ZONE

Delaware Bay

Chesapeake Bay

James

Jamestown

Roanoke Island

Cape Hatteras

Cape Fear

—— 1606 grant to Virginia Company of London. Area between 34° and 41°, 100 miles inland and all islands adjacent or within 100 miles

– – – 1606 grant to Virginia Company of Plymouth. Area between 38° and 45°, 100 miles inland and all islands adjacent or within 100 miles

////// 1620 grant to Council for New England. Area between 40° and 48° including islands and seas adjoining and extending from sea to sea

Neutral Zone. Between 38° and 41° the grants overlapped, but the Charter provided that neither company should settle within 100 miles of the other

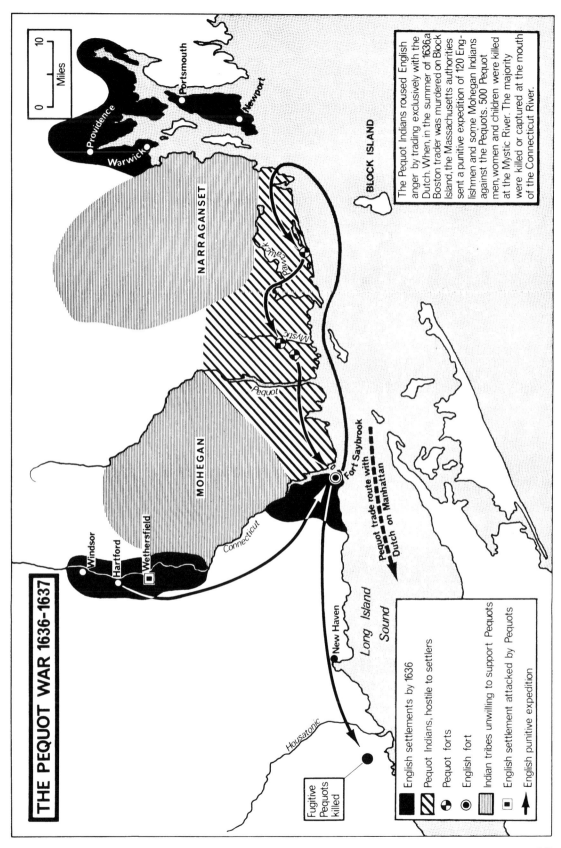

THE PEQUOT WAR 1636–1637

The Pequot Indians roused English anger by trading exclusively with the Dutch. When, in the summer of 1636, a Boston trader was murdered on Block Island, the Massachusetts authorities sent a punitive expedition of 120 Englishmen and some Mohegan Indians against the Pequots. 500 Pequot men, women and children were killed at the Mystic River. The majority were killed or captured at the mouth of the Connecticut River.

Miles
0   10

Providence
Warwick
Portsmouth
Newport

NARRAGANSET

MOHEGAN

Windsor
Hartford
Wethersfield
Connecticut
Pawcatuck
Mystic
Pequot
Fort Saybrook

New Haven

Long Island Sound

Housatonic

BLOCK ISLAND

Pequot trade route with
Dutch on Manhattan

Fugitive Pequots killed

- ■ English settlements by 1636
- ◩ Pequot Indians, hostile to settlers
- ◉ Pequot forts
- ◉ English fort
- ▥ Indian tribes unwilling to support Pequots
- ◘ English settlement attacked by Pequots
- ▲ English punitive expedition

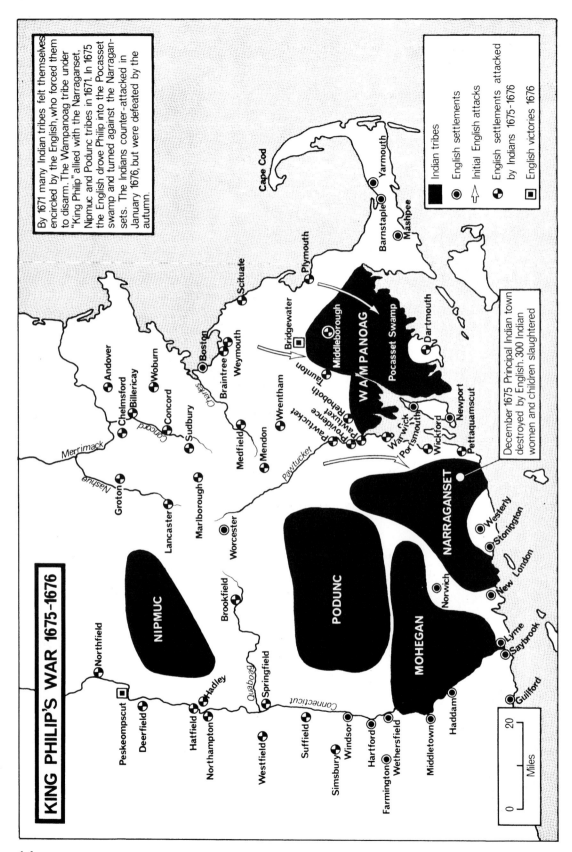

KING PHILIP'S WAR 1675-1676

By 1671 many Indian tribes felt themselves encircled by the English, who forced them to disarm. The Wampanoag tribe under "King Philip" allied with the Narraganset, Nipmuc and Podunc tribes in 1671. In 1675 the English drove Philip into the Pocasset swamp and turned against the Narragansets. The Indians counter-attacked in January 1676, but were defeated by the autumn.

Indian tribes

◉ English settlements

⇨ Initial English attacks

◕ English settlements attacked by Indians 1675-1676

▣ English victories 1676

December 1675 Principal Indian town destroyed by English. 300 Indian women and children slaughtered

Cape Cod

Yarmouth
Mashpee
Barnstaple
Plymouth
Scituate
Bridgewater
Dartmouth
Middleborough
Pocasset Swamp
WAMPANOAG
Boston
Weymouth
Braintree
Wrentham
Taunton
Rehoboth
Newport
Pettaquamscut
Pawtucket
Providence
Pawtuxet
Warwick
Portsmouth
Wickford
Andover
Woburn
Concord
Chelmsford
Billericay
Sudbury
Medfield
Mendon
Marlborough
Worcester
Westerly
Stonington
NARRAGANSET
New London
Norwich
MOHEGAN
Lyme
Saybrook
Guilford
Haddam
Middletown
Wethersfield
Farmington
Hartford
Windsor
Simsbury
Suffield
PODUNC
Brookfield
NIPMUC
Lancaster
Groton
Northfield
Peskeompscut
Deerfield
Hatfield
Northampton
Hadley
Springfield
Westfield

Merrimack
Concord
Nashua
Pawtucker
Charles
Quaboag
Connecticut

0   20
Miles

14

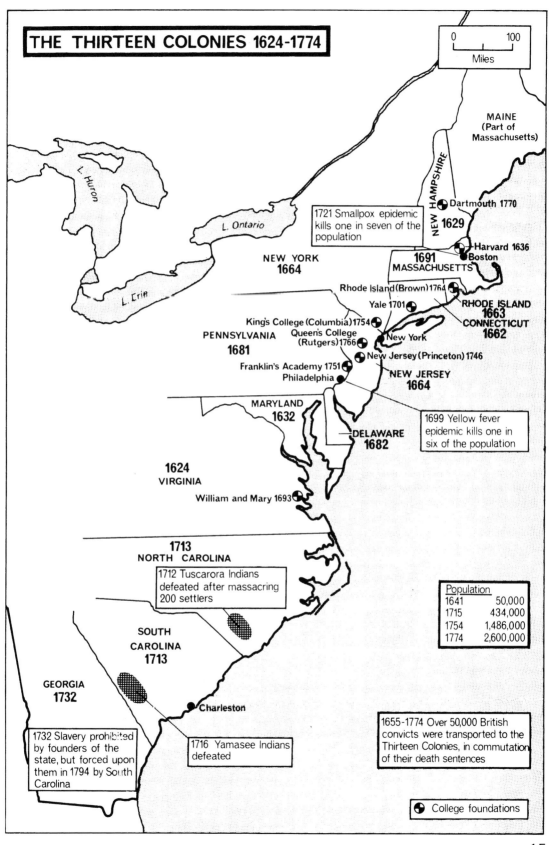

THE THIRTEEN COLONIES 1624-1774

0 ——— 100
Miles

L. Huron

L. Ontario

L. Erie

MAINE
(Part of
Massachusetts)

NEW HAMPSHIRE
1629

Dartmouth 1770

1721 Smallpox epidemic
kills one in seven of the
population

Harvard 1636
Boston

1691
MASSACHUSETTS

NEW YORK
1664

Rhode Island (Brown) 1764

RHODE ISLAND
1663

Yale 1701

CONNECTICUT
1662

King's College (Columbia) 1754

PENNSYLVANIA
1681

Queen's College
(Rutgers) 1766

New York

New Jersey (Princeton) 1746

Franklin's Academy 1751

NEW JERSEY
1664

Philadelphia

MARYLAND
1632

1699 Yellow fever
epidemic kills one in
six of the population

DELAWARE
1682

1624
VIRGINIA

William and Mary 1693

1713
NORTH CAROLINA

1712 Tuscarora Indians
defeated after massacring
200 settlers

SOUTH
CAROLINA
1713

Population	
1641	50,000
1715	434,000
1754	1,486,000
1774	2,600,000

GEORGIA
1732

Charleston

1732 Slavery prohibited
by founders of the
state, but forced upon
them in 1794 by South
Carolina

1716 Yamasee Indians
defeated

1655-1774 Over 50,000 British
convicts were transported to the
Thirteen Colonies, in commutation
of their death sentences

🌓 College foundations

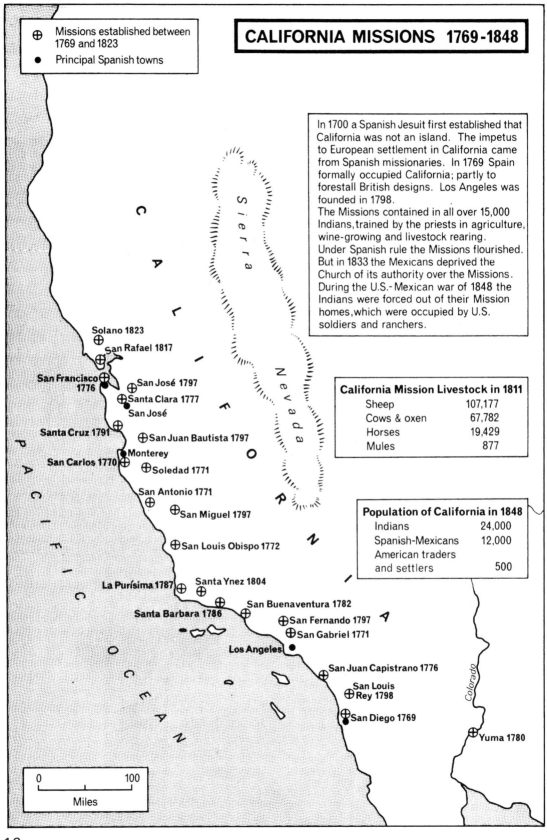

CALIFORNIA MISSIONS 1769-1848

Missions established between 1769 and 1823

Principal Spanish towns

In 1700 a Spanish Jesuit first established that California was not an island. The impetus to European settlement in California came from Spanish missionaries. In 1769 Spain formally occupied California; partly to forestall British designs. Los Angeles was founded in 1798.

The Missions contained in all over 15,000 Indians, trained by the priests in agriculture, wine-growing and livestock rearing.

Under Spanish rule the Missions flourished. But in 1833 the Mexicans deprived the Church of its authority over the Missions. During the U.S.-Mexican war of 1848 the Indians were forced out of their Mission homes, which were occupied by U.S. soldiers and ranchers.

California Mission Livestock in 1811	
Sheep	107,177
Cows & oxen	67,782
Horses	19,429
Mules	877

Population of California in 1848	
Indians	24,000
Spanish-Mexicans	12,000
American traders and settlers	500

Solano 1823
San Rafael 1817
San Francisco 1776
San José 1797
Santa Clara 1777
San José
Santa Cruz 1791
San Juan Bautista 1797
Monterey
San Carlos 1770
Soledad 1771
San Antonio 1771
San Miguel 1797
San Louis Obispo 1772
La Purísima 1787
Santa Ynez 1804
San Buenaventura 1782
Santa Barbara 1786
San Fernando 1797
San Gabriel 1771
Los Angeles
San Juan Capistrano 1776
San Louis Rey 1798
San Diego 1769
Yuma 1780

Sierra Nevada

CALIFORNIA

PACIFIC OCEAN

Colorado

0   100
Miles

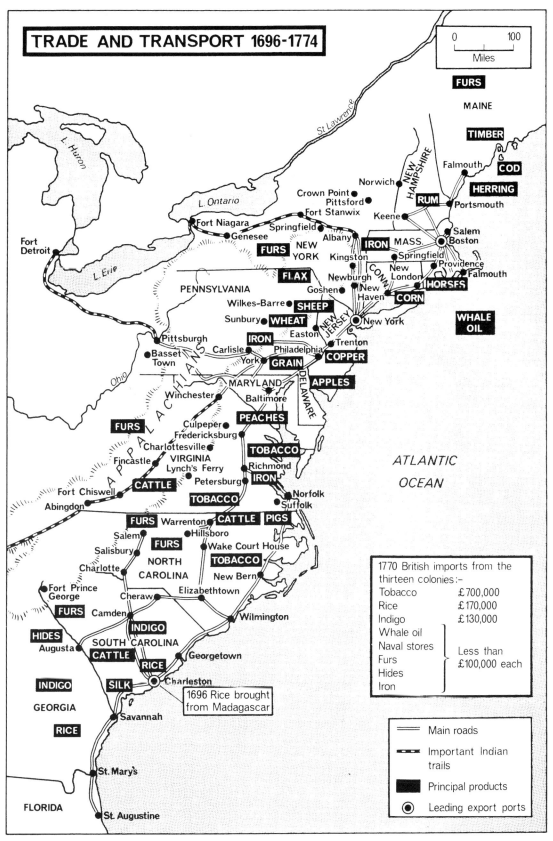

TRADE AND TRANSPORT 1696-1774

0   100
Miles

FURS
MAINE

TIMBER
Falmouth
COD
HERRING
Portsmouth

NEW HAMPSHIRE

Norwich
Crown Point
Pittsford
Fort Stanwix
Keene
RUM

L. Ontario

Fort Niagara
Genesee
Springfield
Albany
Salem
Boston
MASS.

Fort Detroit

L. Erie

FURS
NEW YORK
Kingston
Springfield
Providence
Falmouth

FLAX
Newburgh
New London
HORSES

PENNSYLVANIA
Goshen
New Haven
CORN
CONN

Wilkes-Barre
SHEEP
NEW JERSEY
WHALE OIL

Sunbury
WHEAT
Easton
New York

Pittsburgh
IRON
Trenton
Basset Town
Carlisle
Philadelphia
COPPER
York
GRAIN
APPLES

Ohio

MARYLAND
DELAWARE

Winchester
Baltimore

FURS
Culpeper
PEACHES
Fredericksburg
Charlottesville
Fincastle
VIRGINIA
Lynch's Ferry
TOBACCO
Richmond
IRON

CATTLE
Fort Chiswell
Petersburg
TOBACCO
Norfolk
Abingdon
Suffolk

ATLANTIC OCEAN

FURS
Warrenton
CATTLE
PIGS
Hillsboro
Salem
FURS
Wake Court House
Salisbury
NORTH CAROLINA
TOBACCO
Charlotte
New Bern

Fort Prince George
Cheraw
Elizabethtown

FURS
Camden
Wilmington
HIDES
INDIGO
Augusta
SOUTH CAROLINA
CATTLE
RICE
Georgetown

INDIGO
SILK
Charleston
GEORGIA
1696 Rice brought from Madagascar
Savannah

RICE

St. Mary's

FLORIDA
St. Augustine

1770 British imports from the thirteen colonies:-
Tobacco   £700,000
Rice   £170,000
Indigo   £130,000
Whale oil
Naval stores
Furs   Less than
Hides   £100,000 each
Iron

═══ Main roads

▄▄▄ Important Indian trails

███ Principal products

◉ Leading export ports

17

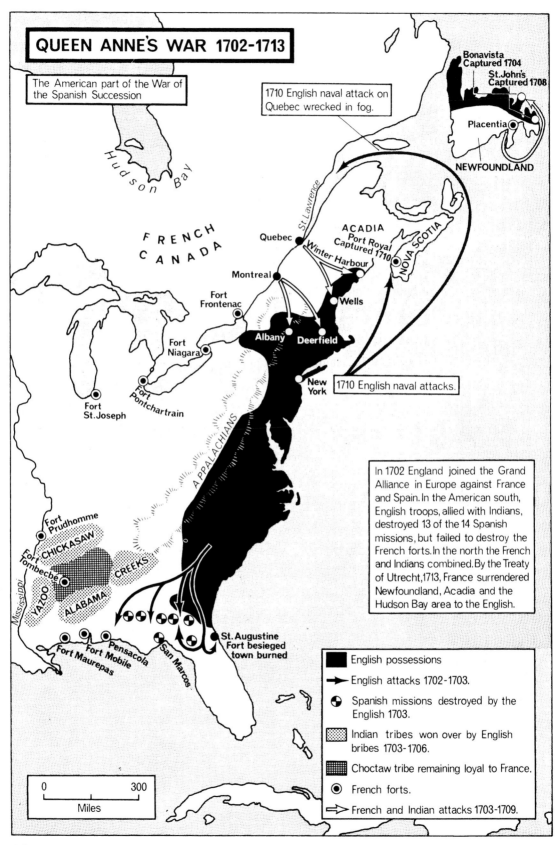

QUEEN ANNE'S WAR 1702-1713

The American part of the War of the Spanish Succession

1710 English naval attack on Quebec wrecked in fog.

Bonavista Captured 1704
St. John's Captured 1708
Placentia
NEWFOUNDLAND

Hudson Bay

FRENCH CANADA

St. Lawrence

Quebec

ACADIA
Port Royal Captured 1710
Winter Harbour

NOVA SCOTIA

Montreal

Fort Frontenac

Wells

Albany   Deerfield

Fort Niagara

APPALACHIANS

Fort Pontchartrain

New York

1710 English naval attacks.

Fort St. Joseph

In 1702 England joined the Grand Alliance in Europe against France and Spain. In the American south, English troops, allied with Indians, destroyed 13 of the 14 Spanish missions, but failed to destroy the French forts. In the north the French and Indians combined. By the Treaty of Utrecht, 1713, France surrendered Newfoundland, Acadia and the Hudson Bay area to the English.

Fort Prudhomme
Fort Tombecbe
CHICKASAW
CREEKS
YAZOO
ALABAMA
Mississippi

Pensacola
Fort Mobile
Fort Maurepas
San Marcos

St. Augustine Fort besieged town burned

	English possessions
→	English attacks 1702-1703.
◔	Spanish missions destroyed by the English 1703.
▒	Indian tribes won over by English bribes 1703-1706.
▓	Choctaw tribe remaining loyal to France.
◉	French forts.
⇨	French and Indian attacks 1703-1709.

0   300
Miles

18

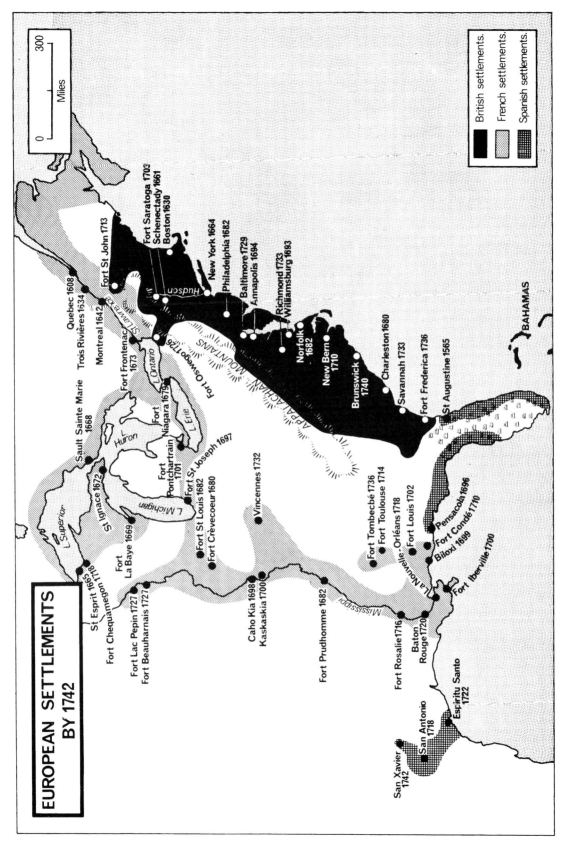

EUROPEAN SETTLEMENTS BY 1742

British settlements.
French settlements.
Spanish settlements.

300
0
Miles

Quebec 1608
Trois Rivières 1634
Montreal 1642
Fort St John 1713
Fort Saratoga 1702
Schenectady 1661
Boston 1630
New York 1664
Philadelphia 1682
Baltimore 1729
Annapolis 1694
Richmond 1733
Williamsburg 1693
Fort Frontenac 1673
Hudson
St Lawrence
L. Ontario
APPALACHIAN MOUNTAINS
Fort Oswego 1725
Norfolk 1682
New Bern 1710
Brunswick 1740
Charleston 1680
Savannah 1733
Fort Frederica 1736
St Augustine 1565
BAHAMAS

Sault Sainte Marie 1668
Fort Niagara 1679
L. Erie
L. Huron
Fort Pontchartrain 1701
Fort St Joseph 1697
St Ignace 1672
L. Michigan
Fort St Louis 1682
Fort Crèvecoeur 1680
Vincennes 1732

L. Superior
St Esprit 1665
Fort Chequamegon
Fort La Baye 1669
Fort Lac Pepin 1727
Fort Beauharnais 1727

Caho Kia 1698
Kaskaskia 1700
Fort Prudhomme 1682
Mississippi

Fort Tombecbé 1736
Fort Toulouse 1714
Fort Louis 1702
La Nouvelle-Orléans 1718
Pensacola 1696
Fort Condé 1710
Biloxi 1699
Fort Iberville 1700

Fort Rosalie 1716
Baton Rouge 1720

Espiritu Santo 1722

San Antonio 1718
San Xavier 1742

19

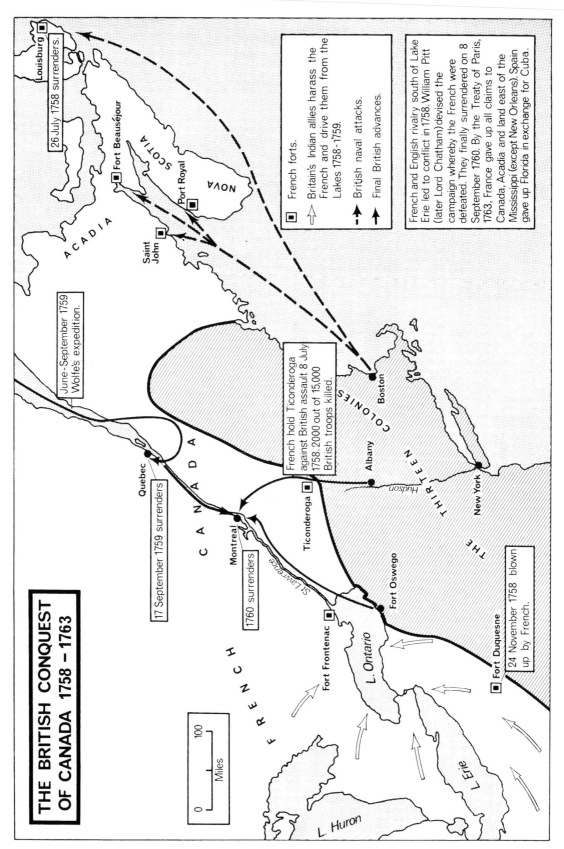

THE BRITISH CONQUEST OF CANADA 1758 – 1763

Louisburg
26 July 1758 surrenders.

Fort Beauséjour

Port Royal

NOVA SCOTIA

Saint John

ACADIA

French forts.

Britain's Indian allies harass the French and drive them from the Lakes 1758-1759.

British naval attacks.

Final British advances.

French and English rivalry south of Lake Erie led to conflict in 1758. William Pitt (later Lord Chatham) devised the campaign whereby the French were defeated. They finally surrendered on 8 September 1760. By the Treaty of Paris, 1763, France gave up all claims to Canada, Acadia and land east of the Mississippi (except New Orleans). Spain gave up Florida in exchange for Cuba.

June-September 1759 Wolfe's expedition.

French hold Ticonderoga against British assault 8 July 1758. 2000 out of 15,000 British troops killed.

Boston

Albany

Hudson

New York

THE THIRTEEN COLONIES

Quebec

17 September 1759 surrenders

Montreal

1760 surrenders

Ticonderoga

St. Lawrence

CANADA

Fort Frontenac

Fort Oswego

L. Ontario

Fort Duquesne

24 November 1758 blown up by French.

FRENCH

Miles
0   100

L. Erie

L. Huron

20

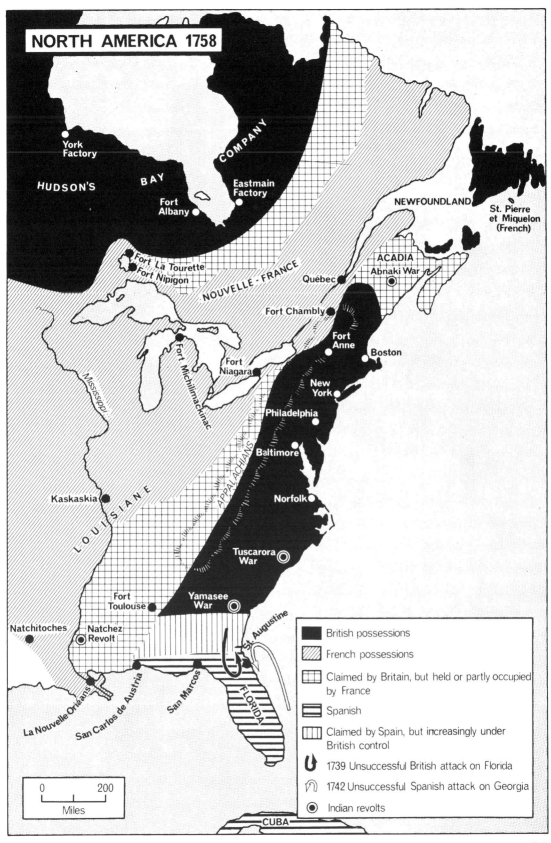

NORTH AMERICA 1758

HUDSON'S BAY COMPANY

York Factory

Eastmain Factory

Fort Albany

NEWFOUNDLAND

St. Pierre et Miquelon (French)

ACADIA

Fort La Tourette
Fort Nipigon

NOUVELLE - FRANCE

Québec

Abnaki War

Fort Chambly

Fort Anne

Boston

Fort Michilimackinac

Fort Niagara

New York

Philadelphia

Mississippi

Baltimore

APPALACHIANS

Kaskaskia

LOUISIANE

Norfolk

Tuscarora War

Fort Toulouse

Yamasee War

Natchitoches

Natchez Revolt

La Nouvelle Orléans

San Carlos de Austria

San Marcos

St. Augustine

FLORIDA

CUBA

■	British possessions
▨	French possessions
⊞	Claimed by Britain, but held or partly occupied by France
▤	Spanish
⊟	Claimed by Spain, but increasingly under British control
↰	1739 Unsuccessful British attack on Florida
↰	1742 Unsuccessful Spanish attack on Georgia
◉	Indian revolts

0   200
Miles

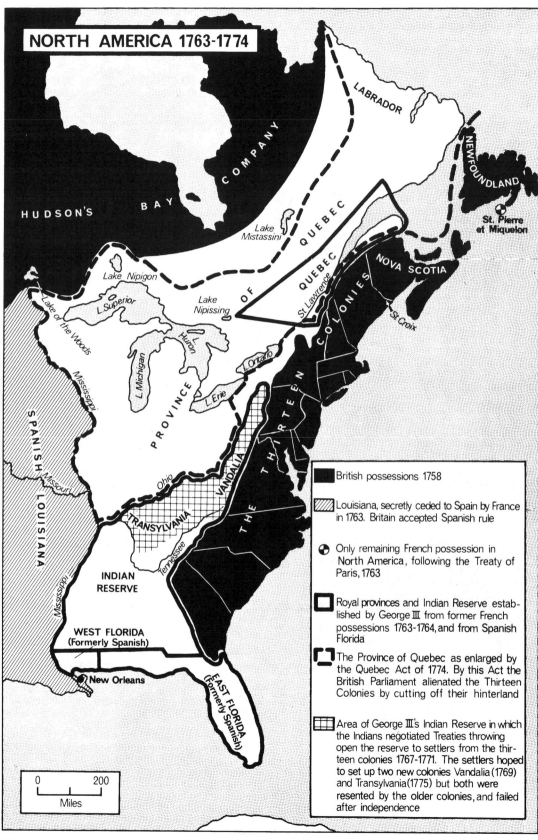

NORTH AMERICA 1763-1774

HUDSON'S BAY COMPANY

LABRADOR

NEWFOUNDLAND

St. Pierre et Miquelon

Lake Mistassini

PROVINCE OF QUEBEC

QUEBEC

St Lawrence

NOVA SCOTIA

St Croix

Lake Nipigon

Lake Nipissing

Lake of the Woods

L. Superior

L. Michigan

L. Huron

L. Ontario

L. Erie

Mississippi

Missouri

SPANISH LOUISIANA

Ohio

VANDALIA

THE THIRTEEN COLONIES

TRANSYLVANIA

Tennessee

INDIAN RESERVE

Mississippi

WEST FLORIDA (Formerly Spanish)

New Orleans

EAST FLORIDA (Formerly Spanish)

British possessions 1758

Louisiana, secretly ceded to Spain by France in 1763. Britain accepted Spanish rule

Only remaining French possession in North America, following the Treaty of Paris, 1763

Royal provinces and Indian Reserve established by George III from former French possessions 1763-1764, and from Spanish Florida

The Province of Quebec as enlarged by the Quebec Act of 1774. By this Act the British Parliament alienated the Thirteen Colonies by cutting off their hinterland

Area of George III's Indian Reserve in which the Indians negotiated Treaties throwing open the reserve to settlers from the thirteen colonies 1767-1771. The settlers hoped to set up two new colonies Vandalia (1769) and Transylvania (1775) but both were resented by the older colonies, and failed after independence

0   200
Miles

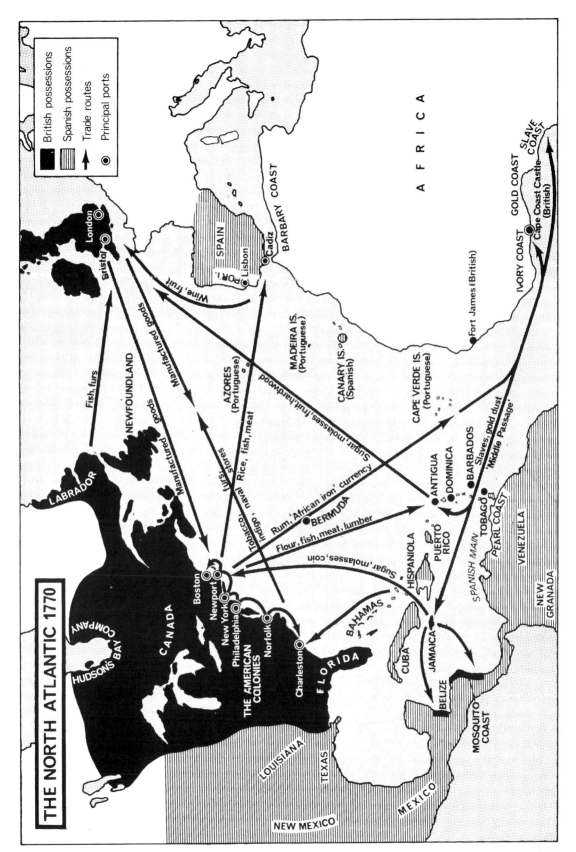

THE NORTH ATLANTIC 1770

Legend:
- ■ British possessions
- ▥ Spanish possessions
- ↑ Trade routes
- ◉ Principal ports

AFRICA

SLAVE COAST

GOLD COAST

IVORY COAST

Cape Coast Castle (British)

Fort James (British)

CAPE VERDE IS. (Portuguese)

CANARY IS. (Spanish)

MADEIRA IS. (Portuguese)

AZORES (Portuguese)

SPAIN

PORT.

Lisbon

Cadiz

BARBARY COAST

London

Bristol

Wine, fruit

Manufactured goods

Manufactured goods

Fish, furs

NEWFOUNDLAND

LABRADOR

HUDSON'S BAY COMPANY

CANADA

THE AMERICAN COLONIES

Boston

Newport

New York

Philadelphia

Norfolk

Charleston

FLORIDA

furs, naval stores

Tobacco, naval stores

Rice, fish, meat

Indigo, 'African iron' currency

Sugar, molasses, fruit, hardwood

Rum, 'African iron' currency

BERMUDA

Flour, fish, meat, lumber

Sugar, molasses, coin

BAHAMAS

CUBA

HISPANIOLA

PUERTO RICO

JAMAICA

BELIZE

MOSQUITO COAST

LOUISIANA

TEXAS

NEW MEXICO

MEXICO

NEW GRANADA

VENEZUELA

SPANISH MAIN

PEARL COAST

TOBAGO

BARBADOS

DOMINICA

ANTIGUA

Slaves, gold dust

'Middle Passage'

23

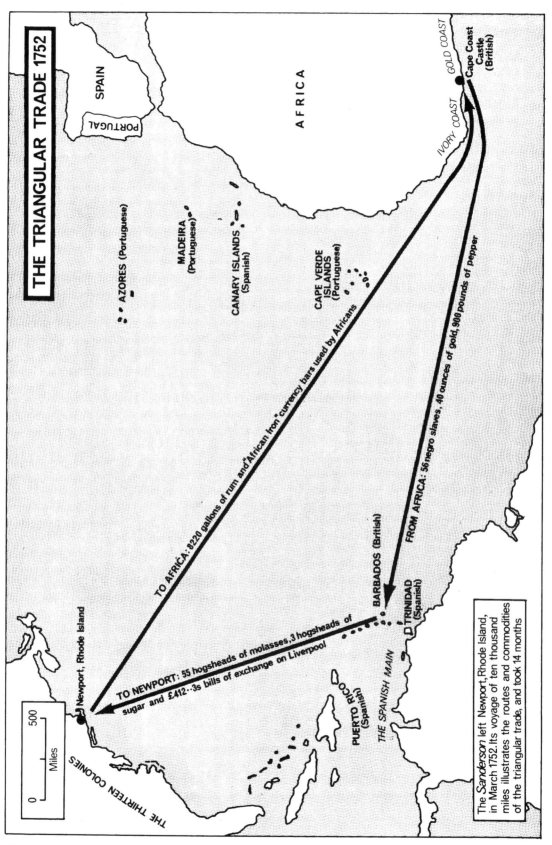

THE TRIANGULAR TRADE 1752

SPAIN

PORTUGAL

AFRICA

GOLD COAST

IVORY COAST

Cape Coast Castle (British)

AZORES (Portuguese)

MADEIRA (Portuguese)

CANARY ISLANDS (Spanish)

CAPE VERDE ISLANDS (Portuguese)

TO AFRICA: 8220 gallons of rum and "African Iron" currency bars used by Africans

FROM AFRICA: 56 negro slaves, 40 ounces of gold, 900 pounds of pepper

BARBADOS (British)

TRINIDAD (Spanish)

Newport, Rhode Island

TO NEWPORT: 55 hogsheads of molasses, 3 hogsheads of sugar and £412 · 3s bills of exchange on Liverpool

PUERTO RICO (Spanish)

THE SPANISH MAIN

500

Miles

0

THE THIRTEEN COLONIES

The *Sanderson* left Newport, Rhode Island, in March 1752. Its voyage of ten thousand miles illustrates the routes and commodities of the triangular trade, and took 14 months

Independence

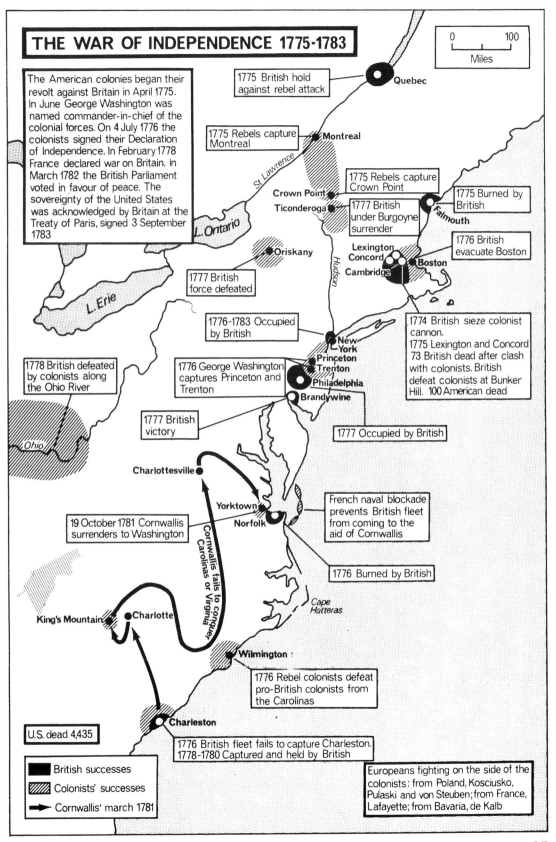

THE WAR OF INDEPENDENCE 1775-1783

0   100
Miles

The American colonies began their revolt against Britain in April 1775. In June George Washington was named commander-in-chief of the colonial forces. On 4 July 1776 the colonists signed their Declaration of Independence. In February 1778 France declared war on Britain. In March 1782 the British Parliament voted in favour of peace. The sovereignty of the United States was acknowledged by Britain at the Treaty of Paris, signed 3 September 1783

1775 British hold against rebel attack

Quebec

1775 Rebels capture Montreal

Montreal

St Lawrence

1775 Rebels capture Crown Point

Crown Point

Ticonderoga

1777 British under Burgoyne surrender

1775 Burned by British

Falmouth

L. Ontario

Oriskany

1777 British force defeated

Hudson

Lexington Concord

Cambridge

Boston

1776 British evacuate Boston

L. Erie

1776-1783 Occupied by British

1774 British sieze colonist cannon.
1775 Lexington and Concord 73 British dead after clash with colonists. British defeat colonists at Bunker Hill. 100 American dead

1778 British defeated by colonists along the Ohio River

New York

Princeton
Trenton

1776 George Washington captures Princeton and Trenton

Philadelphia

Brandywine

Ohio

1777 British victory

1777 Occupied by British

Charlottesville

French naval blockade prevents British fleet from coming to the aid of Cornwallis

Yorktown

Norfolk

19 October 1781 Cornwallis surrenders to Washington

Cornwallis fails to conquer Carolinas or Virginia

1776 Burned by British

Cape Hatteras

King's Mountain

Charlotte

Wilmington

1776 Rebel colonists defeat pro-British colonists from the Carolinas

U.S. dead 4,435

Charleston

1776 British fleet fails to capture Charleston. 1778-1780 Captured and held by British

■ British successes

▨ Colonists' successes

➤ Cornwallis' march 1781

Europeans fighting on the side of the colonists: from Poland, Kosciusko, Pulaski and von Steuben; from France, Lafayette; from Bavaria, de Kalb

25

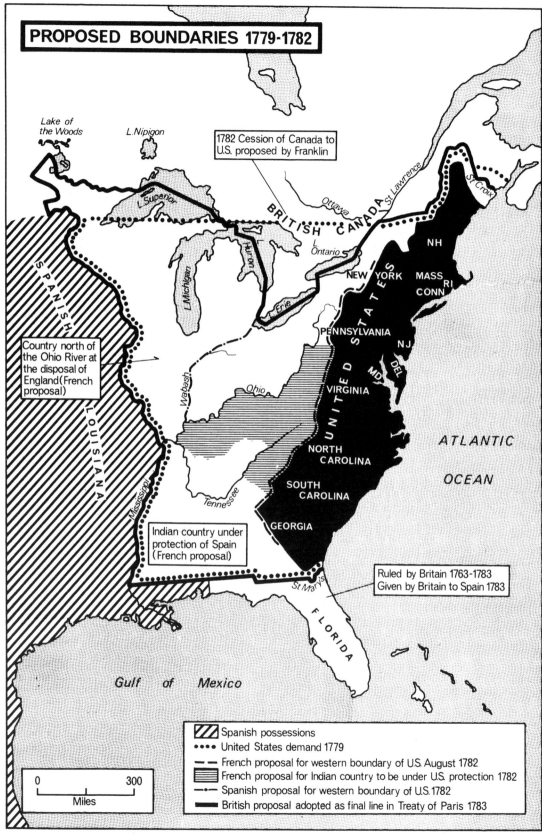

PROPOSED BOUNDARIES 1779-1782

Lake of the Woods

L.Nipigon

1782 Cession of Canada to U.S. proposed by Franklin

L.Superior

BRITISH CANADA

Ottawa

St Lawrence

St Croix

L.Huron

L.Michigan

L. Ontario

NH

NEW YORK

MASS

RI

CONN

Erie

PENNSYLVANIA

NJ

Country north of the Ohio River at the disposal of England(French proposal)

S P A N I S H

Wabash

Ohio

MD

DEL

VIRGINIA

U
N
I
T
E
D

S
T
A
T
E
S

L O U I S I A N A

NORTH CAROLINA

ATLANTIC

OCEAN

Tennessee

SOUTH CAROLINA

Mississippi

Indian country under protection of Spain (French proposal)

GEORGIA

St Mary's

Ruled by Britain 1763-1783
Given by Britain to Spain 1783

F
L
O
R
I
D
A

Gulf of Mexico

0   300
Miles

///// Spanish possessions
•••• United States demand 1779
– – – French proposal for western boundary of U.S. August 1782
▦ French proposal for Indian country to be under U.S. protection 1782
–•– Spanish proposal for western boundary of U.S. 1782
▬▬ British proposal adopted as final line in Treaty of Paris 1783

26

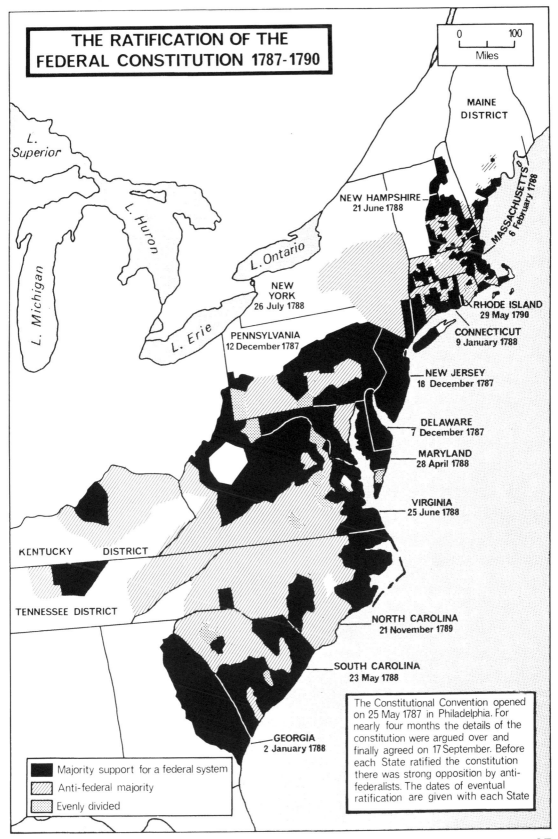

THE RATIFICATION OF THE FEDERAL CONSTITUTION 1787-1790

0 — 100
Miles

MAINE DISTRICT

L. Superior

L. Huron

L. Michigan

L. Ontario

L. Erie

NEW HAMPSHIRE
21 June 1788

MASSACHUSETTS
6 February 1788

NEW YORK
26 July 1788

RHODE ISLAND
29 May 1790

CONNECTICUT
9 January 1788

PENNSYLVANIA
12 December 1787

NEW JERSEY
18 December 1787

DELAWARE
7 December 1787

MARYLAND
28 April 1788

VIRGINIA
25 June 1788

KENTUCKY   DISTRICT

TENNESSEE DISTRICT

NORTH CAROLINA
21 November 1789

SOUTH CAROLINA
23 May 1788

GEORGIA
2 January 1788

■ Majority support for a federal system

▨ Anti-federal majority

▦ Evenly divided

The Constitutional Convention opened on 25 May 1787 in Philadelphia. For nearly four months the details of the constitution were argued over and finally agreed on 17 September. Before each State ratified the constitution there was strong opposition by anti-federalists. The dates of eventual ratification are given with each State

NORTH AMERICA 1783

Legend:
- ■ The United States of America.
- British claims not finally ceded to U.S. until the Jay Treaty of 1795.
- British possessions.
- Spanish possessions.
- Disputed and unsettled frontiers

ALASKA

Kodiak

1784 Russian settlement founded

UNEXPLORED TERRITORY

BAFFIN LAND

NEWFOUNDLAND

Northern limit of Spanish claims

HUDSON BAY

NEW SOUTH WALES

NEW BRITAIN

LABRADOR

Columbia

Snake

ACADIA

CALIFORNIA

CANADA

NOVA SCOTIA

Mississippi

THE UNITED STATES

Rio Grande

TEXAS

FLORIDA

BAHAMAS

MEXICO

CUBA

JAMAICA

BELIZE

MOSQUITO COAST

PANAMA

By the Treaty of Paris, 3 September 1783, Britain recognised the independence of the United States, withdrew all military and naval forces, agreed to fix the boundary of Canada by negotiation, and returned Florida to Spain.

0   1000
Miles

28

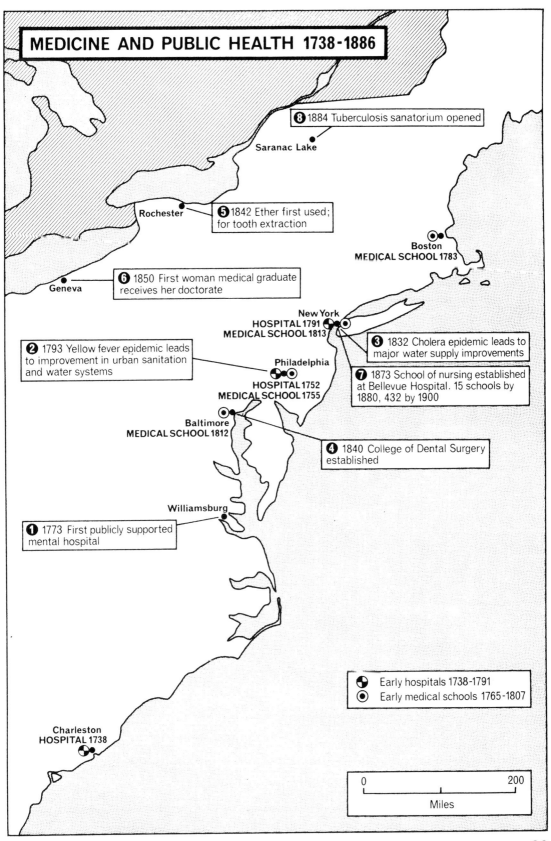

MEDICINE AND PUBLIC HEALTH 1738-1886

8 1884 Tuberculosis sanatorium opened

Saranac Lake

Rochester

5 1842 Ether first used; for tooth extraction

Boston
MEDICAL SCHOOL 1783

6 1850 First woman medical graduate receives her doctorate

Geneva

New York
HOSPITAL 1791
MEDICAL SCHOOL 1813

2 1793 Yellow fever epidemic leads to improvement in urban sanitation and water systems

3 1832 Cholera epidemic leads to major water supply improvements

Philadelphia

7 1873 School of nursing established at Bellevue Hospital. 15 schools by 1880, 432 by 1900

HOSPITAL 1752
MEDICAL SCHOOL 1755

Baltimore
MEDICAL SCHOOL 1812

4 1840 College of Dental Surgery established

Williamsburg

1 1773 First publicly supported mental hospital

| | Early hospitals 1738-1791 |
| | Early medical schools 1765-1807 |

Charleston
HOSPITAL 1738

0   200

Miles

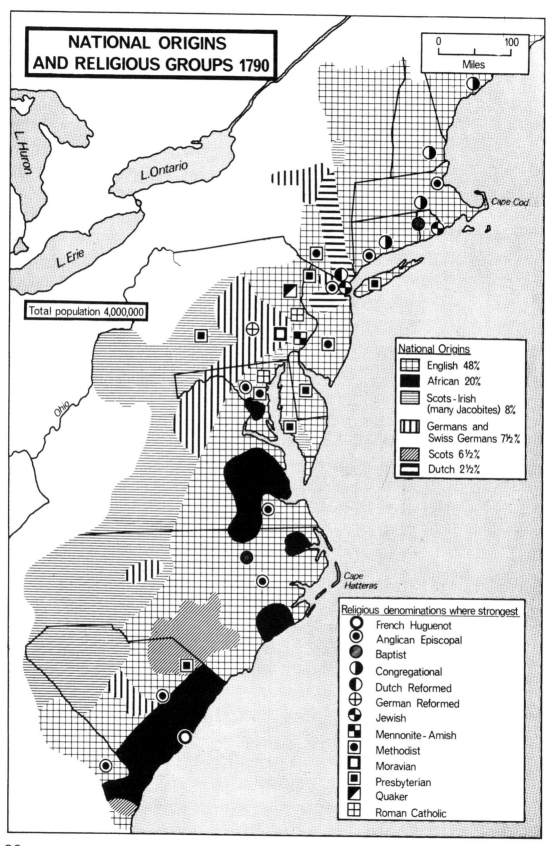

NATIONAL ORIGINS AND RELIGIOUS GROUPS 1790

0   100
Miles

L.Huron

L.Ontario

L.Erie

Cape Cod

Total population 4,000,000

Ohio

Cape Hatteras

National Origins

English 48%	
African 20%	
Scots-Irish (many Jacobites) 8%	
Germans and Swiss Germans 7½%	
Scots 6½%	
Dutch 2½%	

Religious denominations where strongest

- ◐ French Huguenot
- ◉ Anglican Episcopal
- ◐ Baptist
- ◐ Congregational
- ◐ Dutch Reformed
- ⊕ German Reformed
- ✢ Jewish
- ▣ Mennonite-Amish
- ▣ Methodist
- ☐ Moravian
- ▪ Presbyterian
- ◢ Quaker
- ⊞ Roman Catholic

30

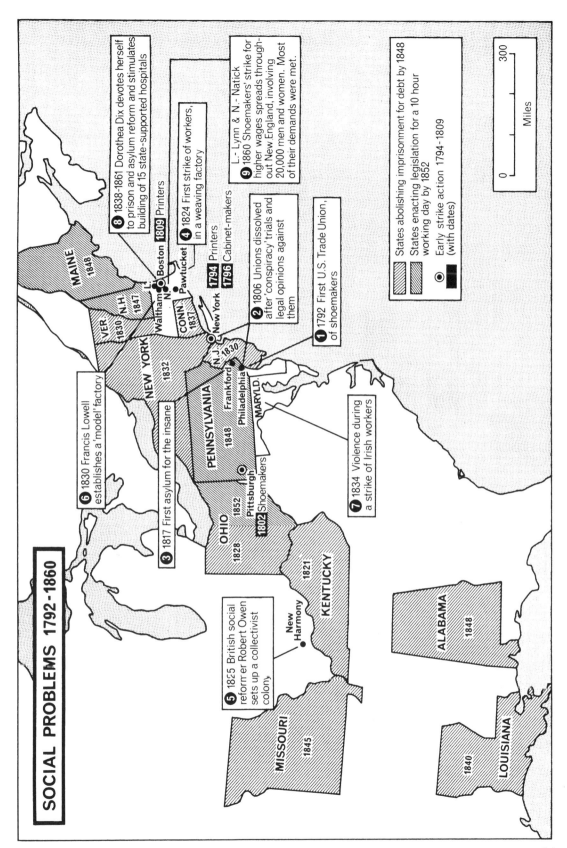

SOCIAL PROBLEMS 1792-1860

8 1838-1861 Dorothea Dix devotes herself to prison and asylum reform and stimulates building of 15 state-supported hospitals

1809 Printers

4 1824 First strike of workers, in a weaving factory

L.- Lynn & N.- Natick
9 1860 Shoemakers' strike for higher wages spreads throughout New England, involving 20,000 men and women. Most of their demands were met.

1794 Printers
1796 Cabinet-makers

2 1806 Unions dissolved after conspiracy 'trials and legal opinions against them

1 1792 First U.S. Trade Union, of shoemakers

6 1830 Francis Lowell establishes a 'model' factory

3 1817 First asylum for the insane

7 1834 Violence during a strike of Irish workers

5 1825 British social reformer Robert Owen sets up a collectivist colony

States abolishing imprisonment for debt by 1848

States enacting legislation for a 10 hour working day by 1852

Early strike action 1794-1809 (with dates)

300

0

Miles

MAINE 1848

N.H. 1830
1847
VER.

Boston
Waltham
N.
Pawtucket

CONN. 1837

NEW YORK 1832

New York
N.J. 1830

PENNSYLVANIA 1848

Frankford
Philadelphia
MARYLD.

Pittsburgh
OHIO 1828
1852
1802 Shoemakers

New Harmony

KENTUCKY 1821

MISSOURI 1845

ALABAMA 1848

LOUISIANA 1840

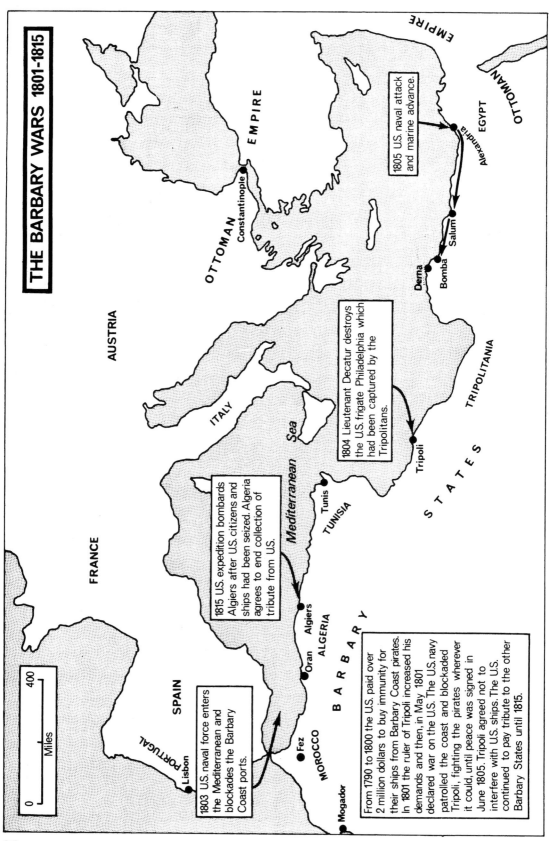

THE BARBARY WARS 1801-1815

OTTOMAN EMPIRE

OTTOMAN EMPIRE

Constantinople

AUSTRIA

ITALY

FRANCE

SPAIN

PORTUGAL

Lisbon

Mogador

MOROCCO

Fez

Oran

Algiers

ALGERIA

Tunis

TUNISIA

Mediterranean Sea

B A R B A R Y   S T A T E S

TRIPOLITANIA

Tripoli

Derna

Bomba

Salum

Alexandria

EGYPT

1805 U.S. naval attack and marine advance.

1804 Lieutenant Decatur destroys the U.S. frigate Philadelphia which had been captured by the Tripolitans.

1815 U.S. expedition bombards Algiers after U.S. citizens and ships had been seized. Algeria agrees to end collection of tribute from U.S.

1803 U.S. naval force enters the Mediterranean and blockades the Barbary Coast ports.

From 1790 to 1800 the U.S. paid over 2 million dollars to buy immunity for their ships from Barbary Coast pirates. In 1801 the ruler of Tripoli increased his demands and then, in May 1801 declared war on the U.S. The U.S. navy patrolled the coast and blockaded Tripoli, fighting the pirates wherever it could, until peace was signed in June 1805. Tripoli agreed not to interfere with U.S. ships. The U.S. continued to pay tribute to the other Barbary States until 1815.

Miles
0   400

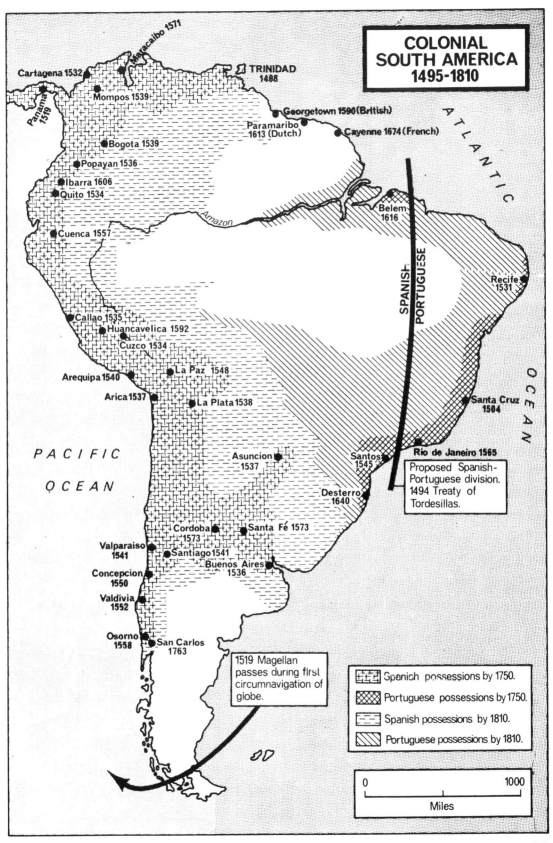

COLONIAL
SOUTH AMERICA
1495-1810

Cartagena 1532

Maracaibo 1571

Mompos 1539

TRINIDAD
1488

Panama
1519

Georgetown 1590 (British)

Paramaribo
1613 (Dutch)

Cayenne 1674 (French)

Bogota 1539

Popayan 1536

Ibarra 1606

Quito 1534

Amazon

Belem
1616

ATLANTIC

Cuenca 1557

SPANISH

PORTUGUESE

Recife
1531

Callao 1535

Huancavelica 1592

Cuzco 1534

Arequipa 1540

La Paz 1548

OCEAN

Arica 1537

La Plata 1538

Santa Cruz
1564

PACIFIC

OCEAN

Asuncion
1537

Santos
1545

Rio de Janeiro 1565

Proposed Spanish-
Portuguese division.
1494 Treaty of
Tordesillas.

Desterro
1640

Cordoba
1573

Santa Fé 1573

Valparaiso
1541

Santiago 1541

Buenos Aires
1536

Concepcion
1550

Valdivia
1552

Osorno
1558

San Carlos
1763

1519 Magellan
passes during first
circumnavigation of
globe.

Spanish possessions by 1750.

Portuguese possessions by 1750.

Spanish possessions by 1810.

Portuguese possessions by 1810.

0   1000

Miles

33

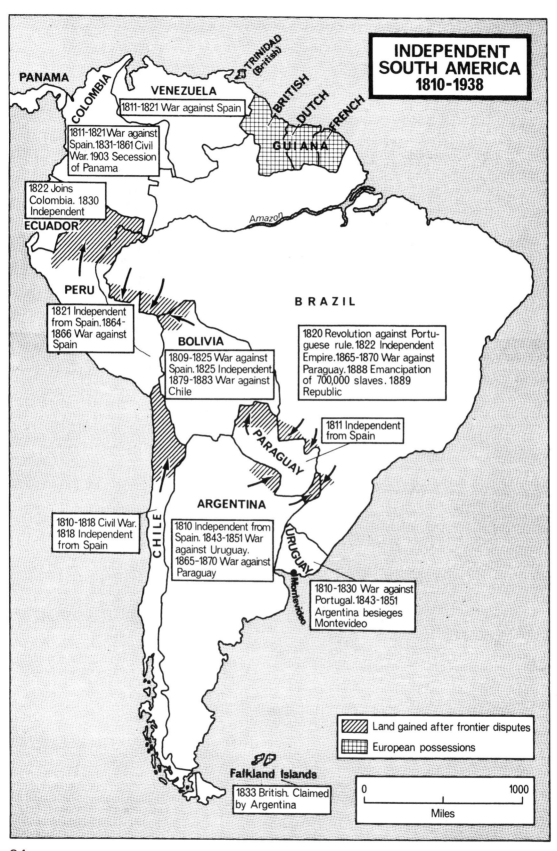

INDEPENDENT SOUTH AMERICA 1810-1938

PANAMA

COLOMBIA

VENEZUELA

1811-1821 War against Spain

1811-1821 War against Spain. 1831-1861 Civil War. 1903 Secession of Panama

1822 Joins Colombia. 1830 Independent

ECUADOR

PERU

1821 Independent from Spain. 1864-1866 War against Spain

BOLIVIA

1809-1825 War against Spain. 1825 Independent. 1879-1883 War against Chile

TRINIDAD (British)

BRITISH

DUTCH

FRENCH

GUIANA

Amazon

B R A Z I L

1820 Revolution against Portuguese rule. 1822 Independent Empire. 1865-1870 War against Paraguay. 1888 Emancipation of 700,000 slaves. 1889 Republic

PARAGUAY

1811 Independent from Spain

CHILE

1810-1818 Civil War. 1818 Independent from Spain

ARGENTINA

1810 Independent from Spain. 1843-1851 War against Uruguay. 1865-1870 War against Paraguay

URUGUAY

Montevideo

1810-1830 War against Portugal. 1843-1851 Argentina besieges Montevideo

Falkland Islands

1833 British. Claimed by Argentina

Land gained after frontier disputes

European possessions

0   1000
Miles

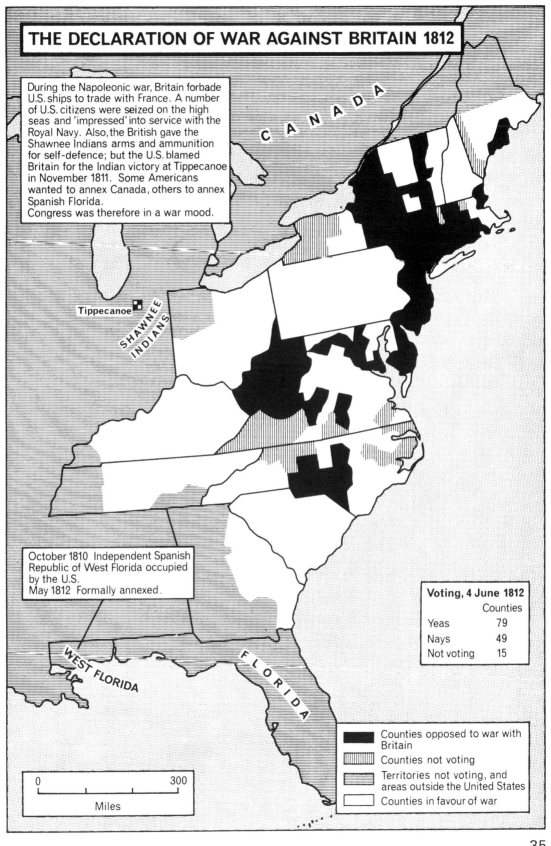

THE DECLARATION OF WAR AGAINST BRITAIN 1812

During the Napoleonic war, Britain forbade U.S. ships to trade with France. A number of U.S. citizens were seized on the high seas and 'impressed' into service with the Royal Navy. Also, the British gave the Shawnee Indians arms and ammunition for self-defence; but the U.S. blamed Britain for the Indian victory at Tippecanoe in November 1811. Some Americans wanted to annex Canada, others to annex Spanish Florida.
Congress was therefore in a war mood.

CANADA

Tippecanoe

SHAWNEE INDIANS

October 1810 Independent Spanish Republic of West Florida occupied by the U.S.
May 1812 Formally annexed.

WEST FLORIDA

FLORIDA

Voting, 4 June 1812

	Counties
Yeas	79
Nays	49
Not voting	15

■ Counties opposed to war with Britain

▥ Counties not voting

▤ Territories not voting, and areas outside the United States

☐ Counties in favour of war

0   300

Miles

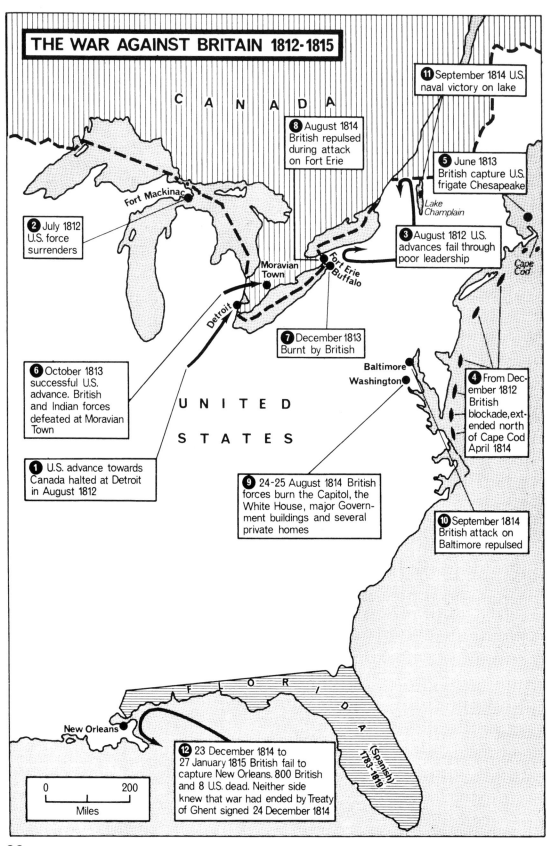

THE WAR AGAINST BRITAIN 1812-1815

C A N A D A

11 September 1814 U.S. naval victory on lake

8 August 1814 British repulsed during attack on Fort Erie

5 June 1813 British capture U.S. frigate Chesapeake

Lake Champlain

Fort Mackinac

2 July 1812 U.S. force surrenders

3 August 1812 U.S. advances fail through poor leadership

Moravian Town

Fort Erie Buffalo

Detroit

Cape Cod

7 December 1813 Burnt by British

6 October 1813 successful U.S. advance. British and Indian forces defeated at Moravian Town

U N I T E D

S T A T E S

Baltimore

Washington

4 From December 1812 British blockade, extended north of Cape Cod April 1814

1 U.S. advance towards Canada halted at Detroit in August 1812

9 24-25 August 1814 British forces burn the Capitol, the White House, major Government buildings and several private homes

10 September 1814 British attack on Baltimore repulsed

F L O R I D A

(Spanish) 1783-1819

New Orleans

12 23 December 1814 to 27 January 1815 British fail to capture New Orleans. 800 British and 8 U.S. dead. Neither side knew that war had ended by Treaty of Ghent signed 24 December 1814

0   200
Miles

Modern Times

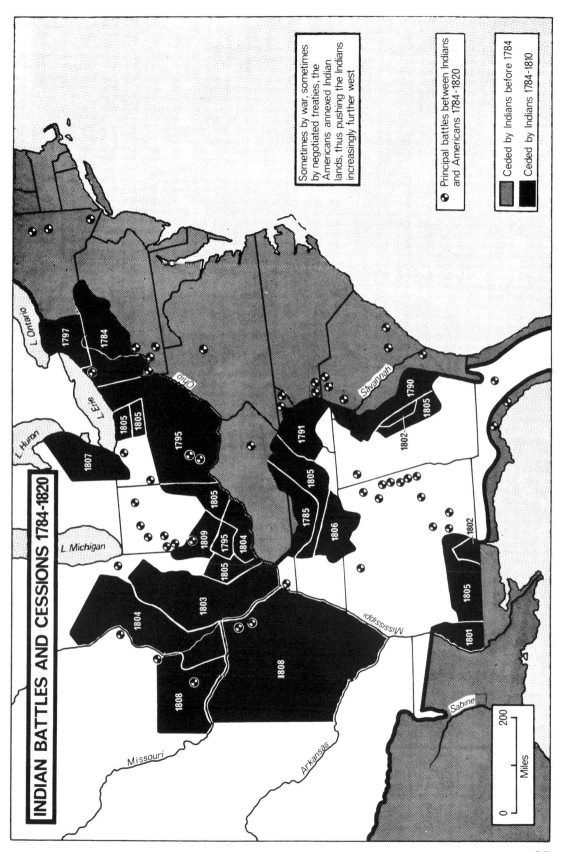

INDIAN BATTLES AND CESSIONS 1784-1820

Sometimes by war, sometimes by negotiated treaties, the Americans annexed Indian lands, thus pushing the Indians increasingly further west

◐ Principal battles between Indians and Americans 1784-1820

▨ Ceded by Indians before 1784

■ Ceded by Indians 1784-1810

L. Ontario

L. Erie

L. Huron

L. Michigan

Ohio

Savannah

Mississippi

Missouri

Arkansas

Sabine

1797
1784
1805
1805
1807
1795
1805
1809
1795
1804
1805
1791
1805
1785
1806
1790
1805
1802
1802
1805
1801
1804
1803
1808
1808

0   200
Miles

37

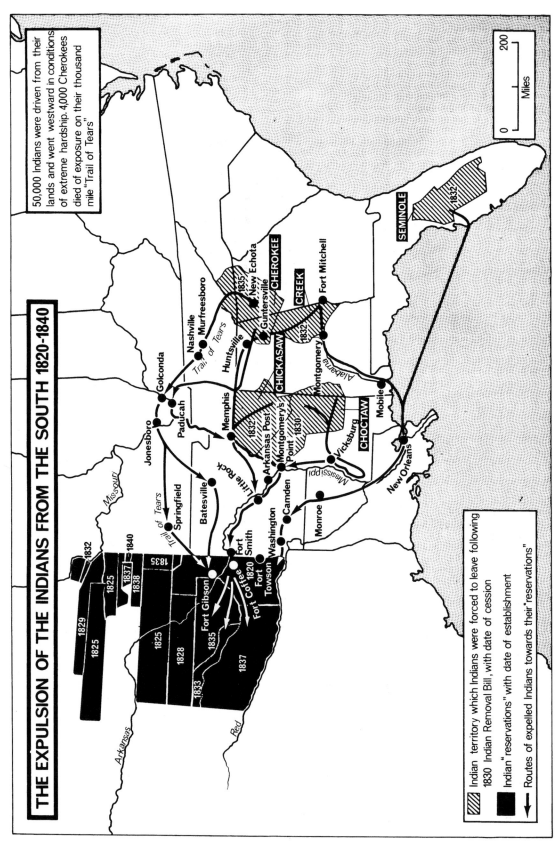

THE EXPULSION OF THE INDIANS FROM THE SOUTH 1820-1840

50,000 Indians were driven from their lands and went westward in conditions of extreme hardship. 4,000 Cherokees died of exposure on their thousand mile "Trail of Tears"

SEMINOLE 1832

CHEROKEE
1835 New Echota
Guntersville
CHICKASAW
1832
CREEK
Fort Mitchell

Murfreesboro
Nashville
Huntsville
Montgomery
Alabama
Mobile

Trail of Tears
Golconda
Paducah
Memphis
1832
Arkansas Post
Montgomery's
Point 1830
CHOCTAW
Vicksburg
Mississippi
New Orleans

Jonesboro
Missouri
Springfield
Batesville
Little Rock
Camden
Monroe

Trail of Tears
Fort Smith
Fort Gibson
Fort Coffee 1820
Fort Towson
Washington

1832
1840
1837
1835
1825
1838
1829
1825
1825
1828
1833
1837

Arkansas
Red

0 — 200 Miles

Indian territory which Indians were forced to leave following 1830 Indian Removal Bill, with date of cession

Indian "reservations" with date of establishment

Routes of expelled Indians towards their "reservations"

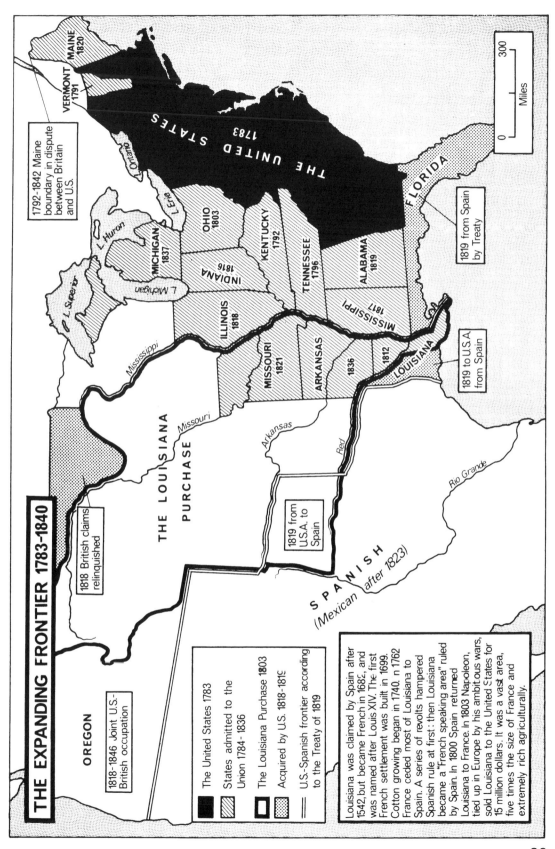

THE EXPANDING FRONTIER 1783-1840

OREGON

1818-1846 Joint U.S.-British occupation

The United States 1783

States admitted to the Union 1784-1836

The Louisiana Purchase 1803

Acquired by U.S. 1818-1819

U.S.-Spanish frontier according to the Treaty of 1819

1818 British claims relinquished

THE LOUISIANA PURCHASE

1819 from U.S.A. to Spain

S P A N I S H
(Mexican after 1823)

Louisiana was claimed by Spain after 1542, but became French in 1682, and was named after Louis XIV. The first French settlement was built in 1699. Cotton growing began in 1740. In 1762 France ceded most of Louisiana to Spain. A series of revolts hampered Spanish rule at first: then Louisiana became a "French speaking area" ruled by Spain. In 1800 Spain returned Louisiana to France. In 1803 Napoleon, tied up in Europe by his ambitious wars, sold Louisiana to the United States for 15 million dollars. It was a vast area, five times the size of France and extremely rich agriculturally.

Rio Grande

Red

Arkansas

Missouri

Mississippi

1819 from U.S.A. to Spain

LOUISIANA 1812

ARKANSAS 1836

MISSOURI 1821

ILLINOIS 1818

MISSISSIPPI 1817

ALABAMA 1819

TENNESSEE 1796

KENTUCKY 1792

INDIANA 1816

OHIO 1803

MICHIGAN 1837

L. Michigan

L. Superior

L. Huron

L. Erie

L. Ontario

THE UNITED STATES 1783

FLORIDA

1819 from Spain by Treaty

MAINE 1820

VERMONT 1791

1792-1842 Maine boundary in dispute between Britain and U.S.

0   300
Miles

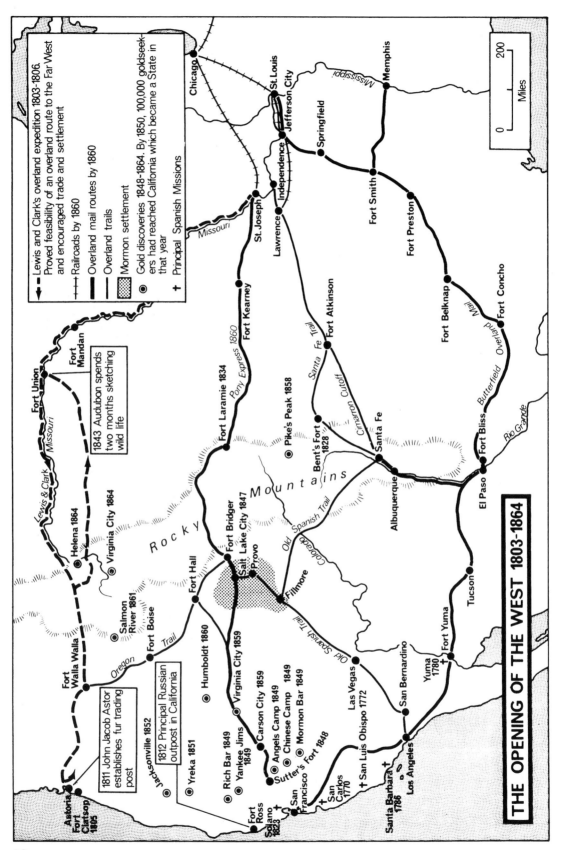

THE OPENING OF THE WEST 1803-1864

Legend:

- - - Lewis and Clark's overland expedition 1803-1806. Proved feasibility of an overland route to the Far West and encouraged trade and settlement
+++ Railroads by 1860
▬▬ Overland mail routes by 1860
— Overland trails
▓ Mormon settlement
◉ Gold discoveries 1848-1864. By 1850, 100,000 goldseekers had reached California which became a State in that year
✝ Principal Spanish Missions

1843 Audubon spends two months sketching wild life

1811 John Jacob Astor establishes fur trading post

1812 Principal Russian outpost in California

Chicago
St. Louis
Memphis
Jefferson City
Springfield
Independence
Fort Smith
Fort Preston
Lawrence
St. Joseph
Missouri
Fort Kearney
Fort Atkinson
Fort Belknap
Fort Concho
Fort Bliss
Santa Fe Trail
Cimarron Cutoff
Santa Fe
Pony Express 1860
Fort Laramie 1834
Pike's Peak 1858
Bent's Fort 1828
Albuquerque
El Paso
Rio Grande
Overland Butterfield Mail
Mississippi
Mountains
Rocky
Fort Bridger
Salt Lake City 1847
Provo
Fillmore
Old Spanish Trail
Colorado
Tucson
Fort Hall
Fort Boise
Salmon River 1861
Virginia City 1864
Helena 1864
Fort Union
Fort Mandan
Lewis & Clark
Missouri
Fort Walla Walla
Oregon Trail
Humboldt 1860
Virginia City 1859
Carson City 1859
Angels Camp 1849
Chinese Camp 1849
Mormon Bar 1849
Sutter's Fort 1848
Yankee Jims 1849
Rich Bar 1849
Yreka 1851
Jacksonville 1852
Fort Ross
Solano 1823
San Francisco 1849
San Carlos 1770
San Luis Obispo 1772
Las Vegas
San Bernardino
Fort Yuma
Yuma 1780
Old Spanish Trail
Santa Barbara 1786
Los Angeles
Astoria Fort Clatsop 1805

0   200
Miles

40

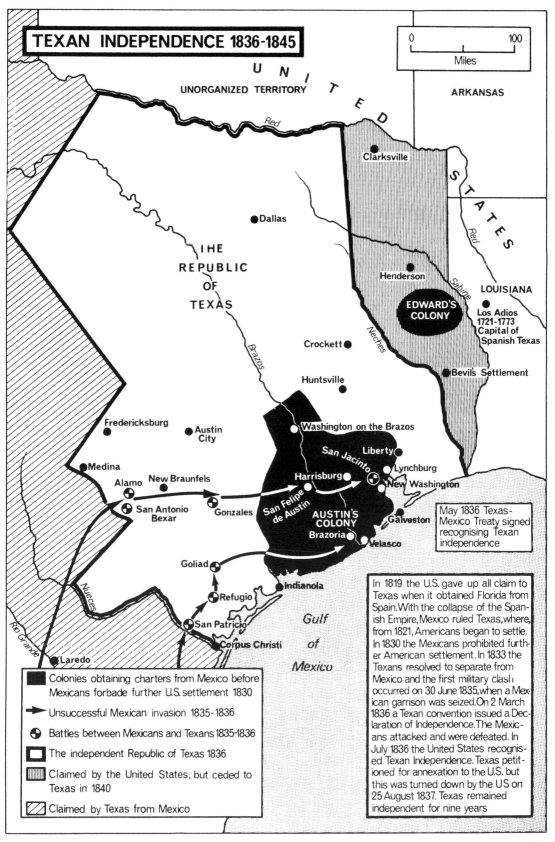

TEXAN INDEPENDENCE 1836-1845

0   100
Miles

U N I T E D

UNORGANIZED TERRITORY

ARKANSAS

Red

Clarksville

S T A T E S

Dallas

THE
REPUBLIC
OF
TEXAS

Henderson

Sabine

Red

LOUISIANA

EDWARD'S
COLONY

Los Adios
1721-1773
Capital of
Spanish Texas

Crockett

Neches

Bevils Settlement

Huntsville

Fredericksburg

Austin
City

Washington on the Brazos

Brazos

San Jacinto

Liberty

Medina

Lynchburg

New Braunfels

Alamo

Harrisburg

New Washington

San Felipe
de Austin

San Antonio
Bexar

Gonzales

AUSTIN'S
COLONY

Galveston

May 1836 Texas-
Mexico Treaty signed
recognising Texan
independence

Brazoria

Velasco

Goliad

Nueces

Indianola

Refugio

San Patricio

Gulf

of

Corpus Christi

Rio Grande

Laredo

Mexico

In 1819 the U.S. gave up all claim to
Texas when it obtained Florida from
Spain. With the collapse of the Spanish Empire, Mexico ruled Texas, where,
from 1821, Americans began to settle.
In 1830 the Mexicans prohibited further American settlement. In 1833 the
Texans resolved to separate from
Mexico and the first military clash
occurred on 30 June 1835, when a Mexican garrison was seized. On 2 March
1836 a Texan convention issued a Declaration of Independence. The Mexicans attacked and were defeated. In
July 1836 the United States recognised Texan Independence. Texas petit-
ioned for annexation to the U.S. but
this was turned down by the US on
25 August 1837. Texas remained
independent for nine years

Colonies obtaining charters from Mexico before
Mexicans forbade further U.S. settlement 1830

Unsuccessful Mexican invasion 1835-1836

Battles between Mexicans and Texans 1835-1836

The independent Republic of Texas 1836

Claimed by the United States, but ceded to
Texas in 1840

Claimed by Texas from Mexico

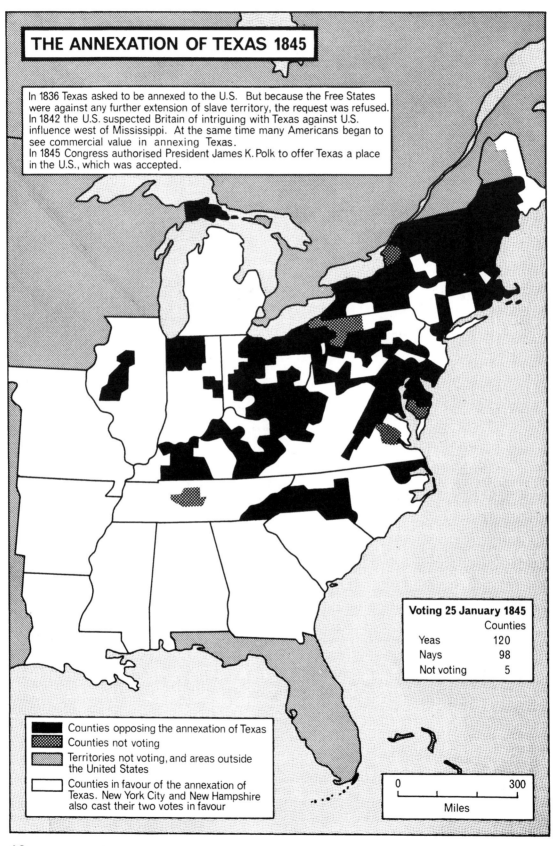

THE ANNEXATION OF TEXAS 1845

In 1836 Texas asked to be annexed to the U.S. But because the Free States were against any further extension of slave territory, the request was refused. In 1842 the U.S. suspected Britain of intriguing with Texas against U.S. influence west of Mississippi. At the same time many Americans began to see commercial value in annexing Texas.
In 1845 Congress authorised President James K. Polk to offer Texas a place in the U.S., which was accepted.

Voting 25 January 1845

	Counties
Yeas	120
Nays	98
Not voting	5

Counties opposing the annexation of Texas
Counties not voting
Territories not voting, and areas outside the United States
Counties in favour of the annexation of Texas. New York City and New Hampshire also cast their two votes in favour

0   300
Miles

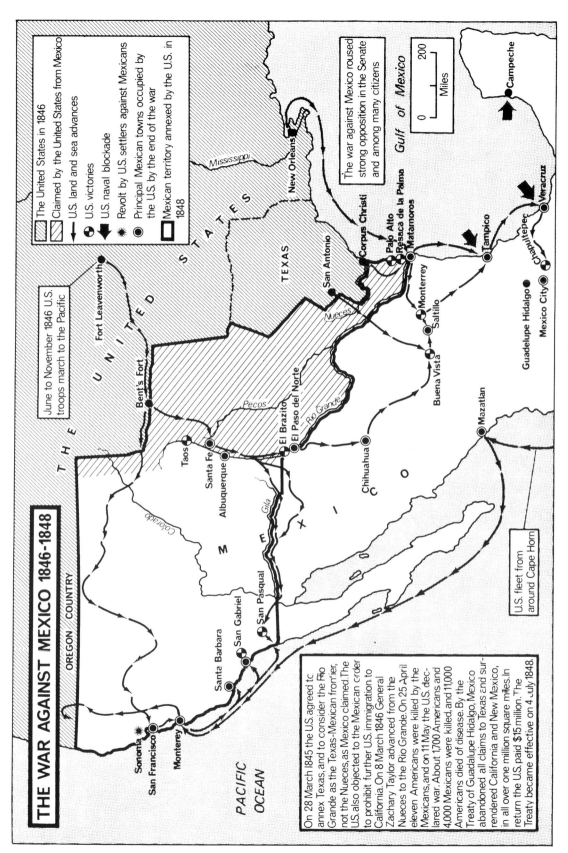

THE WAR AGAINST MEXICO 1846-1848

OREGON COUNTRY

THE UNITED STATES

TEXAS

M E X I C O

PACIFIC OCEAN

Gulf of Mexico

Mississippi

Nueces

Pecos

Rio Grande

Colorado

Gila

Legend:
- The United States in 1846
- Claimed by the United States from Mexico
- ↓ U.S. land and sea advances
- ✚ U.S. victories
- ⬇ U.S. naval blockade
- ✳ Revolt by U.S. settlers against Mexicans
- ● Principal Mexican towns occupied by the U.S. by the end of the war
- ◉ Mexican territory annexed by the U.S. in 1848

The war against Mexico roused strong opposition in the Senate and among many citizens

June to November 1846 U.S. troops march to the Pacific

U.S. fleet from around Cape Horn

Scale: 0 — 200 Miles

Place names:
Fort Leavenworth, Bent's Fort, Santa Fe, Taos, Albuquerque, Santa Barbara, San Gabriel, San Pasqual, Monterey, San Francisco, Sonoma, El Brazito, El Paso del Norte, Chihuahua, Mazatlan, San Antonio, Corpus Christi, Palo Alto, Resaca de la Palma, Matamoros, Monterrey, Saltillo, Buena Vista, Tampico, Veracruz, Chapultepec, Mexico City, Guadalupe Hidalgo, Campeche, New Orleans

On 28 March 1845 the U.S. agreed to annex Texas, and to consider the Rio Grande as the Texas-Mexican frontier, not the Nueces, as Mexico claimed. The U.S. also objected to the Mexican order to prohibit further U.S. immigration to California. On 8 March 1846 General Zachary Taylor advanced from the Nueces to the Rio Grande. On 25 April eleven Americans were killed by the Mexicans, and on 11 May the U.S. declared war. About 1,700 Americans and 4,000 Mexicans were killed, and 11,000 Americans died of disease. By the Treaty of Guadalupe Hidalgo, Mexico abandoned all claims to Texas and surrendered California and New Mexico, in all over one million square miles. In return the U.S. paid $15 million. The Treaty became effective on 4 July 1848.

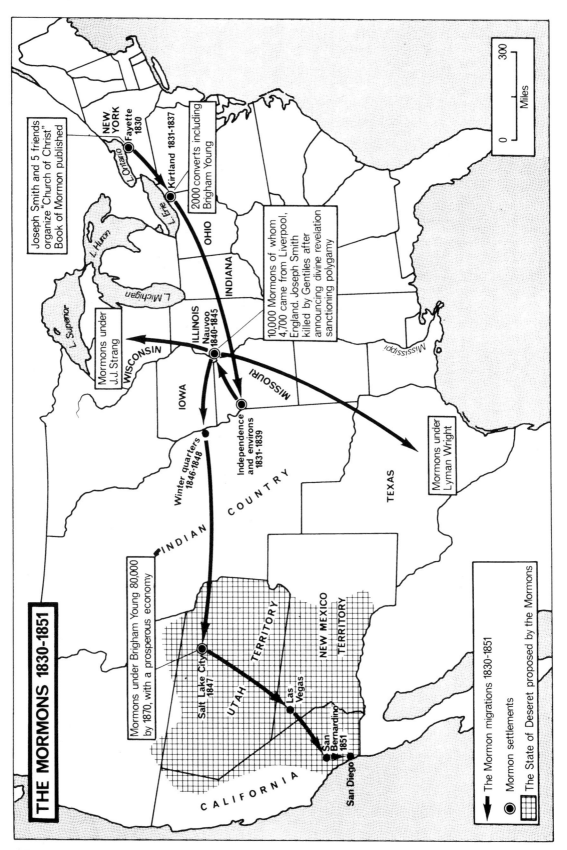

THE MORMONS 1830-1851

0 300
Miles

Joseph Smith and 5 friends organize "Church of Christ" Book of Mormon published

NEW YORK
Fayette 1830

Kirtland 1831-1837

2000 converts including Brigham Young

OHIO

INDIANA

10,000 Mormons of whom 4,700 came from Liverpool, England. Joseph Smith killed by Gentiles after announcing divine revelation sanctioning polygamy

L. Huron

L. Michigan

L. Superior

Mormons under J.J. Strang

WISCONSIN

ILLINOIS
Nauvoo 1840-1845

IOWA

Winter quarters 1846-1848

Independence and environs 1831-1839

MISSOURI

Mississippi

INDIAN   COUNTRY

TEXAS

Mormons under Lyman Wright

Mormons under Brigham Young 80,000 by 1870, with a prosperous economy

Salt Lake City 1847

UTAH
TERRITORY

NEW MEXICO
TERRITORY

Las Vegas

San Bernardino 1851

San Diego

CALIFORNIA

The Mormon migrations 1830-1851

Mormon settlements

The State of Deseret proposed by the Mormons

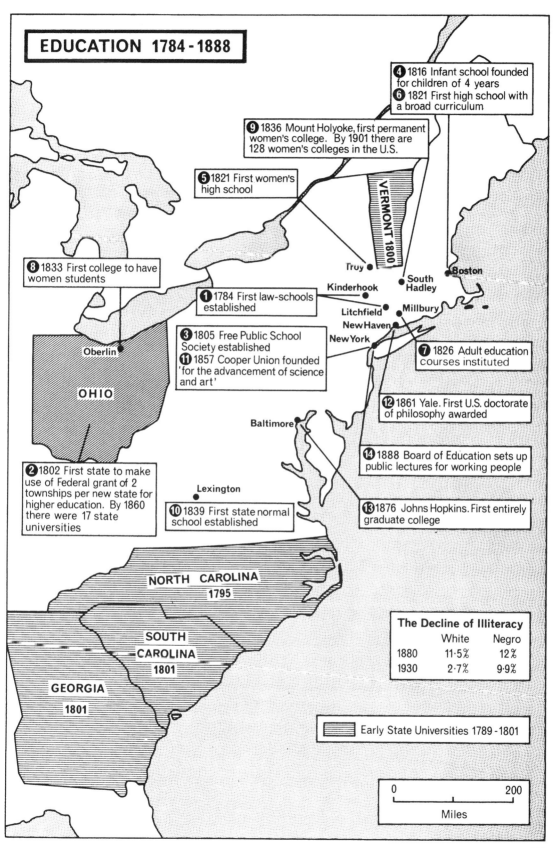

EDUCATION 1784-1888

4 1816 Infant school founded for children of 4 years

6 1821 First high school with a broad curriculum

9 1836 Mount Holyoke, first permanent women's college. By 1901 there are 128 women's colleges in the U.S.

5 1821 First women's high school

VERMONT 1800

8 1833 First college to have women students

1 1784 First law-schools established

3 1805 Free Public School Society established

11 1857 Cooper Union founded 'for the advancement of science and art'

OHIO

Oberlin

Troy ● South Hadley ● Boston ● Kinderhook ● Litchfield Millbury ● New Haven ● New York

7 1826 Adult education courses instituted

12 1861 Yale. First U.S. doctorate of philosophy awarded

Baltimore ●

14 1888 Board of Education sets up public lectures for working people

2 1802 First state to make use of Federal grant of 2 townships per new state for higher education. By 1860 there were 17 state universities

Lexington ●

10 1839 First state normal school established

13 1876 Johns Hopkins. First entirely graduate college

NORTH CAROLINA 1795

SOUTH CAROLINA 1801

GEORGIA 1801

The Decline of Illiteracy		
	White	Negro
1880	11·5%	12%
1930	2·7%	9·9%

Early State Universities 1789-1801

0   200

Miles

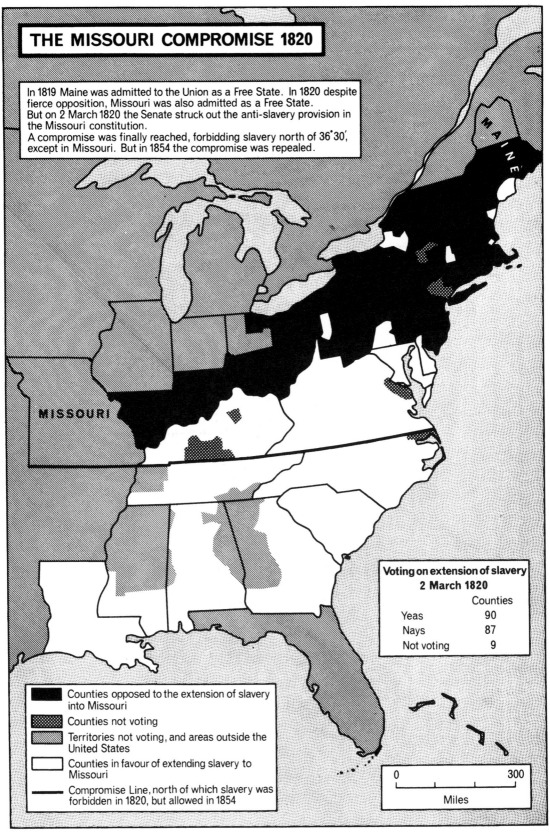

THE MISSOURI COMPROMISE 1820

In 1819 Maine was admitted to the Union as a Free State. In 1820 despite fierce opposition, Missouri was also admitted as a Free State.
But on 2 March 1820 the Senate struck out the anti-slavery provision in the Missouri constitution.
A compromise was finally reached, forbidding slavery north of 36°30′, except in Missouri. But in 1854 the compromise was repealed.

MAINE

MISSOURI

Voting on extension of slavery
2 March 1820

	Counties
Yeas	90
Nays	87
Not voting	9

■ Counties opposed to the extension of slavery into Missouri

▨ Counties not voting

▧ Territories not voting, and areas outside the United States

☐ Counties in favour of extending slavery to Missouri

── Compromise Line, north of which slavery was forbidden in 1820, but allowed in 1854

0　　　　　　300

Miles

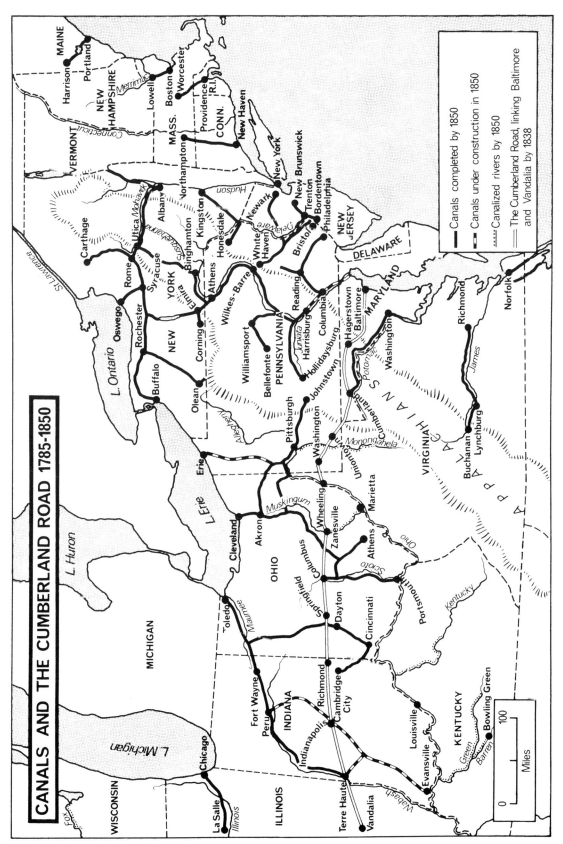

CANALS AND THE CUMBERLAND ROAD 1785-1850

Legend:
- Canals completed by 1850
- Canals under construction in 1850
- Canalized rivers by 1850
- The Cumberland Road, linking Baltimore and Vandalia by 1838

MAINE

Harrison
Portland

NEW HAMPSHIRE

Lowell
Boston
Worcester
R.I.
Providence
MASS.
CONN.
New Haven
New York

VERMONT

Merrimac
Connecticut

Carthage

Utica
Albany
Rome
Mohawk
Syracuse
Schenectady
Binghamton
Elmira
Athens
Kingston
Honesdale
Northampton
Newark
White Haven
Bristol
Trenton
Bordentown
Philadelphia
New Brunswick
NEW JERSEY
DELAWARE

Oswego
Rochester
Buffalo
Olean
NEW YORK
Corning
Wilkes-Barre
Williamsport
Bellefonte
PENNSYLVANIA
Reading
Columbia
Harrisburg
Hollidaysburg
Johnstown
Juniata
Hagerstown
Baltimore
MARYLAND
Washington
Richmond
Norfolk

L. Ontario
L. Erie
Erie
Pittsburgh
Washington
Uniontown
Cumberland
Monongahela
Potomac
James
Buchanan
Lynchburg
VIRGINIA
APPALACHIANS

L. Huron
L. Michigan
Chicago
La Salle
Illinois
Fox
WISCONSIN
MICHIGAN

Cleveland
Akron
Toledo
Maumee
Muskingum
Wheeling
Zanesville
Marietta
Athens
Ohio
Columbus
Springfield
Dayton
Cincinnati
Scioto
Portsmouth
OHIO
Kentucky

Fort Wayne
Peru
INDIANA
Richmond
Cambridge City
Indianapolis
Terre Haute
Vandalia
Louisville
Evansville
Bowling Green
KENTUCKY
Green
Barren
Wabash

Miles
0   100

Allegheny
Susquehanna
Delaware
Hudson

St. Lawrence

47

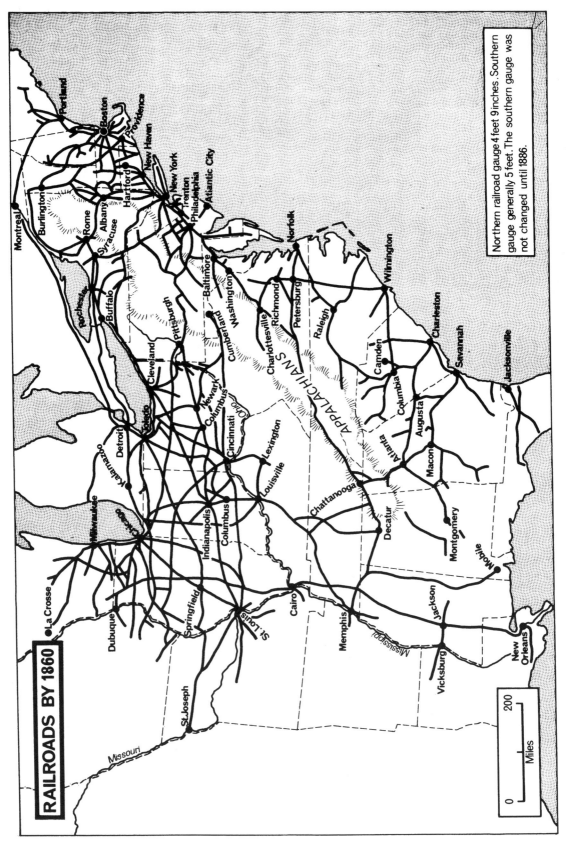

RAILROADS BY 1860

Northern railroad gauge 4 feet 9 inches. Southern gauge generally 5 feet. The southern gauge was not changed until 1886.

Montreal

Portland

Boston

Burlington

Providence

Rome

New Haven

Syracuse

Albany

Hartford

New York

Trenton

Philadelphia

Atlantic City

Norfolk

Baltimore

Washington

Wilmington

Buffalo

Pittsburgh

Cumberland

Charlottesville

Richmond

Petersburg

Raleigh

Charleston

Cleveland

Camden

Savannah

Newark

Columbus

Columbia

Jacksonville

Detroit

Cincinnati

Lexington

Augusta

Toledo

Atlanta

Kalamazoo

Macon

Louisville

APPALACHIANS

Indianapolis

Columbus

Chattanooga

Decatur

Milwaukee

Montgomery

Mobile

La Crosse

Springfield

St. Louis

Cairo

Memphis

Jackson

Illinois

Mississippi

Dubuque

New Orleans

St. Joseph

Vicksburg

Missouri

200

0

Miles

48

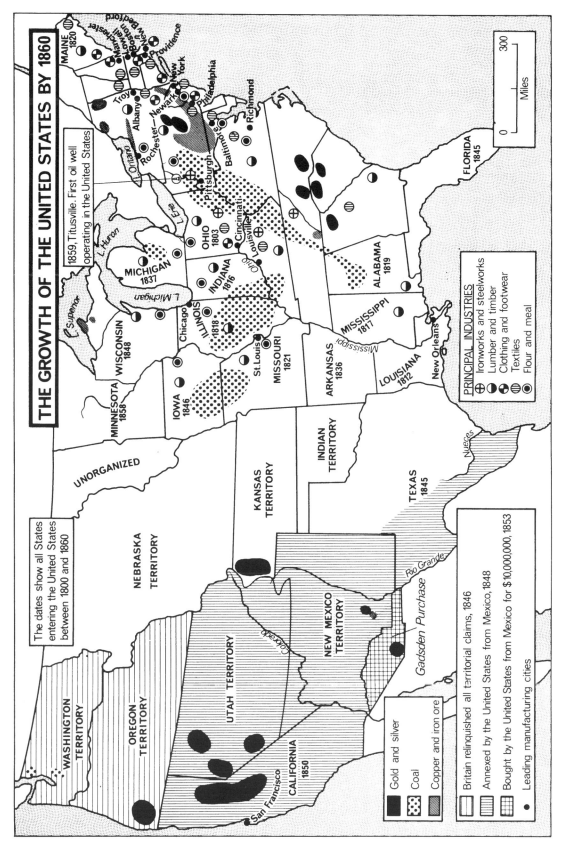

THE GROWTH OF THE UNITED STATES BY 1860

1859, Titusville. First oil well operating in the United States

The dates show all States entering the United States between 1800 and 1860

PRINCIPAL INDUSTRIES
Ironworks and steelworks
Lumber and timber
Clothing and footwear
Textiles
Flour and meal

MAINE 1820
New Bedford
Boston
Lowell
Manchester
Providence
Troy
Albany
New York
Newark
Philadelphia
Baltimore
Richmond
Rochester
Pittsburgh
Cincinnati
Louisville
L. Ontario
L. Erie
L. Huron
L. Michigan
L. Superior

OHIO 1803
MICHIGAN 1837
INDIANA 1816
ILLINOIS 1818
WISCONSIN 1848
MINNESOTA 1858
IOWA 1846
MISSOURI 1821
Chicago
St. Louis
Ohio
Mississippi

ALABAMA 1819
MISSISSIPPI 1817
ARKANSAS 1836
LOUISIANA 1812
FLORIDA 1845
New Orleans

UNORGANIZED
NEBRASKA TERRITORY
KANSAS TERRITORY
INDIAN TERRITORY
TEXAS 1845
Nueces
Rio Grande

WASHINGTON TERRITORY
OREGON TERRITORY
UTAH TERRITORY
NEW MEXICO TERRITORY
CALIFORNIA 1850
San Francisco
Colorado
Gadsden Purchase

Gold and silver
Coal
Copper and iron ore

Britain relinquished all territorial claims, 1846
Annexed by the United States from Mexico, 1848
Bought by the United States from Mexico for $10,000,000, 1853
Leading manufacturing cities

0   300
Miles

49

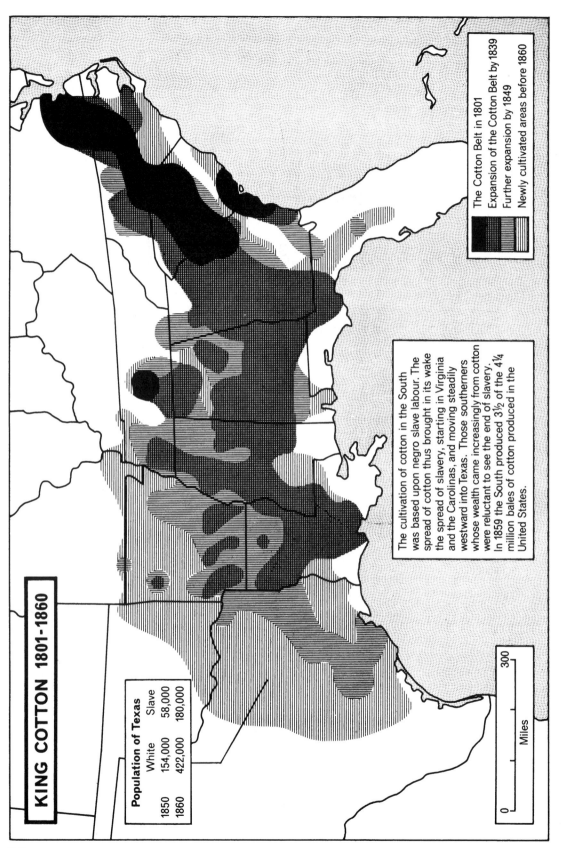

KING COTTON 1801-1860

Population of Texas

	White	Slave
1850	154,000	58,000
1860	422,000	180,000

The cultivation of cotton in the South was based upon negro slave labour. The spread of cotton thus brought in its wake the spread of slavery, starting in Virginia and the Carolinas, and moving steadily westward into Texas. Those southerners whose wealth came increasingly from cotton were reluctant to see the end of slavery. In 1859 the South produced 3½ of the 4¼ million bales of cotton produced in the United States.

The Cotton Belt in 1801
Expansion of the Cotton Belt by 1839
Further expansion by 1849
Newly cultivated areas before 1860

Miles

0   300

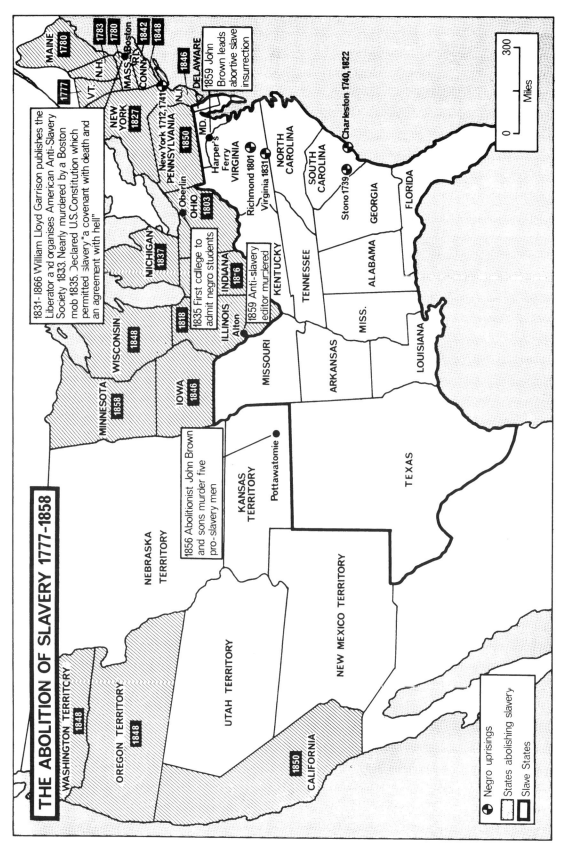

THE ABOLITION OF SLAVERY 1777-1858

1831-1866 William Lloyd Garrison publishes the Liberator a nd organises American Anti-Slavery Society 1833. Nearly murdered by a Boston mob 1835. Declared U.S.Constitution which permitted slavery "a covenant with death and an agreement with hell"

1859 John Brown leads abortive slave insurrection

1835 First college to admit negro students

1859 Anti-slavery editor murdered

1856 Abolitionist John Brown and sons murder five pro-slavery men

MAINE 1780

N.H.

VT. 1777

MASS. 1783 1780
Boston
R.I. 1842
CONN. 1848

NEW YORK 1827

PENNSYLVANIA 1850
New York 1712, 1741

DELAWARE 1846

N.J.

MD.

Harper's Ferry
VIRGINIA
Richmond 1801
Virginia 1831

NORTH CAROLINA

Charleston 1740, 1822

SOUTH CAROLINA

Stono 1739

GEORGIA

FLORIDA

Oberlin
OHIO 1803

MICHIGAN 1837

INDIANA 1816

ILLINOIS
Alton

WISCONSIN 1848

IOWA 1846

MINNESOTA 1858

KENTUCKY

TENNESSEE

ALABAMA

MISS.

ARKANSAS

MISSOURI

LOUISIANA

Pottawatomie

KANSAS TERRITORY

TEXAS

NEBRASKA TERRITORY

WASHINGTON TERRITORY 1848

OREGON TERRITORY 1848

UTAH TERRITORY

NEW MEXICO TERRITORY

CALIFORNIA 1850

300

0   Miles

● Negro uprisings
☐ States abolishing slavery
▣ Slave States

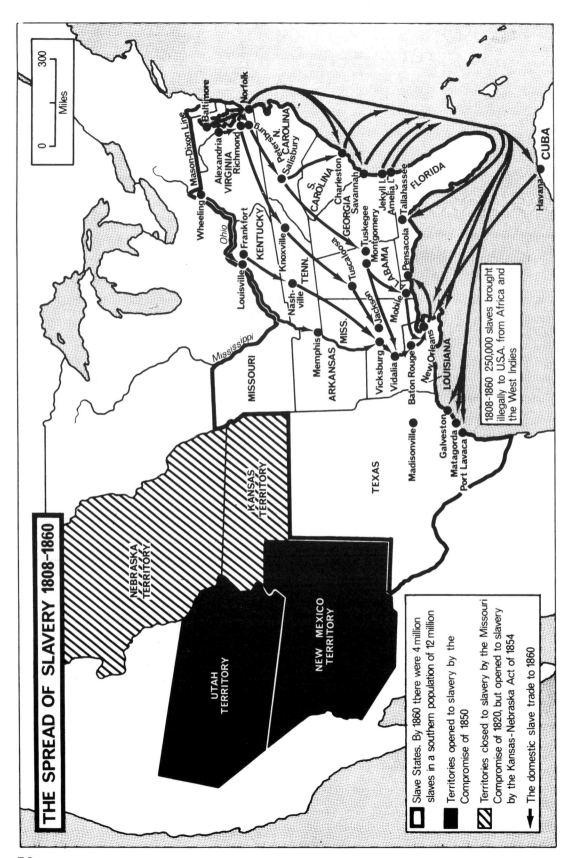

THE SPREAD OF SLAVERY 1808–1860

300

0

Miles

Mason–Dixon Line

Baltimore
Norfolk
Alexandria
Richmond
VIRGINIA
Petersburg
N. CAROLINA
Salisbury
S. CAROLINA
Charleston
Savannah
GEORGIA
Tuskegee
Montgomery
ALABAMA
Tuscaloosa
Jekyll I.
Amelia I.
Pensacola
FLORIDA
Tallahassee
Mobile

Wheeling
Ohio
Frankfort
KENTUCKY
Louisville
Knoxville
TENN.
Nashville
Memphis
MISS.
Jackson
Vicksburg
Vidalia
Baton Rouge
New Orleans
LOUISIANA

Mississippi

MISSOURI

ARKANSAS

Madisonville
Galveston
Matagorda
Port Lavaca

TEXAS

CUBA

Havana

1808–1860 250,000 slaves brought
illegally to U.S.A. from Africa and
the West Indies

NEBRASKA
TERRITORY

KANSAS
TERRITORY

UTAH
TERRITORY

NEW MEXICO
TERRITORY

☐ Slave States. By 1860 there were 4 million
slaves in a southern population of 12 million

■ Territories opened to slavery by the
Compromise of 1850

▨ Territories closed to slavery by the Missouri
Compromise of 1820, but opened to slavery
by the Kansas-Nebraska Act of 1854

→ The domestic slave trade to 1860

52

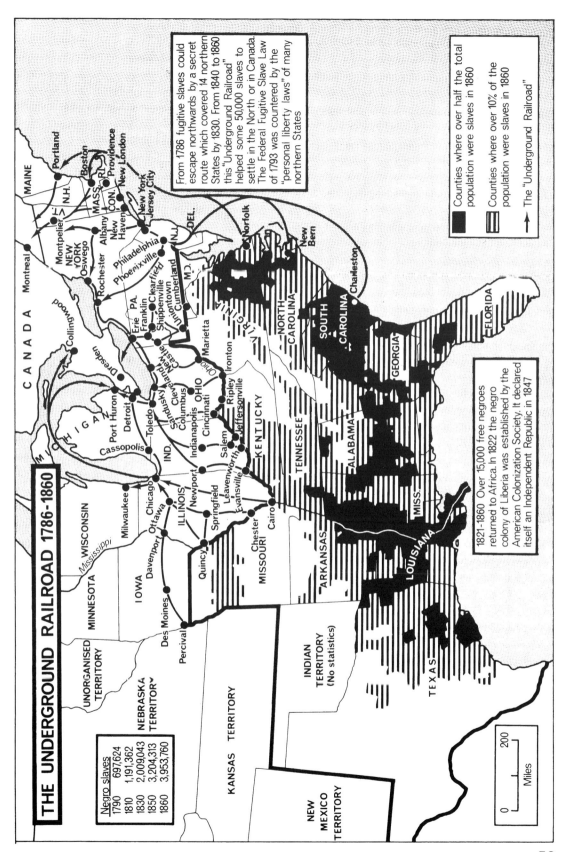

THE UNDERGROUND RAILROAD 1786-1860

Negro slaves
1790	697,624
1810	1,191,362
1830	2,009,043
1850	3,204,313
1860	3,953,760

From 1786 fugitive slaves could escape northwards by a secret route which covered 14 northern States by 1830. From 1840 to 1860 this "Underground Railroad" helped some 50,000 slaves to settle in the North or in Canada. The Federal Fugitive Slave Law of 1793 was countered by the "personal liberty laws" of many northern States

1821-1860 Over 15,000 free negroes returned to Africa. In 1822 the negro colony of Liberia was established by the American Colonization Society. It declared itself an Independent Republic in 1847

Counties where over half the total population were slaves in 1860

Counties where over 10% of the population were slaves in 1860

The "Underground Railroad"

0   200
Miles

CANADA

MAINE
N.H.
MASS.
CON.
R.I.
Portland
Boston
Providence
New London
New York City
Jersey City
Montpelier
NEW YORK
Albany
Oswego
Rochester
New Haven
Montreal
Collingwood
Dresden
Port Huron
Detroit
MICHIGAN
Cassopolis
Milwaukee
Chicago
Ottawa
ILLINOIS
Davenport
IOWA
Des Moines
Percival
WISCONSIN
MINNESOTA
UNORGANISED TERRITORY
NEBRASKA TERRITORY
Mississippi
Sandusky
Cleveland
Toledo
Columbus
Indianapolis
IND.
OHIO
Cincinnati
Ripley
Jeffersonville
Salem
Newport
Springfield
Evansville
Leavenworth
KANSAS TERRITORY
Quincy
Chester
MISSOURI
Cairo
Erie
PA.
Franklin
Shippenville
Clearfield
Phoenixville
Philadelphia
Uniontown
Cumberland
DEL.
N.J.
MD.
Marietta
Ironton
Ohio
KENTUCKY
TENNESSEE
ARKANSAS
INDIAN TERRITORY (No statistics)
TEXAS
LOUISIANA
MISS.
ALABAMA
GEORGIA
FLORIDA
SOUTH CAROLINA
NORTH CAROLINA
VIRGINIA
Norfolk
New Bern
Charleston
NEW MEXICO TERRITORY

53

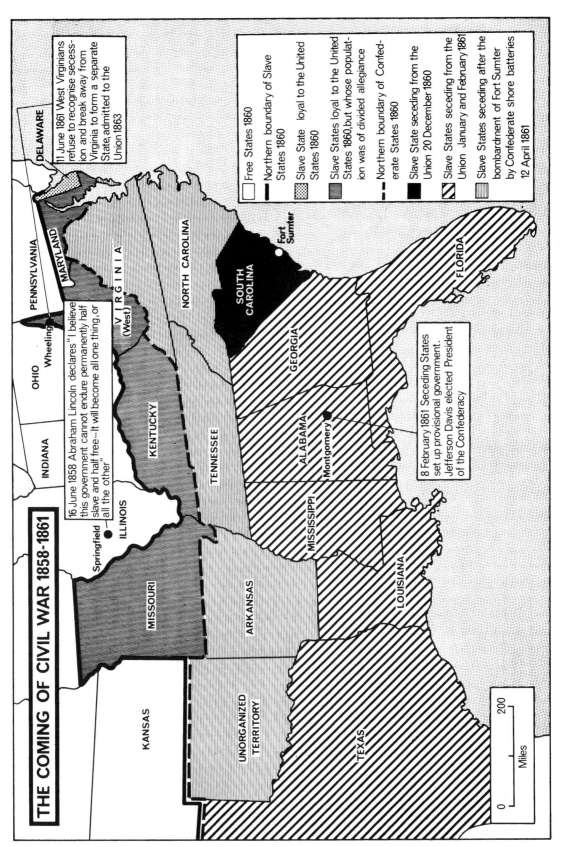

THE COMING OF CIVIL WAR 1858-1861

Legend:

Free States 1860

Northern boundary of Slave States 1860

Slave State loyal to the United States 1860

Slave States loyal to the United States 1860, but whose population was of divided allegiance

Northern boundary of Confederate States 1860

Slave State seceding from the Union 20 December 1860

Slave States seceding from the Union January and February 1861

Slave States seceding after the bombardment of Fort Sumter by Confederate shore batteries 12 April 1861

11 June 1861 West Virginians refuse to recognise secession and break away from Virginia to form a separate State, admitted to the Union 1863

16 June 1858 Abraham Lincoln declares "I believe this government cannot endure permanently half slave and half free...It will become all one thing, or all the other"

8 February 1861 Seceding States set up provisional government. Jefferson Davis elected President of the Confederacy

DELAWARE

PENNSYLVANIA

OHIO
Wheeling

INDIANA

ILLINOIS
Springfield

MISSOURI

KANSAS

UNORGANIZED TERRITORY

ARKANSAS

TENNESSEE

KENTUCKY

VIRGINIA
(West)

MARYLAND

NORTH CAROLINA

SOUTH CAROLINA

Fort Sumter

GEORGIA

ALABAMA

MISSISSIPPI
Montgomery

LOUISIANA

TEXAS

FLORIDA

0   200
Miles

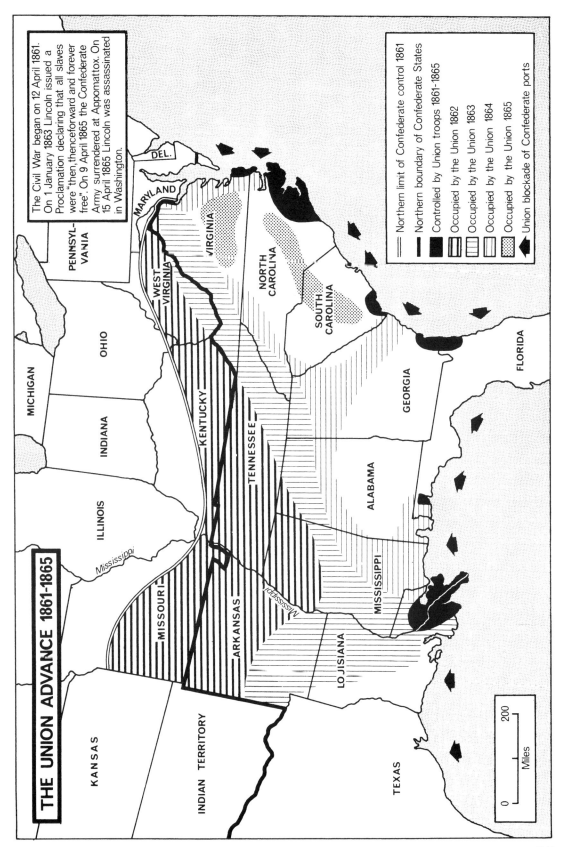

THE UNION ADVANCE 1861-1865

The Civil War began on 12 April 1861. On 1 January 1863 Lincoln issued a Proclamation declaring that all slaves were "then, thenceforward and forever free". On 9 April 1865 the Confederate Army surrendered at Appomattox. On 15 April 1865 Lincoln was assassinated in Washington.

Northern limit of Confederate control 1861
Northern boundary of Confederate States
Controlled by Union troops 1861-1865
Occupied by the Union 1862
Occupied by the Union 1863
Occupied by the Union 1864
Occupied by the Union 1865
Union blockade of Confederate ports

MICHIGAN
PENNSYLVANIA
DEL.
MARYLAND
OHIO
INDIANA
ILLINOIS
KANSAS
INDIAN TERRITORY
MISSOURI
ARKANSAS
TEXAS
LOUISIANA
MISSISSIPPI
ALABAMA
GEORGIA
FLORIDA
TENNESSEE
KENTUCKY
WEST VIRGINIA
VIRGINIA
NORTH CAROLINA
SOUTH CAROLINA
LOUISIANA

Mississippi
Mississippi

0   200
Miles

55

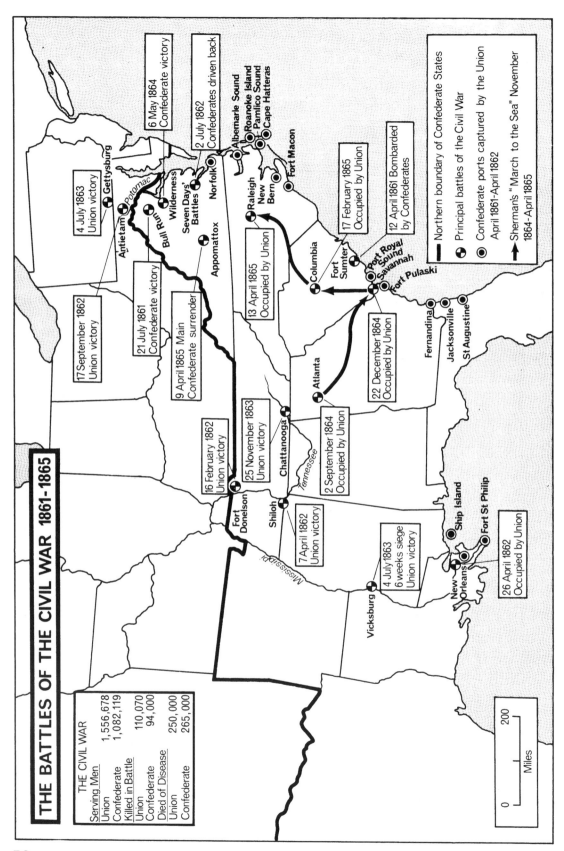

THE BATTLES OF THE CIVIL WAR 1861-1865

THE CIVIL WAR
Serving Men
Union   1,556,678
Confederate   1,082,119
Killed in Battle
Union   110,070
Confederate   94,000
Died of Disease
Union   250,000
Confederate   265,000

4 July 1863
Union victory

6 May 1864
Confederate victory

2 July 1862
Confederates driven back

17 February 1865
Occupied by Union

12 April 1861 Bombarded
by Confederates

Gettysburg

Antietam
Bull Run
Wilderness
Seven Days'
Battles
Norfolk
Raleigh
New
Bern
Columbia
Fort
Sumter
Port Royal
Sound
Savannah
Fort Pulaski

Appomattox

Potomac

Albemarle Sound
Roanoke Island
Pamlico Sound
Cape Hatteras
Fort Macon

17 September 1862
Union victory

21 July 1861
Confederate victory

9 April 1865 Main
Confederate surrender

13 April 1865
Occupied by Union

22 December 1864
Occupied by Union

Fernandina
Jacksonville
St Augustine

16 February 1862
Union victory

25 November 1863
Union victory

2 September 1864
Occupied by Union

Atlanta

Fort
Donelson
Chattanooga

Tennessee

Shiloh

7 April 1862
Union victory

Ship Island
Fort St Philip

New
Orleans

26 April 1862
Occupied by Union

4 July 1863
6 weeks siege
Union victory

Vicksburg

Mississippi

— Northern boundary of Confederate States

◑ Principal battles of the Civil War

◉ Confederate ports captured by the Union
  April 1861-April 1862

→ Sherman's "March to the Sea" November
  1864-April 1865

0   200
Miles

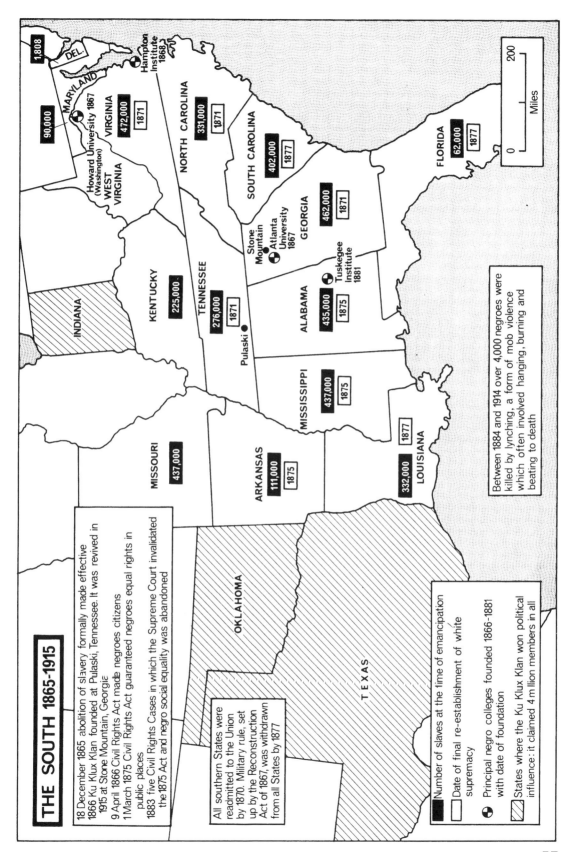

THE SOUTH 1865-1915

18 December 1865 abolition of slavery formally made effective
1866 Ku Klux Klan founded at Pulaski, Tennessee. It was revived in 1915 at Stone Mountain, Georgia
9 April 1866 Civil Rights Act made negroes citizens
1 March 1875 Civil Rights Act guaranteed negroes equal rights in public places
1883 five Civil Rights Cases in which the Supreme Court invalidated the 1875 Act and negro social equality was abandoned

All southern States were readmitted to the Union by 1870. Military rule, set up by the Reconstruction Act of 1867, was withdrawn from all States by 1877

Between 1884 and 1914 over 4,000 negroes were killed by lynching, a form of mob violence which often involved hanging, burning and beating to death

■ Number of slaves at the time of emancipation
□ Date of final re-establishment of white supremacy
◕ Principal negro colleges founded 1866-1881 with date of foundation
▨ States where the Ku Klux Klan won political influence: it claimed 4 million members in all

TEXAS

OKLAHOMA

MISSOURI 437,000

ARKANSAS 111,000 1875

LOUISIANA 332,000 1877

MISSISSIPPI 437,000 1875

TENNESSEE 276,000 1871

Pulaski ●

KENTUCKY 225,000

INDIANA

ALABAMA 435,000 1875

Tuskegee Institute 1881 ◕

GEORGIA 462,000 1871

Stone Mountain ●
Atlanta University 1867 ◕

SOUTH CAROLINA 402,000 1877

NORTH CAROLINA 331,000 1871

VIRGINIA 472,000 1871

WEST VIRGINIA

Howard University (Washington) 1867

MARYLAND 90,000

DEL. 1,808

Hampton Institute 1868 ◕

FLORIDA 62,000 1877

0 ___ 200
Miles

57

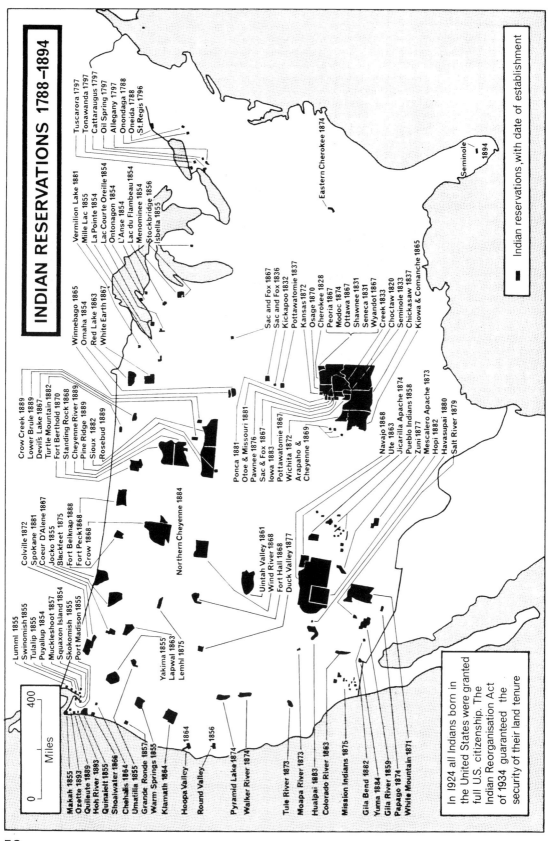

INDIAN RESERVATIONS 1788–1894

Makah 1855
Ozette 1893
Quileute 1889
Hoh River 1893
Quinaielt 1855
Shoalwater 1866
Chehalis 1864
Umatilla 1855
Grande Ronde 1857
Warm Springs 1855
Klamath 1864

Hoopa Valley

Round Valley

Pyramid Lake 1874
Walker River 1874

Tule River 1873

Moapa River 1873

Huaipai 1883
Colorado River 1863

Mission Indians 1875

Gila Bend 1882
Yuma 1884
Gila River 1859
Papago 1874
White Mountain 1871

Lummi 1855
Swinomish 1855
Tulalip 1855
Muckleshoot 1857
Squaxon Island 1854
Skokomish 1855
Port Madison 1855

Colville 1872
Spokane 1881
Coeur D'Alene 1867
Jocko 1855
Blackfeet 1875
Fort Belknap 1888
Fort Peck 1868
Crow 1868

Yakima 1855
Lapwal 1863
Lemhi 1875

1864

1856

Northern Cheyenne 1884

Uintah Valley 1861
Wind River 1868
Fort Hall 1868
Duck Valley 1877

Crow Creek 1889
Lower Brule 1889
Devils Lake 1867
Turtle Mountain 1882
Fort Berthold 1870
Standing Rock 1868
Cheyenne River 1889
Pine Ridge 1889
Sioux 1882
Rosebud 1889

Ponca 1881
Otoe & Missouri 1881
Pawnee 1876
Sac & Fox 1867
Iowa 1883
Pottawatomie 1867
Wichita 1872
Arapaho &
Cheyenne 1869

Winnebago 1865
Omaha 1854
Red Lake 1863
White Earth 1867

Sac and Fox 1867
Sac and Fox 1836
Kickapoo 1832
Pottawatomie 1837
Kansas 1872
Osage 1870
Cherokee 1828
Peoria 1867
Modoc 1874
Ottawa 1867
Shawnee 1831
Seneca 1831
Wyandot 1867
Creek 1833
Choctaw 1820
Seminole 1833
Chickasaw 1837
Kiowa & Comanche 1865

Vermilion Lake 1881
Mille Lac 1855
La Pointe 1854
Lac Courte Oreille 1854
Ontonagon 1854
L'Anse 1854
Lac du Flambeau 1854
Menomine 1854
Stockbridge 1856
Isbella 1855

Tuscarora 1797
Tonawanda 1797
Cattaraugus 1797
Oil Spring 1797
Allegany 1797
Onondaga 1788
Oneida 1788
St. Regis 1796

Navajo 1868
Ute 1863
Jicarilla Apache 1874
Pueblo Indians 1858
Zuni 1877
Mescalero Apache 1873
Hopi 1882
Havasupai 1880
Salt River 1879

Eastern Cherokee 1874

Seminole
1894

0   400
Miles

In 1924 all Indians born in
the United States were granted
full U.S. citizenship. The
Indian Reorganisation Act
of 1934 guaranteed the
security of their land tenure

■   Indian reservations, with date of establishment

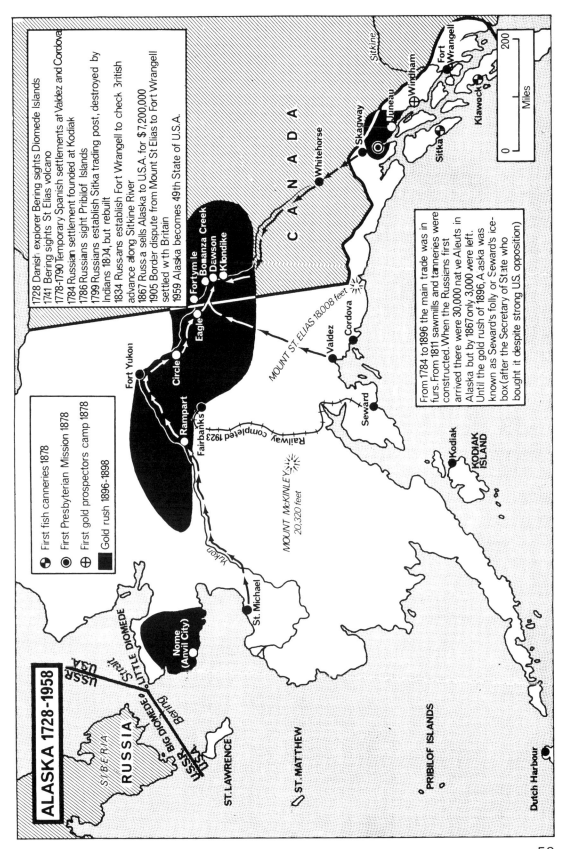

ALASKA 1728-1958

1728 Danish explorer Bering sights Diomede Islands
1741 Bering sights St Elias volcano
1778-1790 Temporary Spanish settlements at Valdez and Cordova
1784 Russian settlement founded at Kodiak
1786 Russians sight Pribilof Islands
1799 Russians establish Sitka trading post, destroyed by Indians 1804, but rebuilt
1834 Russians establish Fort Wrangell to check British advance along Sitkine River
1867 Russia sells Alaska to U.S.A. for $7,200,000
1905 Border dispute from Mount St Elias to Fort Wrangell settled with Britain
1959 Alaska becomes 49th State of U.S.A.

☉ First fish canneries 1878
◉ First Presbyterian Mission 1878
⊕ First gold prospectors camp 1878
■ Gold rush 1896-1898

From 1784 to 1896 the main trade was in furs. From 1811 sawmills and tanneries were constructed. When the Russians first arrived there were 30,000 native Aleuts in Alaska but by 1867 only 3,000 were left. Until the gold rush of 1896, Alaska was known as Seward's folly or Seward's icebox (after the Secretary of State who bought it despite strong U.S. opposition)

0   200
Miles

SOCIAL DISCONTENT 1876-1932

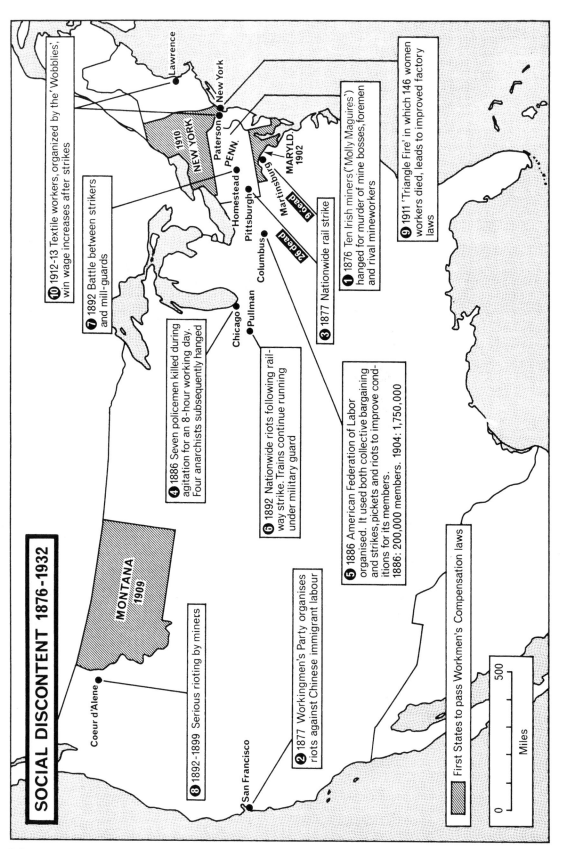

10 1912-13 Textile workers, organized by the 'Wobblies', win wage increases after strikes

7 1892 Battle between strikers and mill-guards

4 1886 Seven policemen killed during agitation for an 8-hour working day. Four anarchists subsequently hanged

6 1892 Nationwide riots following railway strike. Trains continue running under military guard

9 1911 'Triangle Fire' in which 146 women workers died, leads to improved factory laws

1 1876 Ten Irish miners ('Molly Maguires') hanged for murder of mine bosses, foremen and rival mineworkers

3 1877 Nationwide rail strike

5 1886 American Federation of Labor organised. It used both collective bargaining and strikes, pickets and riots to improve conditions for its members.
1886: 200,000 members. 1904: 1,750,000

8 1892-1899 Serious rioting by miners

2 1877 Workingmen's Party organises riots against Chinese immigrant labour

Lawrence
New York
Paterson
PENN.
1910
NEW YORK
Homestead
Pittsburgh
MARYLD.
1902
Martinsburg
9 dead
28 dead
Columbus
Pullman
Chicago
MONTANA
1909
Coeur d'Alene
San Francisco

First States to pass Workmen's Compensation laws

Miles
0   500

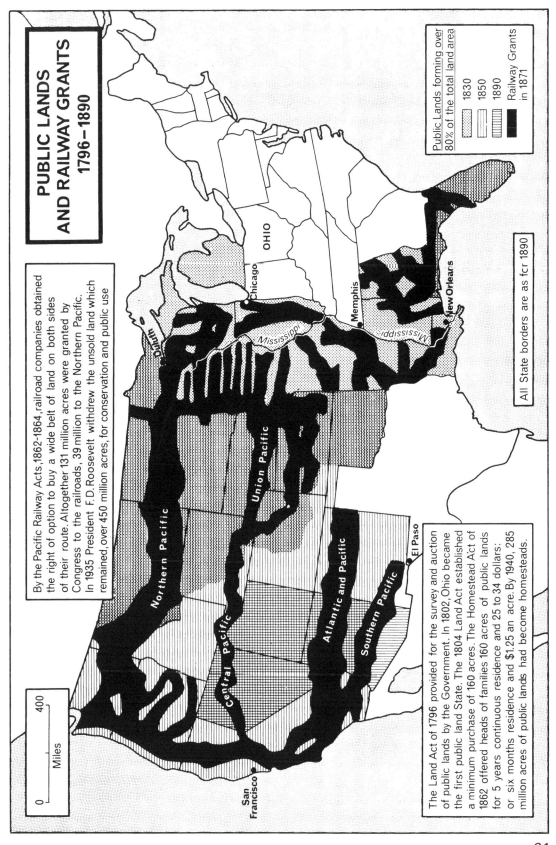

PUBLIC LANDS AND RAILWAY GRANTS 1796–1890

By the Pacific Railway Acts,1862-1864, railroad companies obtained the right of option to buy a wide belt of land on both sides of their route. Altogether 131 million acres were granted by Congress to the railroads, 39 million to the Northern Pacific. In 1935 President F.D. Roosevelt withdrew the unsold land which remained, over 450 million acres, for conservation and public use

The Land Act of 1796 provided for the survey and auction of public lands by the Government. In 1802, Ohio became the first public land State. The 1804 Land Act established a minimum purchase of 160 acres. The Homestead Act of 1862 offered heads of families 160 acres of public lands for 5 years continuous residence and 25 to 34 dollars; or six months residence and $1.25 an acre. By 1940, 285 million acres of public lands had become homesteads.

Public Lands forming over 80% of the total land area
- 1830
- 1850
- 1890
- Railway Grants in 1871

All State borders are as for 1890

Miles
0   400

Northern Pacific
Central Pacific
Union Pacific
Atlantic and Pacific
Southern Pacific

San Francisco
Duluth
Chicago
OHIO
Memphis
Mississippi
Mississippi
New Orleans
El Paso

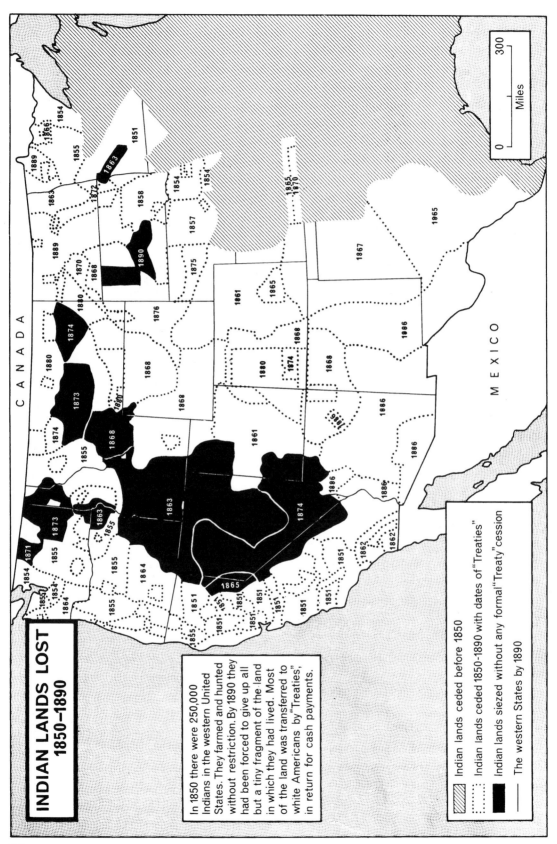

INDIAN LANDS LOST 1850–1890

In 1850 there were 250,000 Indians in the western United States. They farmed and hunted without restriction. By 1890 they had been forced to give up all but a tiny fragment of the land in which they had lived. Most of the land was transferred to white Americans by "Treaties", in return for cash payments.

CANADA

MEXICO

Miles

0   300

Indian lands ceded before 1850

Indian lands ceded 1850–1890 with dates of "Treaties"

Indian lands siezed without any formal "Treaty" cession

The western States by 1890

1854
1866
1889
1855
1863
1851
1872
1863
1858
1854
1854
1889
1857
1870
1868
1890
1875
1880
1874
1876
1865
1870
1865
1880
1873
1868
1855
1868
1861
1865
1867
1868
1868
1855
1855
1863
1855
1874
1880
1868
1874
1868
1873
1863
1871
1854
1855
1855
1855
1864
1861
1886
1866
1886
1865
1874
1886
1886
1886
1854
1854
1864
1855
1851
1865
1851
1851
1851
1851
1862
1862
1855
1855
1851
1851
1851

62

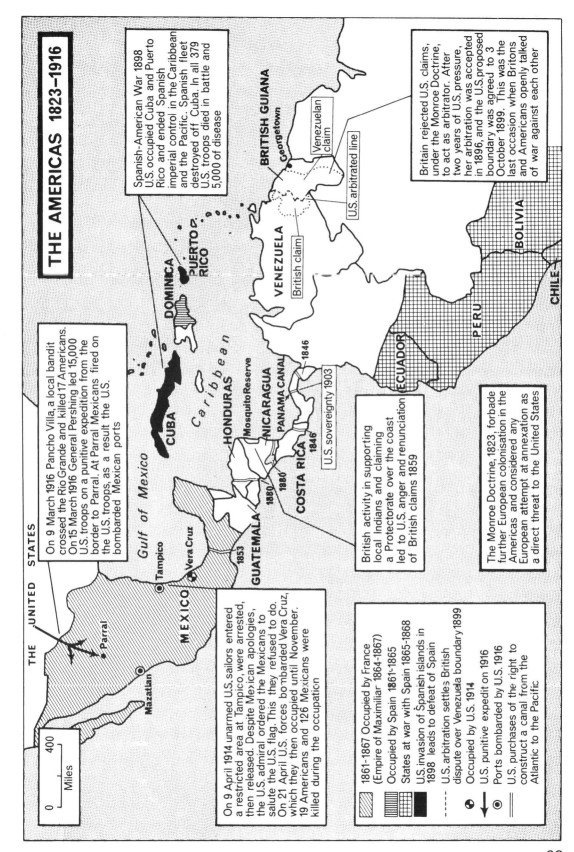

THE AMERICAS 1823–1916

Spanish-American War 1898 U.S. occupied Cuba and Puerto Rico and ended Spanish imperial control in the Caribbean and the Pacific. Spanish fleet destroyed off Cuba. In all 379 U.S. troops died in battle and 5,000 of disease

Britain rejected U.S. claims, under the Monroe Doctrine, to act as arbitrator. After two years of U.S. pressure, her arbitration was accepted in 1896, and the U.S. proposed boundary was agreed to 3 October 1899. This was the last occasion when Britons and Americans openly talked of war against each other

BRITISH GUIANA

Georgetown

Venezuelan claim

U.S. arbitrated line

VENEZUELA

British claim

DOMINECA

PUERTO RICO

CUBA

Caribbean

1846

British activity in supporting local Indians and claiming a Protectorate over the coast led to U.S. anger and renunciation of British claims 1859

ECUADOR

PERU

BOLIVIA

CHILE

HONDURAS

MosquitoReserve

NICARAGUA

PANAMA CANAL

COSTA RICA

1846

1880

1880

U.S. sovereignty 1903

GUATEMALA

1853

Gulf of Mexico

Tampico

Vera Cruz

MEXICO

Mazatlan

Parral

THE UNITED STATES

On 9 March 1916 Pancho Villa, a local bandit crossed the Rio Grande and killed 17 Americans. On 15 March 1916 General Pershing led 15,000 U.S. troops on a punitive expedition from the border to Parral. At Parral Mexicans fired on the U.S. troops, as a result the U.S. bombarded Mexican ports

On 9 April 1914 unarmed U.S. sailors entered a restricted area at Tampico, were arrested, then released. Despite Mexican apologies, the U.S. admiral ordered the Mexicans to salute the U.S. flag. This they refused to do. On 21 April U.S. forces bombarded Vera Cruz, which they then occupied until November. 19 Americans and 126 Mexicans were killed during the occupation

0   400
Miles

1861-1867 Occupied by France (Empire of Maximilian 1864-1867)

Occupied by Spain 1861-1865

States at war with Spain 1865-1868

U.S. invasion of Spanish islands in 1898 leads to defeat of Spain

----- U.S. arbitration settles British dispute over Venezuela boundary 1899

◑ Occupied by U.S. 1914

↓ U.S. punitive expedit on 1916

◉ Ports bombarded by U.S. 1916

═ U.S. purchases of the right to construct a canal from the Atlantic to the Pacific

The Monroe Doctrine, 1823, forbade further European colonisation in the Americas and considered any European attempt at annexation as a direct threat to the United States

63

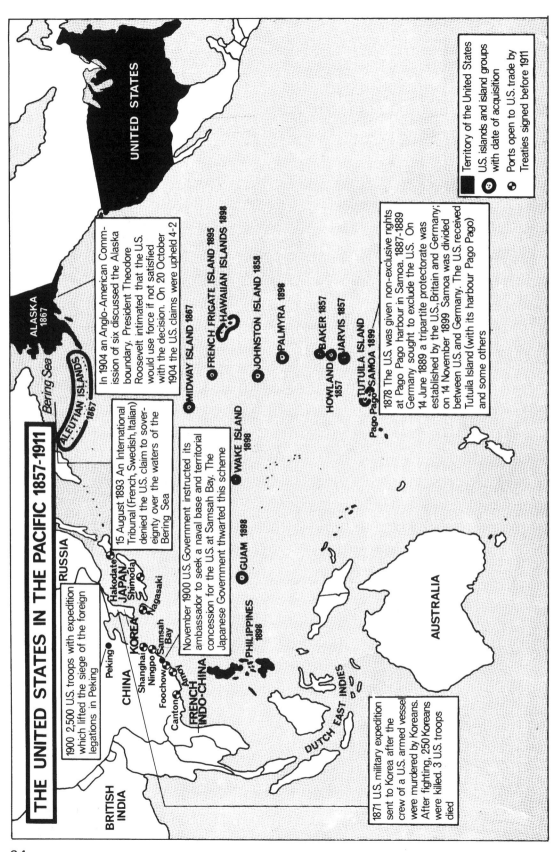

THE UNITED STATES IN THE PACIFIC 1857-1911

1900 2,500 U.S. troops with expedition which lifted the siege of the foreign legations in Peking

15 August 1893 An International Tribunal (French, Swedish, Italian) denied the U.S. claim to sovereignty over the waters of the Bering Sea

November 1900 U.S. Government instructed its ambassador to seek a naval base and territorial concession for the U.S. at Samsah Bay. The Japanese Government thwarted this scheme

In 1904 an Anglo-American Commission of six discussed the Alaska boundary. President Theodore Roosevelt intimated that the U.S. would use force if not satisfied with the decision. On 20 October 1904 the U.S. claims were upheld 4-2

1878 The U.S. was given non-exclusive rights at Pago Pago harbour in Samoa. 1887-1889 Germany sought to exclude the U.S. On 14 June 1889 a tripartite protectorate was established by the U.S., Britain and Germany; on 14 November 1899 Samoa was divided between U.S. and Germany. The U.S. received Tutuila Island (with its harbour Pago Pago) and some others

1871 U.S. military expedition sent to Korea after the crew of a U.S. armed vessel were murdered by Koreans. After fighting, 250 Koreans were killed. 3 U.S. troops died

UNITED STATES

ALASKA 1867

ALEUTIAN ISLANDS 1867

Bering Sea

RUSSIA

BRITISH INDIA

CHINA

Peking

Shanghai

Ningpo

Foochow

Amoy

Canton

FRENCH INDO-CHINA

KOREA

Samsah Bay

JAPAN

Hakodate

Shimoda

Nagasaki

PHILIPPINES 1898

GUAM 1898

WAKE ISLAND 1898

MIDWAY ISLAND 1867

FRENCH FRIGATE ISLAND 1895

HAWAIIAN ISLANDS 1898

JOHNSTON ISLAND 1858

PALMYRA 1898

HOWLAND 1857

BAKER 1857

JARVIS 1857

TUTUILA ISLAND

Pago Pago SAMOA 1899

DUTCH EAST INDIES

AUSTRALIA

Territory of the United States

U.S. islands and island groups with date of acquisition

Ports open to U.S. trade by Treaties signed before 1911

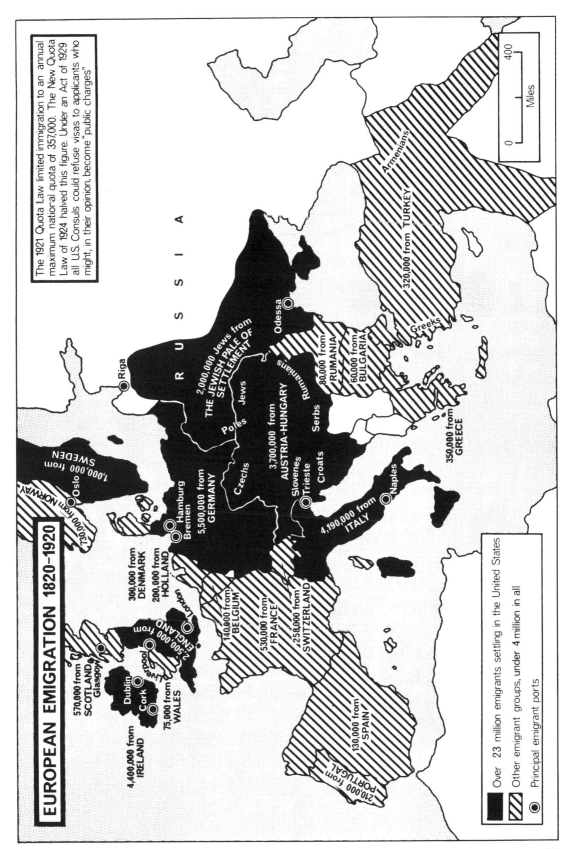

EUROPEAN EMIGRATION 1820–1920

The 1921 Quota Law limited immigration to an annual maximum national quota of 357,000. The New Quota Law of 1924 halved this figure. Under an Act of 1929 all U.S. Consuls could refuse visas to applicants who might, in their opinion, become "public charges"

730,000 from NORWAY

1,000,000 from SWEDEN

570,000 from SCOTLAND, Glasgow

4,400,000 from IRELAND

75,000 from WALES

2,500,000 from ENGLAND

300,000 from DENMARK

200,000 from HOLLAND

140,000 from BELGIUM

530,000 from FRANCE

258,000 from SWITZERLAND

130,000 from SPAIN

210,000 from PORTUGAL

5,500,000 from GERMANY

2,000,000 Jews from THE JEWISH PALE OF SETTLEMENT

Poles   Jews

Czechs

3,700,000 from AUSTRIA-HUNGARY

Slovenes

Croats   Serbs

Rumanians

4,190,000 from ITALY

80,000 from RUMANIA

60,000 from BULGARIA

350,000 from GREECE

Greeks

320,000 from TURKEY

Armenians

R U S S I A

Riga   Odessa   Oslo   Hamburg   Bremen   Trieste   Naples   London   Liverpool   Dublin   Cork

Miles   0   400

Over 23 million emigrants settling in the United States

Other emigrant groups, under 4 million in all

Principal emigrant ports

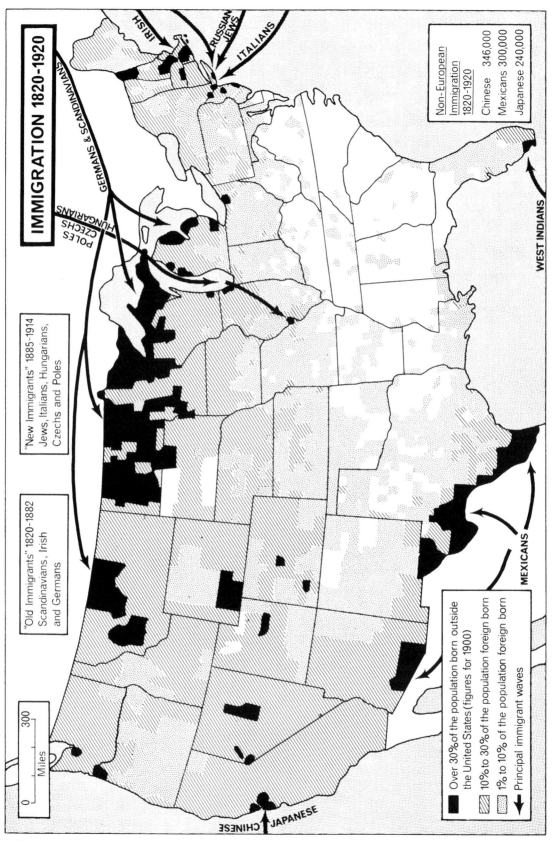

IMMIGRATION 1820-1920

IRISH
RUSSIAN JEWS
ITALIANS
GERMANS & SCANDINAVIANS
SCANDINAVIANS
POLES CZECHS HUNGARIANS

Non-European
Immigration
1820-1920

Chinese 346,000
Mexicans 300,000
Japanese 240,000

WEST INDIANS

"New Immigrants" 1885-1914
Jews, Italians, Hungarians,
Czechs and Poles

"Old Immigrants" 1820-1882
Scandinavians, Irish
and Germans

MEXICANS

300

Miles

0

CHINESE JAPANESE

▉ Over 30% of the population born outside
the United States (figures for 1900)

▨ 10% to 30% of the population foreign born

░ 1% to 10% of the population foreign born

→ Principal immigrant waves

66

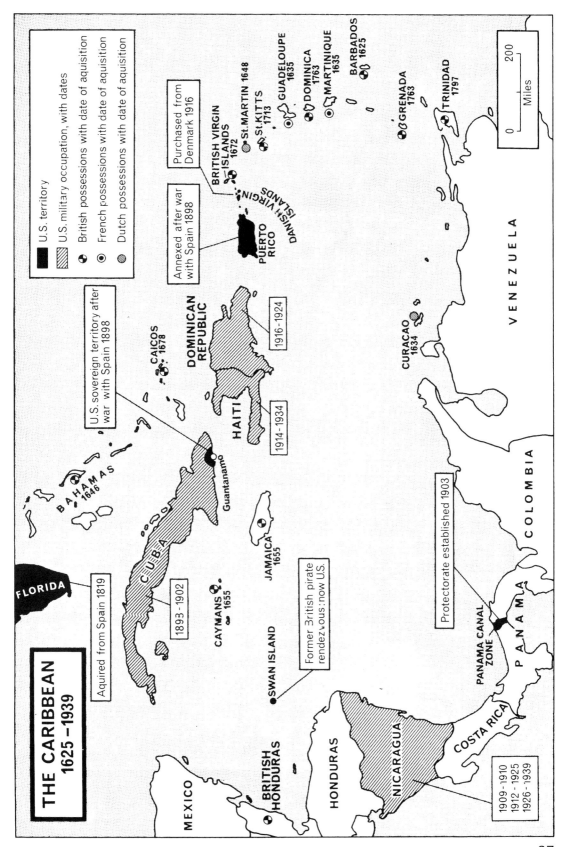

THE CARIBBEAN
1625 – 1939

U.S. territory
U.S. military occupation, with dates
British possessions with date of aquisition
French possessions with date of aquisition
Dutch possessions with date of aquisition

Aquired from Spain 1819

U.S. sovereign territory after war with Spain 1898

Former British pirate rendezvous: now U.S.

Protectorate established 1903

Annexed after war with Spain 1898

Purchased from Denmark 1916

200
Miles
0

MEXICO
BRITISH HONDURAS
HONDURAS
NICARAGUA
COSTA RICA
PANAMA
PANAMA CANAL ZONE
COLOMBIA
VENEZUELA

FLORIDA
BAHAMAS 1646
CUBA
Guantanamo
CAYMANS 1655
JAMAICA 1655
SWAN ISLAND
CAICOS 1678
HAITI
DOMINICAN REPUBLIC
PUERTO RICO
DANISH VIRGIN ISLANDS
BRITISH VIRGIN ISLANDS 1672
St. MARTIN 1648
St. KITTS 1713
GUADELOUPE 1635
DOMINICA 1763
MARTINIQUE 1635
BARBADOS 1625
GRENADA 1763
TRINIDAD 1797
CURACAO 1634

1893 - 1902
1914 - 1934
1916 - 1924
1909 - 1910
1912 - 1925
1926 - 1939

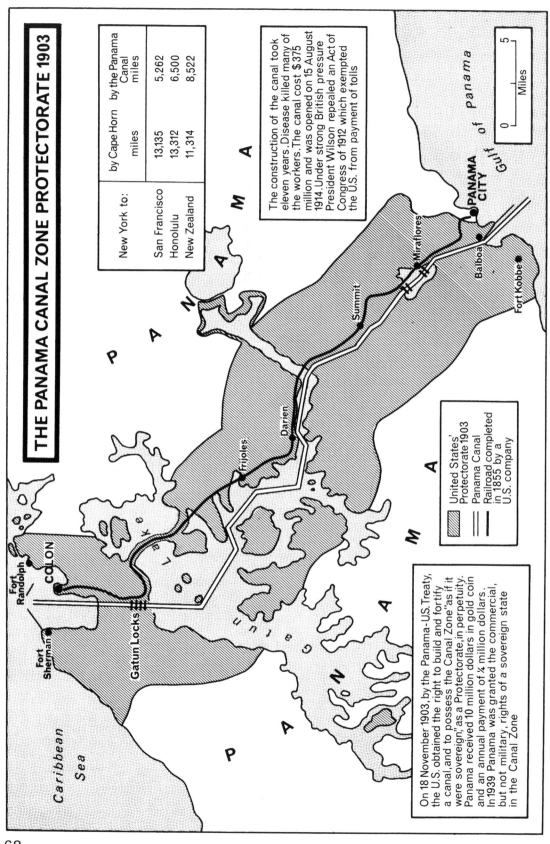

THE PANAMA CANAL ZONE PROTECTORATE 1903

New York to:	by Cape Horn miles	by the Panama Canal miles
San Francisco	13,135	5,262
Honolulu	13,312	6,500
New Zealand	11,314	8,522

The construction of the canal took eleven years. Disease killed many of the workers. The canal cost $375 million and was opened on 15 August 1914. Under strong British pressure President Wilson repealed an Act of Congress of 1912 which exempted the U.S. from payment of tolls

On 18 November 1903, by the Panama-U.S. Treaty, the U.S. obtained the right to build and fortify a canal, and to possess the Canal Zone "as if it were sovereign," as a Protectorate, in perpetuity. Panama received 10 million dollars in gold coin and an annual payment of ¼ million dollars. In 1939 Panama was granted the commercial, but not military, rights of a sovereign state in the Canal Zone

Legend:
- United States' Protectorate 1903
- Panama Canal
- Railroad completed in 1855 by a U.S. company

Caribbean Sea

Fort Sherman
Fort Randolph
COLON
Gatun Locks

Frijoles

Darien

Summit

Miraflores

Balboa

PANAMA CITY

Fort Kobbe

Gulf of Panama

P A N A M A

0   5
Miles

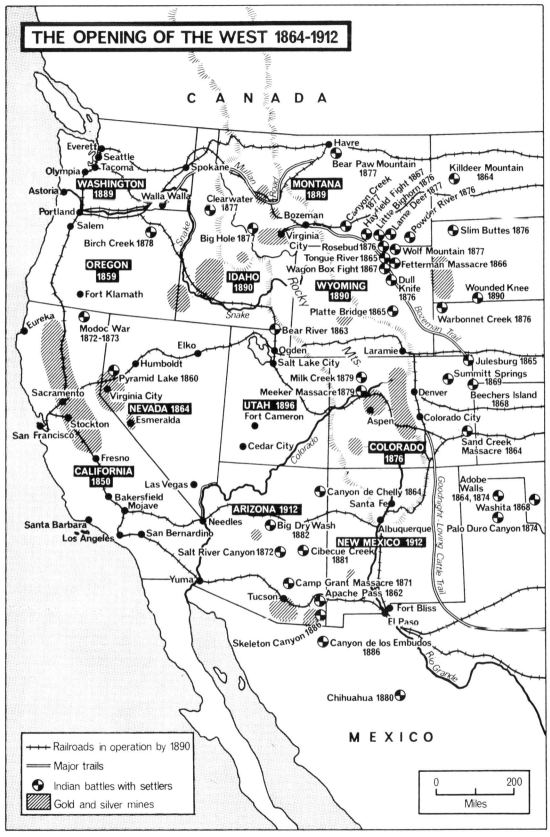

THE OPENING OF THE WEST 1864-1912

CANADA

Everett
Seattle
Tacoma
Olympia
Astoria
Portland
Salem

WASHINGTON 1889

Spokane
Walla Walla

Mullan Road

Clearwater 1877

MONTANA 1889

Havre
Bear Paw Mountain 1877

Killdeer Mountain 1864

Canyon Creek 1877
Hayfield Fight 1867
Little Bighorn 1876
Lame Deer 1877
Powder River 1876

Bozeman

Slim Buttes 1876

Virginia City
Big Hole 1877

Rosebud 1876
Tongue River 1865
Wagon Box Fight 1867

Wolf Mountain 1877
Fetterman Massacre 1866

OREGON 1859

Birch Creek 1878

Fort Klamath

IDAHO 1890

Snake

Snake

Rocky

WYOMING 1890

Dull Knife 1876

Wounded Knee 1890

Platte Bridge 1865

Warbonnet Creek 1876

Bozeman Trail

Eureka

Modoc War 1872-1873

Elko

Humboldt
Pyramid Lake 1860

Sacramento

Virginia City

NEVADA 1864

Esmeralda

Stockton

San Francisco

Fresno

CALIFORNIA 1850

Bakersfield
Mojave

Santa Barbara
Los Angeles

San Bernardino

Needles

Bear River 1863

Ogden
Salt Lake City

Milk Creek 1879
Meeker Massacre 1879

Laramie

Mts.

Julesburg 1865

Summitt Springs 1869

Denver

Beechers Island 1868

UTAH 1896
Fort Cameron

Aspen

Colorado City

Sand Creek Massacre 1864

Cedar City

Colorado

COLORADO 1876

Las Vegas

Canyon de Chelly 1864

Santa Fe

ARIZONA 1912

Big Dry Wash 1882

Salt River Canyon 1872

Cibecue Creek 1881

Albuquerque

NEW MEXICO 1912

Adobe Walls 1864, 1874

Washita 1868

Palo Duro Canyon 1874

Goodnight - Loving Cattle Trail

Yuma

Camp Grant Massacre 1871
Apache Pass 1862

Tucson

Fort Bliss

El Paso

Skeleton Canyon 1886

Canyon de los Embudos 1886

Rio Grande

Chihuahua 1880

MEXICO

Railroads in operation by 1890
Major trails
Indian battles with settlers
Gold and silver mines

0   200
Miles

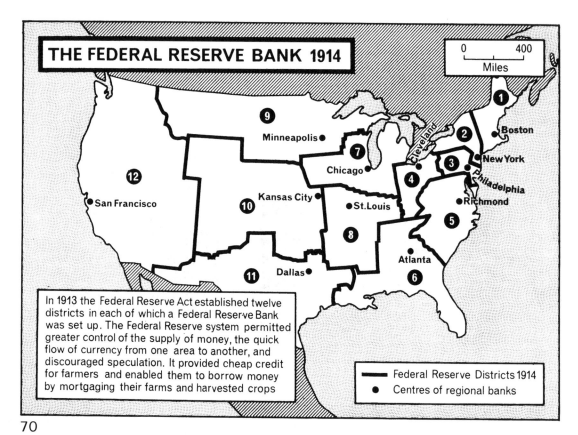

THE FEDERAL RESERVE BANK 1914

0 — 400
Miles

①
②
Boston
New York
③
Cleveland
④
Philadelphia
⑤
Richmond
⑥
Atlanta
⑦
⑧
St. Louis
⑨
Minneapolis
⑩
Kansas City
⑪
Dallas
⑫
San Francisco
Chicago

In 1913 the Federal Reserve Act established twelve districts in each of which a Federal Reserve Bank was set up. The Federal Reserve system permitted greater control of the supply of money, the quick flow of currency from one area to another, and discouraged speculation. It provided cheap credit for farmers and enabled them to borrow money by mortgaging their farms and harvested crops

—— Federal Reserve Districts 1914
● Centres of regional banks

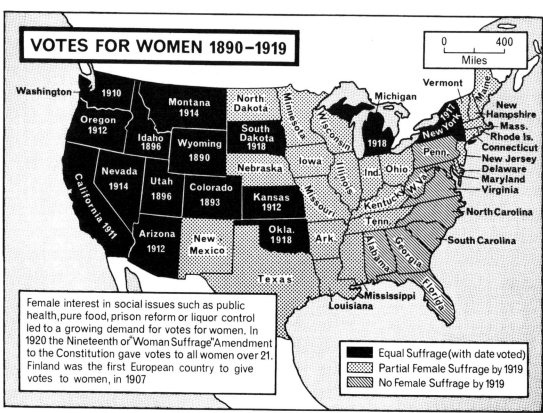

VOTES FOR WOMEN 1890–1919

0 — 400
Miles

Washington 1910
Oregon 1912
Idaho 1896
Montana 1914
Wyoming 1890
North Dakota
South Dakota 1918
Minnesota
Wisconsin
Michigan
Vermont
Maine
New Hampshire
Mass.
Rhode Is.
New York 1917
1918
Penn.
Connecticut
New Jersey
Delaware
Maryland
Virginia
Nevada 1914
Utah 1896
Colorado 1893
Nebraska
Iowa
Illinois
Ind.
Ohio
W. Va.
Kentucky
North Carolina
California 1911
Arizona 1912
New Mexico
Kansas 1912
Okla. 1918
Missouri
Tenn.
Ark
Alabama
Georgia
South Carolina
Texas
Mississippi
Louisiana
Florida

Female interest in social issues such as public health, pure food, prison reform or liquor control led to a growing demand for votes for women. In 1920 the Nineteenth or "Woman Suffrage" Amendment to the Constitution gave votes to all women over 21. Finland was the first European country to give votes to women, in 1907

■ Equal Suffrage (with date voted)
▦ Partial Female Suffrage by 1919
▨ No Female Suffrage by 1919

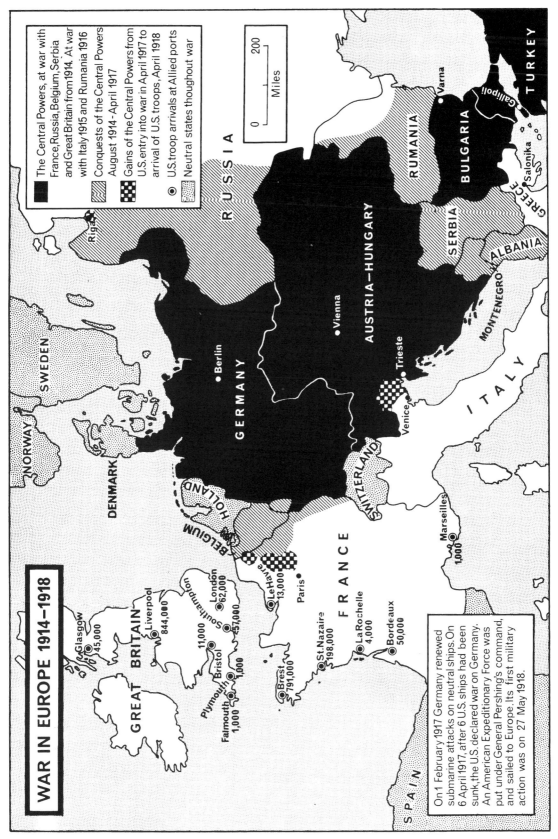

WAR IN EUROPE 1914–1918

The Central Powers, at war with France, Russia, Belgium, Serbia and Great Britain from 1914. At war with Italy 1915 and Rumania 1916

Conquests of the Central Powers August 1914 – April 1917

Gains of the Central Powers from U.S. entry into war in April 1917 to arrival of U.S. troops, April 1918

⊙ U.S. troop arrivals at Allied ports

Neutral states thoughout war

0 | 200
Miles

On 1 February 1917 Germany renewed submarine attacks on neutral ships. On 6 April 1917, after 6 U.S. ships had been sunk, the U.S. declared war on Germany. An American Expeditionary Force was put under General Pershing's command, and sailed to Europe. Its first military action was on 27 May 1918.

NORWAY

SWEDEN

DENMARK

HOLLAND

BELGIUM

GREAT BRITAIN

Glasgow 45,000

Liverpool 844,000

Southampton 57,000

Bristol 11,000

London 62,000

Plymouth 1,000

Falmouth 1,000

Le Havre 13,000

Brest 791,000

St. Nazaire 198,000

La Rochelle 4,000

Bordeaux 50,000

Marseilles 1,000

FRANCE

Paris

SPAIN

GERMANY

Berlin

SWITZERLAND

Vienna

AUSTRIA–HUNGARY

Trieste

Venice

ITALY

RUSSIA

Riga

RUMANIA

SERBIA

MONTENEGRO

ALBANIA

BULGARIA

Varna

Gallipoli

GREECE

Salonika

TURKEY

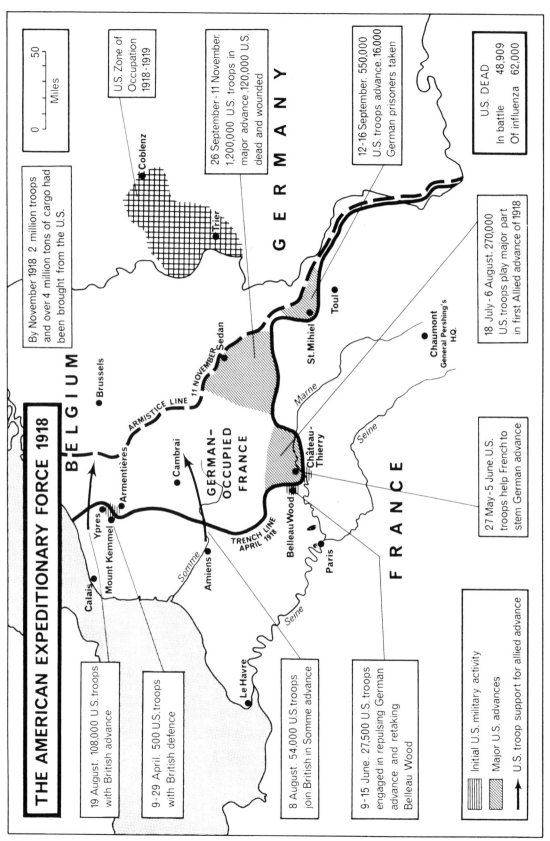

THE AMERICAN EXPEDITIONARY FORCE 1918

U.S. Zone of Occupation 1918-1919

26 September-11 November. 1,200,000 U.S. troops in major advance.120,000 U.S. dead and wounded

12-16 September. 550,000 U.S. troops advance.16,000 German prisoners taken

U.S. DEAD
In battle 48,909
Of influenza 62,000

By November 1918 2 million troops and over 4 million tons of cargo had been brought from the U.S.

18 July- 6 August. 270,000 U.S. troops play major part in first Allied advance of 1918

27 May-5 June. U.S. troops help French to stem German advance

19 August. 108,000 U.S.troops with British advance

9-29 April. 500 U.S.troops with British defence

8 August. 54,000 U.S.troops join British in Somme advance

9-15 June. 27,500 U.S. troops engaged in repulsing German advance and retaking Belleau Wood

GERMANY

BELGIUM

FRANCE

GERMAN-OCCUPIED FRANCE

Coblenz

Trier

Brussels

Sedan

ARMISTICE LINE   11 NOVEMBER

Armentières

Cambrai

Château-Thierry

Belleau Wood

Paris

Ypres

Mount Kemmel

Calais

Amiens

Le Havre

Toul

St. Mihiel

Chaumont
General Pershing's
H.Q.

TRENCH LINE
APRIL 1918

Marne

Seine

Seine

Somme

Seine

0   50
Miles

Initial U.S. military activity

Major U.S. advances

U.S. troop support for allied advance

73

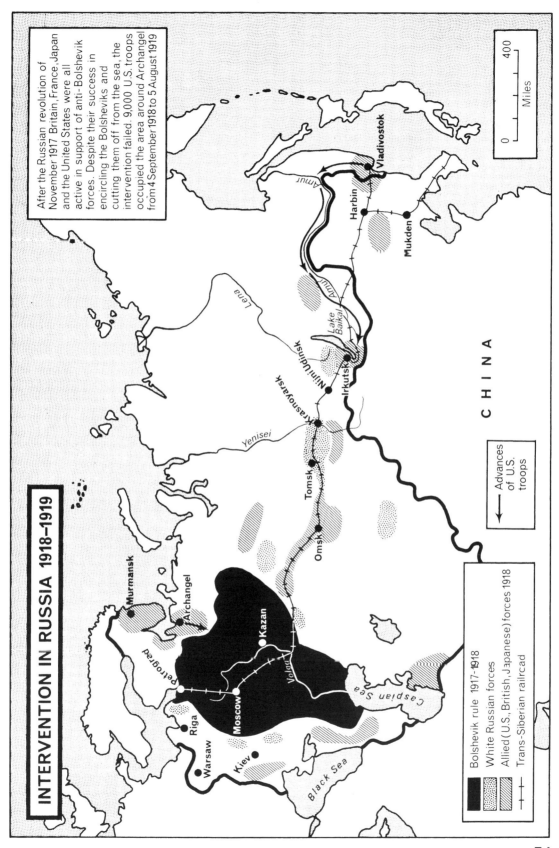

INTERVENTION IN RUSSIA 1918–1919

After the Russian revolution of November 1917 Britain, France, Japan and the United States were all active in support of anti-Bolshevik forces. Despite their success in encircling the Bolsheviks and cutting them off from the sea, the intervention failed. 9,000 U.S. troops occupied the area around Archangel from 4 September 1918 to 5 August 1919

400

0

Miles

Vladivostok

Harbin

Mukden

Amur

Amur

Lena

Lake Baikal

Nijni Udinsk

Irkutsk

Krasnoyarsk

Yenisei

Tomsk

Omsk

C H I N A

Advances of U.S. troops

Murmansk

Archangel

Kazan

Petrograd

Moscow

Volga

Riga

Warsaw

Kiev

Black Sea

Caspian Sea

Bolshevik rule 1917–1918

White Russian forces

Allied (U.S., British, Japanese) forces 1918

Trans-Siberian railroad

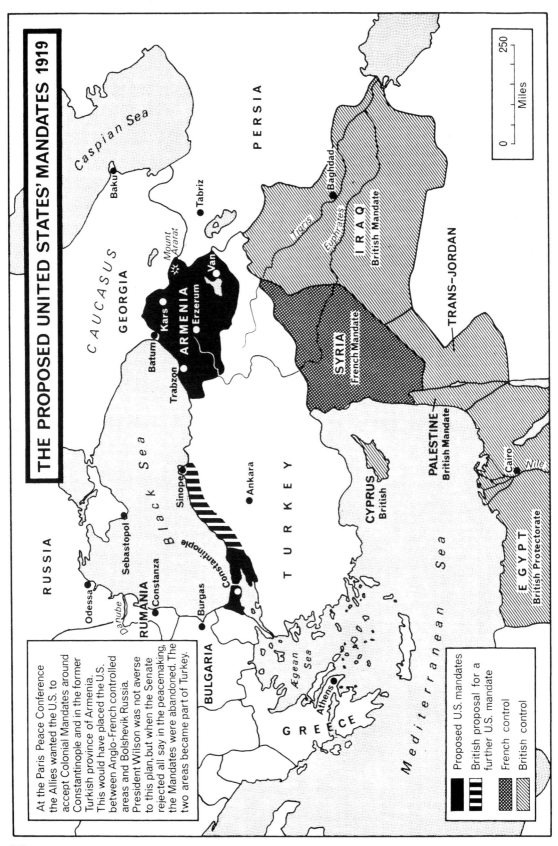

THE PROPOSED UNITED STATES' MANDATES 1919

250

Miles

0

Caspian Sea

PERSIA

Baku

Tabriz

Mount Ararat

Baghdad

Tigris

Euphrates

IRAQ
British Mandate

TRANS-JORDAN

GEORGIA

CAUCASUS

Van

ARMENIA

Kars

Erzerum

Batum

Trabzon

SYRIA
French Mandate

RUSSIA

Black Sea

Sinope

Ankara

CYPRUS
British

PALESTINE
British Mandate

Cairo

Nile

Odessa

Sebastopol

Constanza

Burgas

RUMANIA

Danube

Constantinople

TURKEY

Mediterranean Sea

EGYPT
British Protectorate

BULGARIA

Aegean Sea

Athens

GREECE

At the Paris Peace Conference the Allies wanted the U.S. to accept Colonial Mandates around Constantinople and in the former Turkish province of Armenia. This would have placed the U.S. between Anglo-French controlled areas and Bolshevik Russia. President Wilson was not averse to this plan, but when the Senate rejected all say in the peacemaking, the Mandates were abandoned. The two areas became part of Turkey.

Proposed U.S. mandates

British proposal for a further U.S. mandate

French control

British control

75

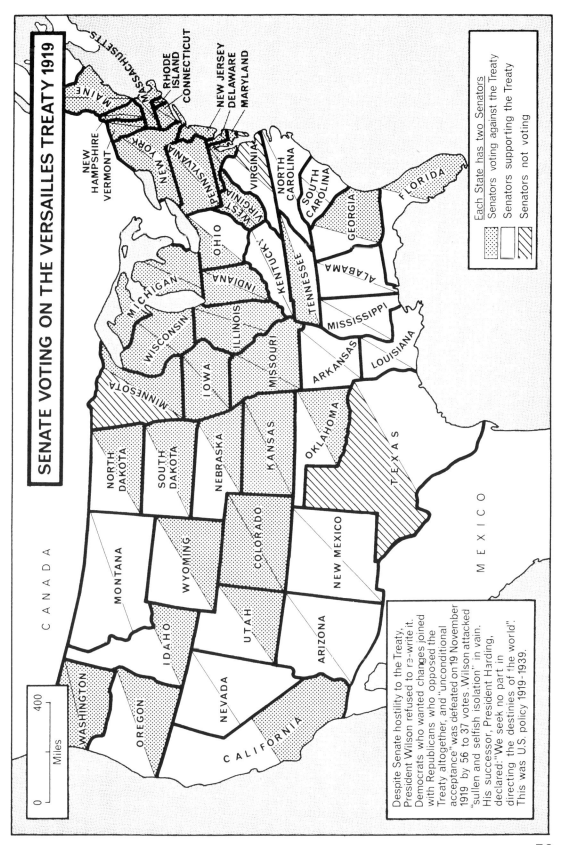

SENATE VOTING ON THE VERSAILLES TREATY 1919

CANADA

MEXICO

Each State has two Senators
Senators voting against the Treaty
Senators supporting the Treaty
Senators not voting

WASHINGTON
OREGON
CALIFORNIA
NEVADA
IDAHO
MONTANA
WYOMING
UTAH
ARIZONA
NEW MEXICO
COLORADO
NORTH DAKOTA
SOUTH DAKOTA
NEBRASKA
KANSAS
OKLAHOMA
TEXAS
MINNESOTA
IOWA
MISSOURI
ARKANSAS
LOUISIANA
WISCONSIN
MICHIGAN
ILLINOIS
INDIANA
OHIO
KENTUCKY
TENNESSEE
MISSISSIPPI
ALABAMA
GEORGIA
FLORIDA
SOUTH CAROLINA
NORTH CAROLINA
VIRGINIA
WEST VIRGINIA
PENNSYLVANIA
NEW YORK
MAINE
NEW HAMPSHIRE
VERMONT
MASSACHUSETTS
RHODE ISLAND
CONNECTICUT
NEW JERSEY
DELAWARE
MARYLAND

0   400
Miles

Despite Senate hostility to the Treaty,
President Wilson refused to re-write it.
Democrats who wanted changes joined
with Republicans who opposed the
Treaty altogether, and "unconditional
acceptance" was defeated on 19 November
1919 by 56 to 37 votes. Wilson attacked
"sullen and selfish isolation" in vain.
His successor, President Harding,
declared:"We seek no part in
directing the destinies of the world".
This was U.S. policy 1919-1939.

76

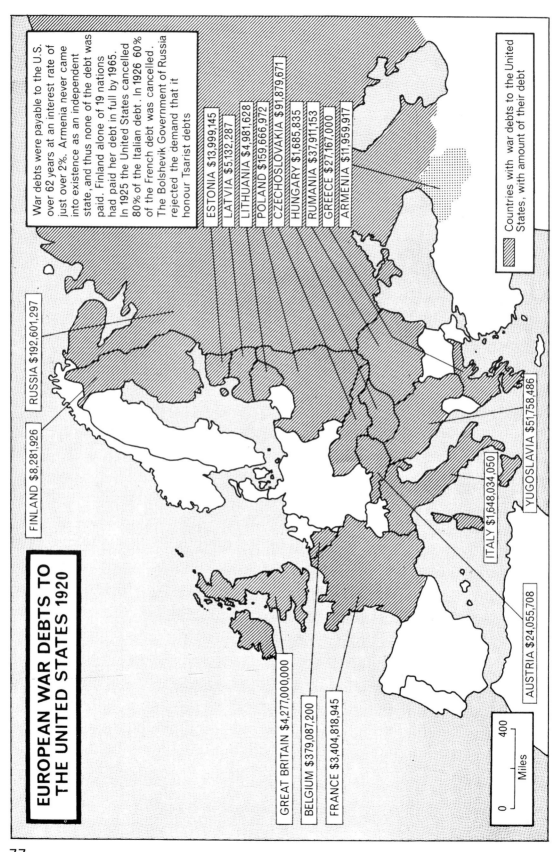

EUROPEAN WAR DEBTS TO THE UNITED STATES 1920

War debts were payable to the U.S. over 62 years at an interest rate of just over 2%. Armenia never came into existence as an independent state, and thus none of the debt was paid. Finland alone of 19 nations had paid her debt in full by 1965. In 1925 the United States cancelled 80% of the Italian debt. In 1926 60% of the French debt was cancelled. The Bolshevik Government of Russia rejected the demand that it honour Tsarist debts

ESTONIA $13,999,145
LATVIA $5,132,287
LITHUANIA $4,981,628
POLAND $159,666,972
CZECHOSLOVAKIA $91,879,671
HUNGARY $1,685,835
RUMANIA $37,911,153
GREECE $27,167,000
ARMENIA $11,959,917

RUSSIA $192,601,297
FINLAND $8,281,926

ITALY $1,648,034,050
YUGOSLAVIA $51,758,486
AUSTRIA $24,055,708

GREAT BRITAIN $4,277,000,000
BELGIUM $379,087,200
FRANCE $3,404,818,945

Countries with war debts to the United States, with amount of their debt

400
0
Miles

77

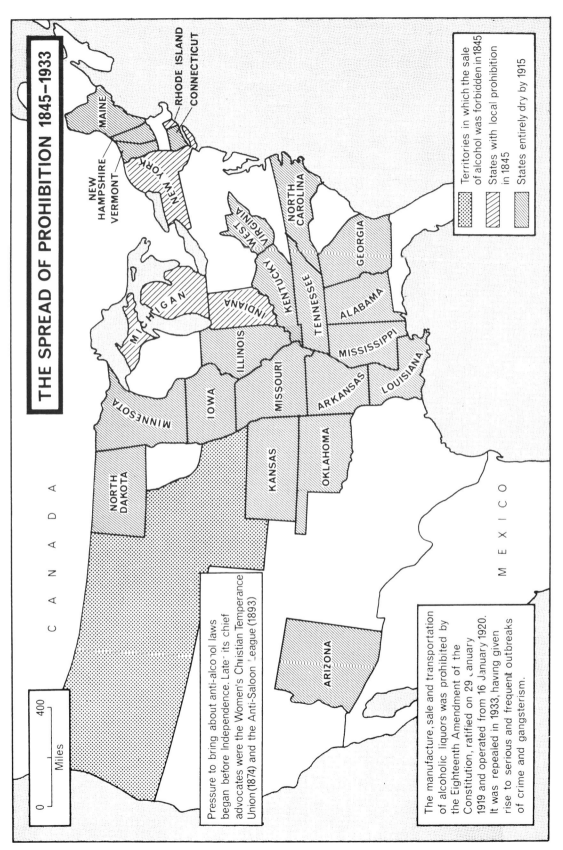

THE SPREAD OF PROHIBITION 1845–1933

RHODE ISLAND
CONNECTICUT

MAINE

NEW
HAMPSHIRE
VERMONT

NEW YORK

NORTH
CAROLINA

GEORGIA

WEST VIRGINIA

KENTUCKY

TENNESSEE

ALABAMA

MISSISSIPPI

MICHIGAN

INDIANA

ILLINOIS

IOWA

MISSOURI

ARKANSAS

LOUISIANA

MINNESOTA

NORTH
DAKOTA

KANSAS

OKLAHOMA

ARIZONA

C A N A D A

M E X I C O

Territories in which the sale
of alcohol was forbidden in 1845

States with local prohibition
in 1845

States entirely dry by 1915

400

0

Miles

Pressure to bring about anti-alcohol laws
began before Independence. Later its chief
advocates were the Women's Christian Temperance
Union (1874) and the Anti-Saloon League (1893)

The manufacture, sale and transportation
of alcoholic liquors was prohibited by
the Eighteenth Amendment of the
Constitution, ratified on 29 January
1919 and operated from 16 January 1920.
It was repealed in 1933, having given
rise to serious and frequent outbreaks
of crime and gangsterism.

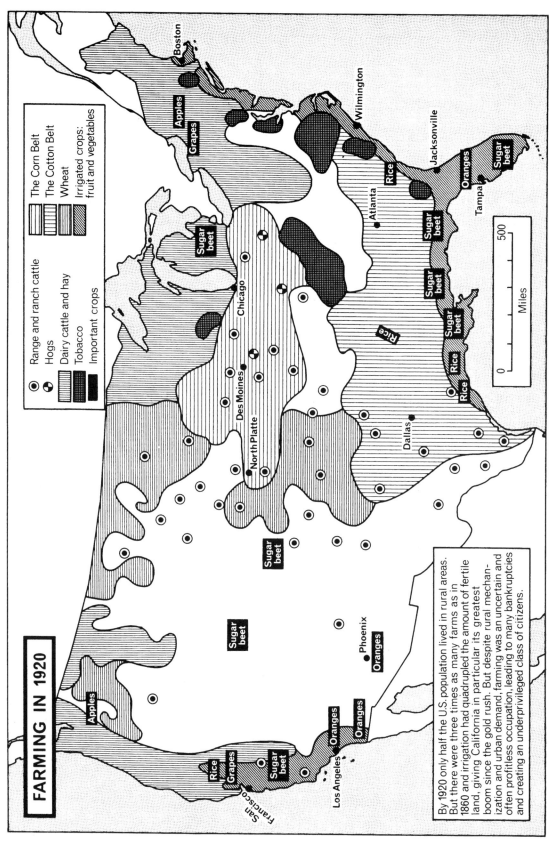

FARMING IN 1920

Legend:

The Corn Belt
The Cotton Belt
Wheat
Irrigated crops:
fruit and vegetables

Range and ranch cattle
Hogs
Dairy cattle and hay
Tobacco
Important crops

Labels on map:

Boston
Apples
Grapes
Wilmington
Jacksonville
Rice
Oranges
Sugar beet
Tampa
Atlanta
Sugar beet
Sugar beet
Sugar beet
Rice
Rice
Rice
Rice
Dallas
Chicago
Des Moines
North Platte
Sugar beet
Sugar beet
Phoenix
Oranges
Apples
Oranges
Oranges
Rice
Grapes
Sugar beet
Los Angeles
San Francisco

500

Miles

0

By 1920 only half the U.S. population lived in rural areas. But there were three times as many farms as in 1860 and irrigation had quadrupled the amount of fertile land, giving California in particular its greatest boom since the gold rush. But despite rural mechanization and urban demand, farming was an uncertain and often profitless occupation, leading to many bankruptcies and creating an underprivileged class of citizens.

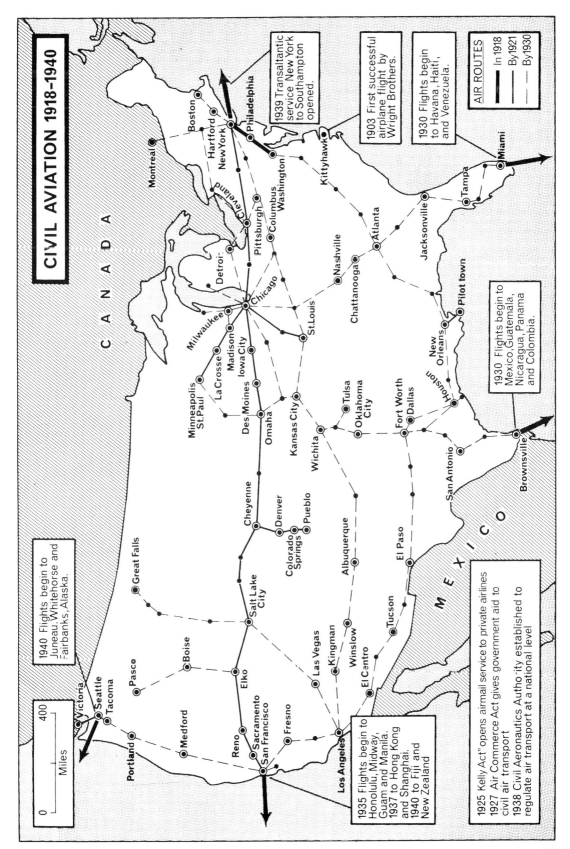

CIVIL AVIATION 1918-1940

CANADA

MEXICO

AIR ROUTES
In 1918
By 1921
By 1930

1939 Transaltantic service New York to Southampton opened.

1903 First successfull airplane flight by Wright Brothers.

1930 Flights begin to Havana, Haiti, and Venezuela.

1930 Flights begin to Mexico, Guatemala, Nicaragua, Panama and Colombia.

1940 Flights begin to Juneau, Whitehorse and Fairbanks, Alaska.

1935 Flights begin to Honolulu, Midway, Guam and Manila. 1937 to Hong Kong and Shanghai. 1940 to Fiji and New Zealand

1925 "Kelly Act" opens airmail service to private airlines
1927 Air Commerce Act gives government aid to civil air transport
1938 Civil Aeronautics Authority established to regulate air transport at a national level

Boston
Hartford
New York
Philadelphia
Washington
Montreal
Cleveland
Pittsburgh
Columbus
Kittyhawk
Detroit
Chicago
Nashville
Atlanta
Chattanooga
Jacksonville
Tampa
Miami
Pilot town
St.Louis
New Orleans
Milwaukee
Madison
Iowa City
La Crosse
Minneapolis St.Paul
Des Moines
Omaha
Kansas City
Wichita
Tulsa
Oklahoma City
Fort Worth
Dallas
Houston
Great Falls
Cheyenne
Denver
Pueblo
Colorado Springs
Albuquerque
El Paso
San Antonio
Brownsville
Salt Lake City
Las Vegas
Kingman
Winslow
El Centro
Tucson
Pasco
Boise
Medford
Victoria
Seattle
Tacoma
Portland
Reno
Elko
Sacramento
San Francisco
Fresno
Los Angeles

0   400
Miles

80

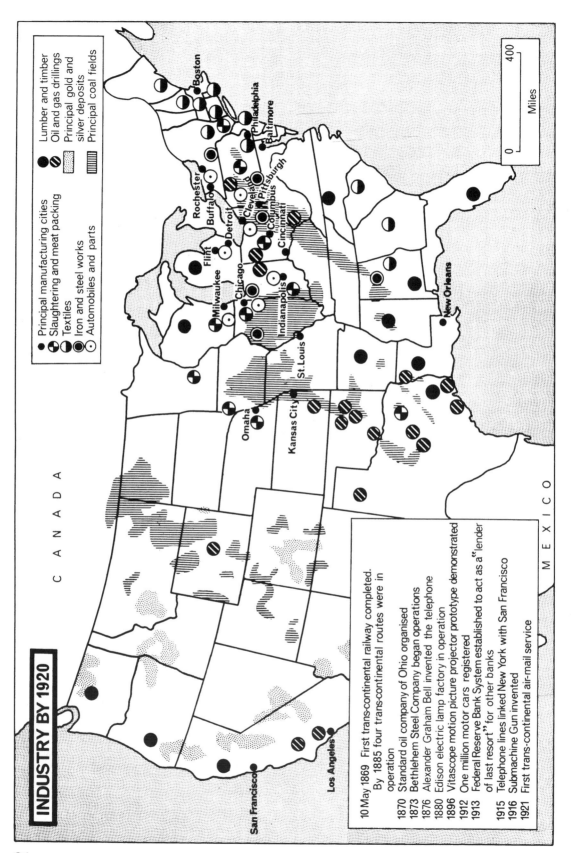

INDUSTRY BY 1920

Legend:

- Principal manufacturing cities
- Slaughtering and meat packing
- Textiles
- Iron and steel works
- Automobiles and parts
- Lumber and timber
- Oil and gas drillings
- Principal gold and silver deposits
- Principal coal fields

CANADA

MEXICO

Boston
Philadelphia
Baltimore
Rochester
Buffalo
Cleveland
Pittsburgh
Detroit
Columbus
Cincinnati
Flint
Milwaukee
Chicago
Indianapolis
St. Louis
Omaha
Kansas City
New Orleans
San Francisco
Los Angeles

Miles
0   400

10 May 1869   First trans-continental railway completed.
              By 1885 four trans-continental routes were in
              operation
1870   Standard oil company of Ohio organised
1873   Bethlehem Steel Company began operations
1876   Alexander Graham Bell invented the telephone
1880   Edison electric lamp factory in operation
1896   Vitascope motion picture projector prototype demonstrated
1912   One million motor cars registered
1913   Federal Reserve Bank System established to act as a "lender
       of last resort" for other banks
1915   Telephone lines linked New York with San Francisco
1916   Submachine Gun invented
1921   First trans-continental air-mail service

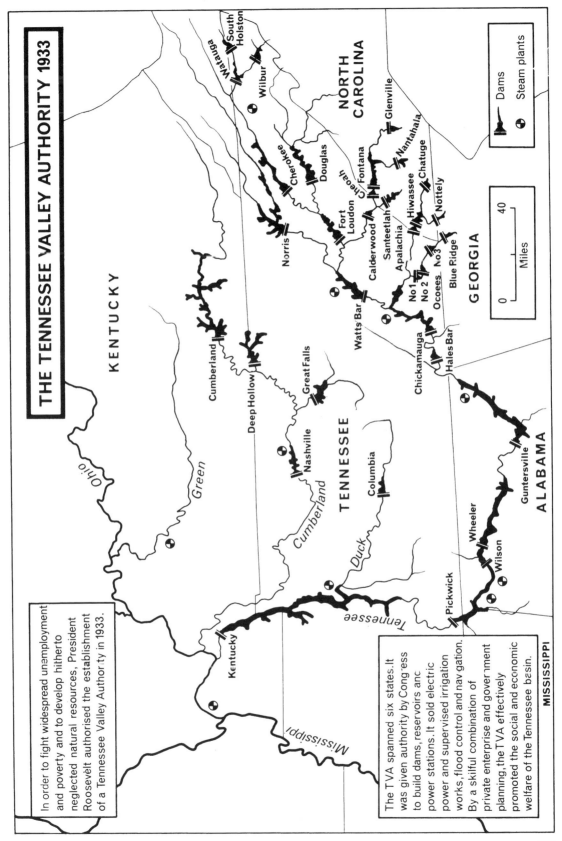

THE TENNESSEE VALLEY AUTHORITY 1933

In order to fight widespread unemployment and poverty and to develop hitherto neglected natural resources, President Roosevelt authorised the establishment of a Tennessee Valley Authority in 1933.

The TVA spanned six states. It was given authority by Congress to build dams, reservoirs and power stations. It sold electric power and supervised irrigation works, flood control and navigation. By a skilful combination of private enterprise and government planning, the TVA effectively promoted the social and economic welfare of the Tennessee basin.

▲ Dams
⊕ Steam plants

0   40
Miles

KENTUCKY

TENNESSEE

NORTH CAROLINA

GEORGIA

ALABAMA

MISSISSIPPI

Ohio

Green

Cumberland

Duck

Tennessee

Mississippi

Watauga
South Holston
Wilbur
Cherokee
Douglas
Cheoah
Fontana
Glenville
Nantahala
Chatuge
Hiwassee
Nottely
Fort Loudon
Calderwood
Santeetlah
Apalachia
Blue Ridge
No 1
No 2
Ocoee
No 3
Norris
Watts Bar
Chickamauga
Hales Bar
Cumberland
Deep Hollow
Great Falls
Nashville
Columbia
Wheeler
Wilson
Guntersville
Pickwick
Kentucky

82

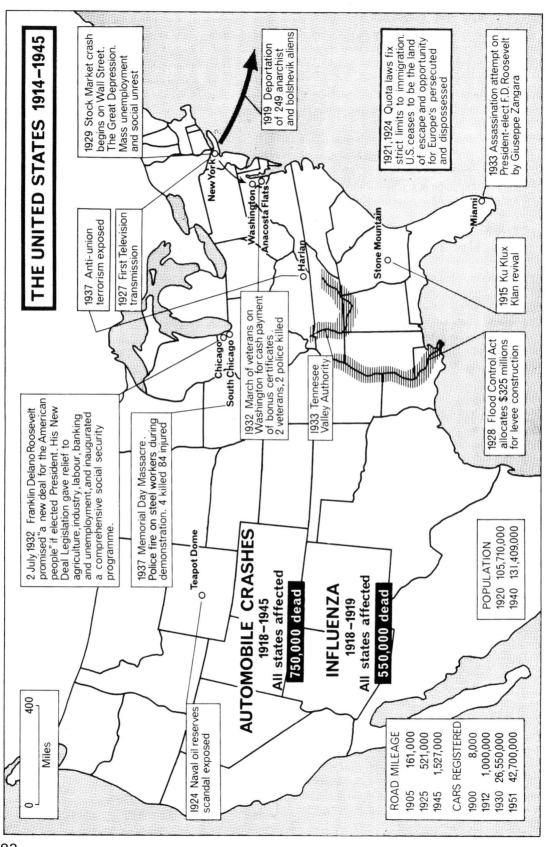

THE UNITED STATES 1914–1945

1929 Stock Market crash begins on Wall Street. The Great Depression. Mass unemployment and social unrest

1919 Deportation of 249 anarchist and bolshevik aliens

1921, 1924 Quota laws fix strict limits to immigration. U.S. ceases to be the land of escape and opportunity for Europe's persecuted and dispossessed

1933 Assassination attempt on President-elect F.D. Roosevelt by Giuseppe Zangara

1937 Anti-union terrorism exposed

1927 First Television transmission

New York

Washington
Anacosta Flats

Harlan

Stone Mountain

Miami

1915 Ku Klux Klan revival

2 July 1932 Franklin Delano Roosevelt promised "a new deal for the American people" if elected President. His New Deal Legislation gave relief to agriculture, industry, labour, banking and unemployment, and inaugurated a comprehensive social security programme.

1937 Memorial Day Massacre. Police fire on steel workers during demonstration. 4 killed 84 injured

Chicago
South Chicago

1932 March of veterans on Washington for cash payment of bonus certificates 2 veterans, 2 police killed

1933 Tennessee Valley Authority

1928 Flood Control Act allocates $325 millions for levee construction

Teapot Dome

AUTOMOBILE CRASHES
1918–1945
All states affected
750,000 dead

INFLUENZA
1918–1919
All states affected
550,000 dead

1924 Naval oil reserves scandal exposed

Miles	
0	400

POPULATION	
1920	105,710,000
1940	131,409,000

ROAD MILEAGE	
1905	161,000
1925	521,000
1945	1,527,000

CARS REGISTERED	
1900	8,000
1912	1,000,000
1930	26,550,000
1951	42,700,000

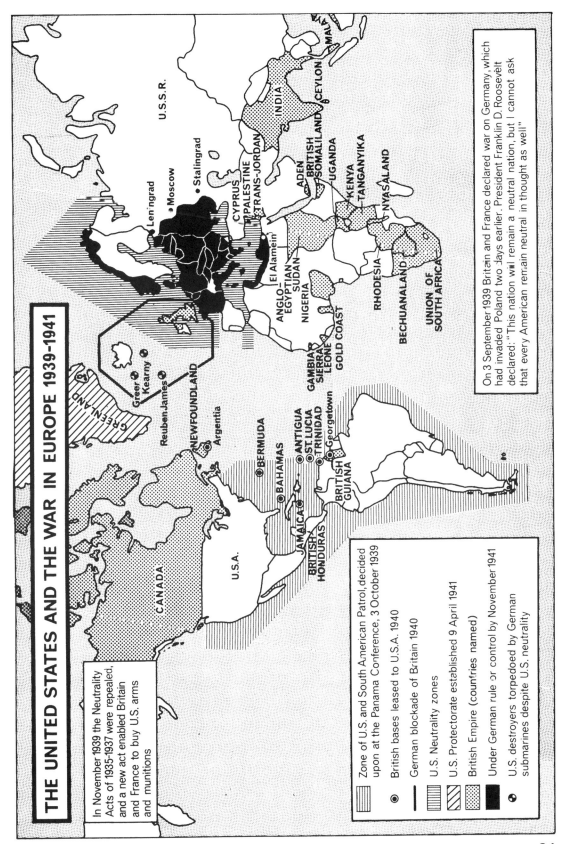

THE UNITED STATES AND THE WAR IN EUROPE 1939-1941

In November 1939 the Neutrality Acts of 1935-1937 were repealed, and a new act enabled Britain and France to buy U.S. arms and munitions

On 3 September 1939 Britain and France declared war on Germany, which had invaded Poland two days earlier. President Franklin D. Roosevelt declared: "This nation will remain a neutral nation, but I cannot ask that every American remain neutral in thought as well"

Zone of U.S. and South American Patrol, decided upon at the Panama Conference, 3 October 1939

⊙ British bases leased to U.S.A. 1940

——— German blockade of Britain 1940

U.S. Neutrality zones

U.S. Protectorate established 9 April 1941

British Empire (countries named)

Under German rule or control by November 1941

⊕ U.S. destroyers torpedoed by German submarines despite U.S. neutrality

U.S.S.R.

Leningrad • Moscow • Stalingrad

CYPRUS
PALESTINE
TRANS-JORDAN
ADEN
BRITISH SOMALILAND
CEYLON
INDIA
MALA
UGANDA
KENYA
TANGANYIKA
NYASALAND
ANGLO-EGYPTIAN SUDAN
NIGERIA
RHODESIA
BECHUANALAND
UNION OF SOUTH AFRICA
GAMBIA
SIERRA LEONE
GOLD COAST
El Alamein

GREENLAND

Greer ⊕
Kearny ⊕
Reuben James ⊕
NEWFOUNDLAND
Argentia

BERMUDA
BAHAMAS
JAMAICA
BRITISH HONDURAS
ANTIGUA
ST LUCIA
TRINIDAD
Georgetown
BRITISH GUIANA

CANADA

U.S.A.

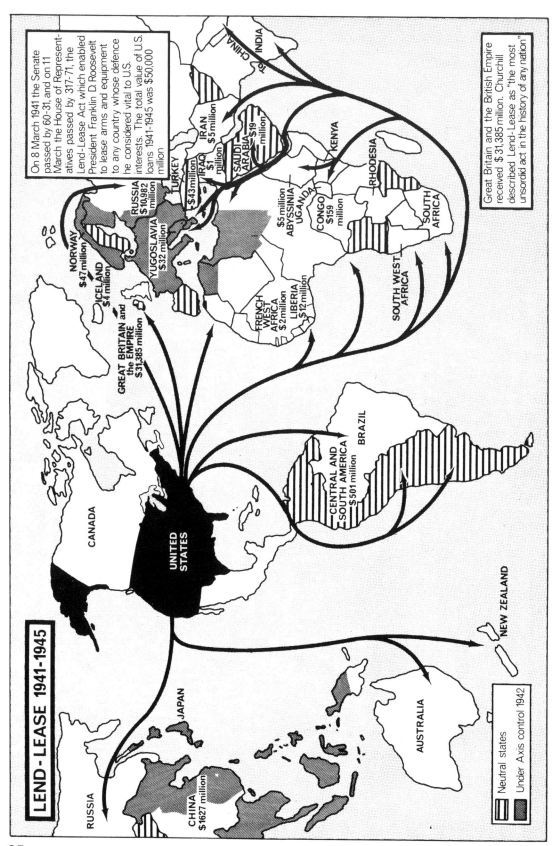

LEND-LEASE 1941-1945

On 8 March 1941 the Senate passed by 60-31, and on 11 March the House of Representatives passed by 317-71, the Lend-Lease Act which enabled President Franklin D. Roosevelt to lease arms and equipment to any country whose defence he considered vital to U.S. interests. The total value of U.S. loans 1941-1945 was $50,000 million

Great Britain and the British Empire received $31,385 million. Churchill described Lend-Lease as "the most unsordid act in the history of any nation"

CHINA
To INDIA
INDIA
TURKEY $43 million
IRAN $5 million
IRAQ $1 million
SAUDI ARABIA $19 million
KENYA
RHODESIA
ABYSSINIA $5 million
UGANDA
CONGO $159 million
SOUTH AFRICA
SOUTH WEST AFRICA
RUSSIA $10,982 million
YUGOSLAVIA $32 million
NORWAY $47 million
ICELAND $4 million
GREAT BRITAIN and the EMPIRE $31,385 million
FRENCH WEST AFRICA $2 million
LIBERIA $12 million

CANADA
UNITED STATES

CENTRAL AND SOUTH AMERICA $501 million
BRAZIL

NEW ZEALAND
AUSTRALIA

RUSSIA
JAPAN
CHINA $1627 million

Neutral states
Under Axis control 1942

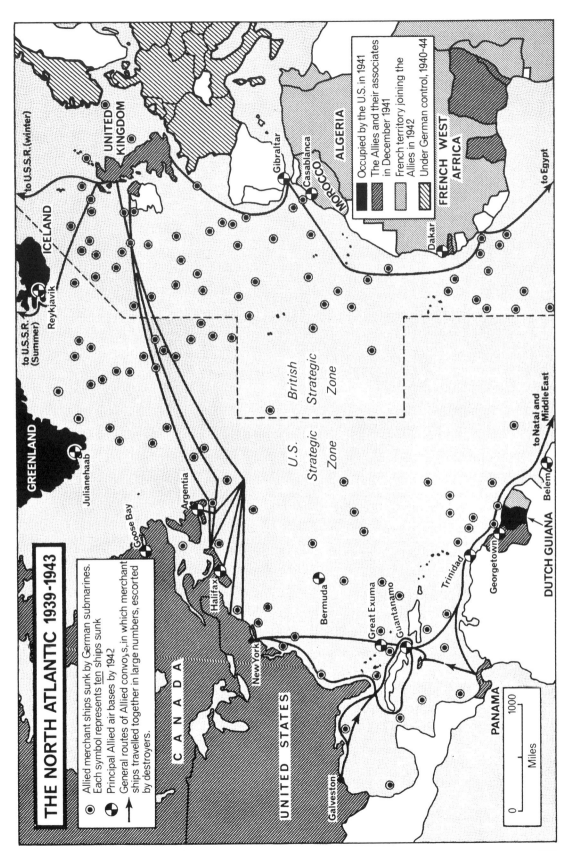

THE NORTH ATLANTIC 1939-1943

⊙ Allied merchant ships sunk by German submarines.
Each symbol represents <u>ten</u> ships sunk

◑ Principal Allied air bases by 1942

↑ General routes of Allied convoys, in which merchant
ships travelled together in large numbers, escorted
by destroyers.

Occupied by the U.S. in 1941

The Allies and their associates
in December 1941

French territory joining the
Allies in 1942

Under German control, 1940-44

FRENCH WEST
AFRICA

ALGERIA

MOROCCO

Gibraltar

Casablanca

Dakar

to Egypt

to U.S.S.R. (winter)

to U.S.S.R.
(Summer)

UNITED
KINGDOM

ICELAND

Reykjavik

GREENLAND

Julianehaab

Goose Bay

Argentia

Halifax

CANADA

New York

UNITED STATES

Galveston

PANAMA

British
Strategic
Zone

U.S.
Strategic
Zone

Bermuda

Great Exuma

Guantanamo

Trinidad

Georgetown

DUTCH GUIANA

Belem

to Natal and
Middle East

Miles

0   1000

86

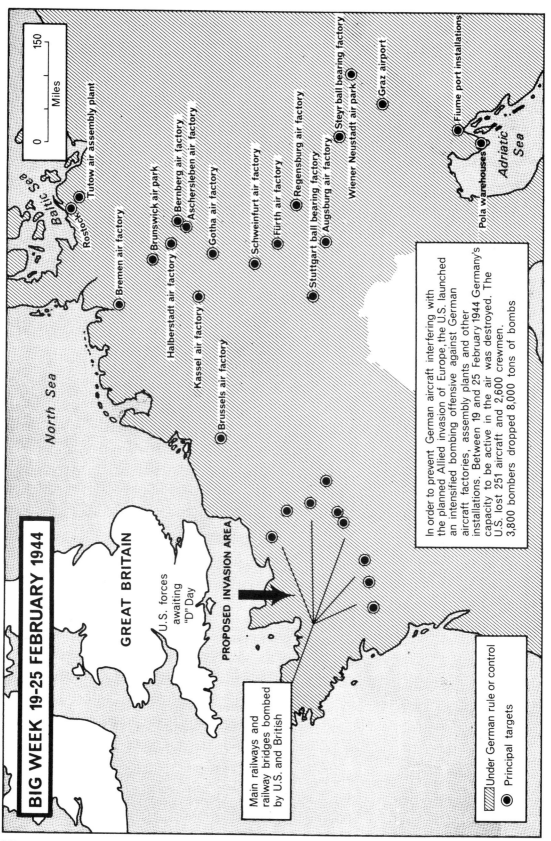

BIG WEEK 19-25 FEBRUARY 1944

150

Miles

0

Baltic Sea

North Sea

GREAT BRITAIN

U.S. forces awaiting "D" Day

PROPOSED INVASION AREA

Adriatic Sea

Tutow air assembly plant

Rostock

Bremen air factory

Brunswick air park

Bernberg air factory

Aschersleben air factory

Halberstadt air factory

Gotha air factory

Kassel air factory

Schweinfurt air factory

Furth air factory

Brussels air factory

Regensburg air factory

Stuttgart ball bearing factory

Augsburg air factory

Steyr ball bearing factory

Wiener Neustadt air park

Graz airport

Fiume port installations

Pola warehouses

In order to prevent German aircraft interfering with the planned Allied invasion of Europe, the U.S. launched an intensified bombing offensive against German aircraft factories, assembly plants and other installations. Between 19 and 25 February 1944 Germany's capacity to be active in the air was destroyed. The U.S. lost 251 aircraft and 2,600 crewmen. 3,800 bombers dropped 8,000 tons of bombs

Main railways and railway bridges bombed by U.S. and British

▨ Under German rule or control

● Principal targets

87

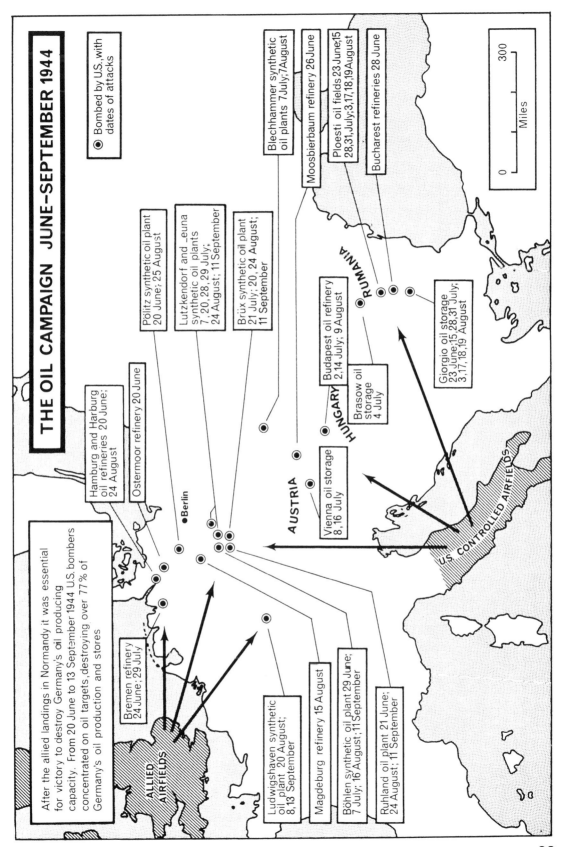

THE OIL CAMPAIGN JUNE–SEPTEMBER 1944

◉ Bombed by U.S.,with dates of attacks

After the allied landings in Normandy it was essential for victory to destroy Germany's oil producing capacity. From 20 June to 13 September 1944 U.S. bombers concentrated on oil targets,destroying over 77% of Germany's oil production and stores

Hamburg and Harburg oil refineries 20 June; 24 August

Ostermoor refinery 20 June

Pölitz synthetic oil plant 20 June; 25 August

Lutzkendorf and _euna synthetic oil plants 7,20,28,29 July; 24 August; 11 September

Brüx synthetic oil plant 21 July; 20, 24 August; 11 September

Blechhammer synthetic oil plants 7 July;7August

Moosbierbaum refinery 26June

Ploesti oil fields 23 June;15 28,31,July;3,17,18,19August

Bucharest refineries 28 June

Budapest oil refinery 2,14 July; 9 August

Brasow oil storage 4 July

Giorgio oil storage 23 June;15,28,31 July; 3,17,18,19 August

Vienna oil storage 8,16 July

•Berlin

RUMANIA

HUNGARY

AUSTRIA

U.S. CONTROLLED AIRFIELDS

ALLIED AIRFIELDS

Bremen refinery 24 June; 29 July

Ludwigshaven synthetic oil plant 20 August; 8,13 September

Magdeburg refinery 15 August

Böhlen synthetic oil plant 29 June; 7 July; 16 August;11September

Ruhland oil plant 21 June; 24 August; 11 September

0   300
        Miles

88

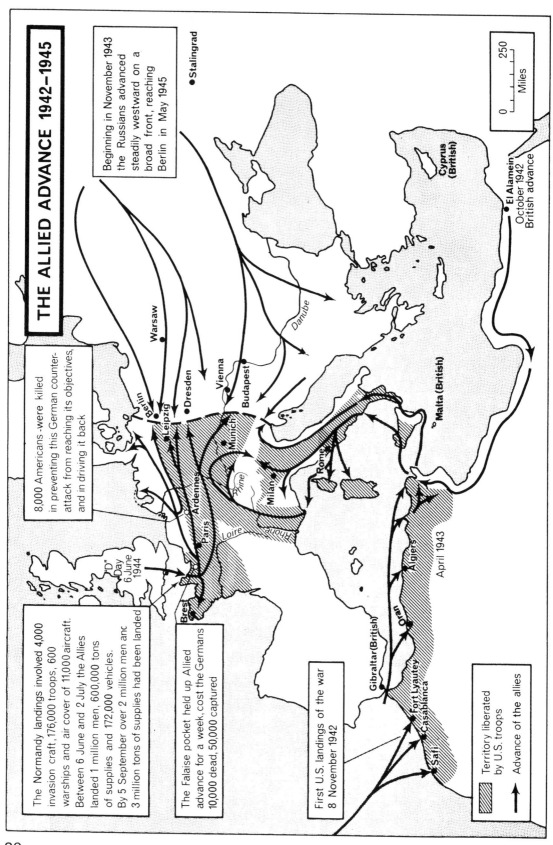

THE ALLIED ADVANCE 1942–1945

Beginning in November 1943 the Russians advanced steadily westward on a broad front, reaching Berlin in May 1945

8,000 Americans were killed in preventing this German counter-attack from reaching its objectives, and in driving it back

The Normandy landings involved 4,000 invasion craft, 176,000 troops, 600 warships and air cover of 11,000 aircraft. Between 6 June and 2 July the Allies landed 1 million men, 600,000 tons of supplies and 172,000 vehicles. By 5 September over 2 million men and 3 million tons of supplies had been landed

The Falaise pocket held up Allied advance for a week, cost the Germans 10,000 dead, 50,000 captured

First U.S. landings of the war 8 November 1942

El Alamein October 1942 British advance

"D" Day 6 June 1944

April 1943

Stalingrad

Warsaw

Vienna

Dresden

Leipzig

Berlin

Budapest

Munich

Ardennes

Paris

Brest

Milan

Rome

Danube

Rhône

Rhine

Loire

Garonne

Cyprus (British)

Malta (British)

Gibraltar (British)

Algiers

Oran

Fort Lyautey

Casablanca

Safi

0   250
Miles

Territory liberated by U.S. troops

Advance of the allies

89

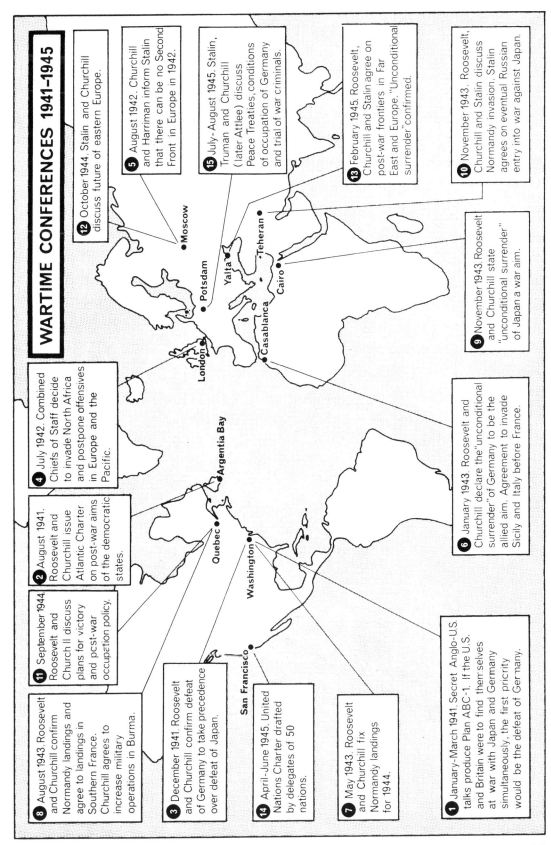

WARTIME CONFERENCES 1941–1945

12 October 1944. Stalin and Churchill discuss future of eastern Europe.

5 August 1942. Churchill and Harriman inform Stalin that there can be no Second Front in Europe in 1942.

15 July–August 1945. Stalin, Truman and Churchill (later Attlee) discuss Peace Treaties, conditions of occupation of Germany and trial of war criminals.

13 February 1945. Roosevelt, Churchill and Stalin agree on post-war frontiers in Far East and Europe. "Unconditional surrender" confirmed.

10 November 1943. Roosevelt, Churchill and Stalin discuss Normandy invasion. Stalin agrees on eventual Russian entry into war against Japan.

9 November 1943. Roosevelt and Churchill state "unconditional surrender" of Japan a war aim.

4 July 1942. Combined Chiefs of Staff decide to invade North Africa and postpone offensives in Europe and the Pacific.

2 August 1941. Roosevelt and Churchill issue Atlantic Charter on post-war aims of the democratic states.

6 January 1943. Roosevelt and Churchill declare the "unconditional surrender" of Germany to be the allied aim. Agreement to invade Sicily and Italy before France.

11 September 1944. Roosevelt and Church II discuss plans for victory and post-war occupation policy.

8 August 1943. Roosevelt and Churchill confirm Normandy landings and agree to landings in Southern France. Churchill agrees to increase military operations in Burma.

3 December 1941. Roosevelt and Churchill confirm defeat of Germany to take precedence over defeat of Japan.

14 April–June 1945. United Nations Charter drafted by delegates of 50 nations.

7 May 1943. Roosevelt and Churchill fix Normandy landings for 1944.

1 January–March 1941. Secret Anglo-U.S. talks produce Plan ABC-1. If the U.S. and Britain were to find themselves at war with Japan and Germany simultaneously, the first priority would be the defeat of Germany.

Moscow · Potsdam · Yalta · Teheran · Cairo · Casablanca · London · Argentia Bay · Quebec · Washington · San Francisco

90

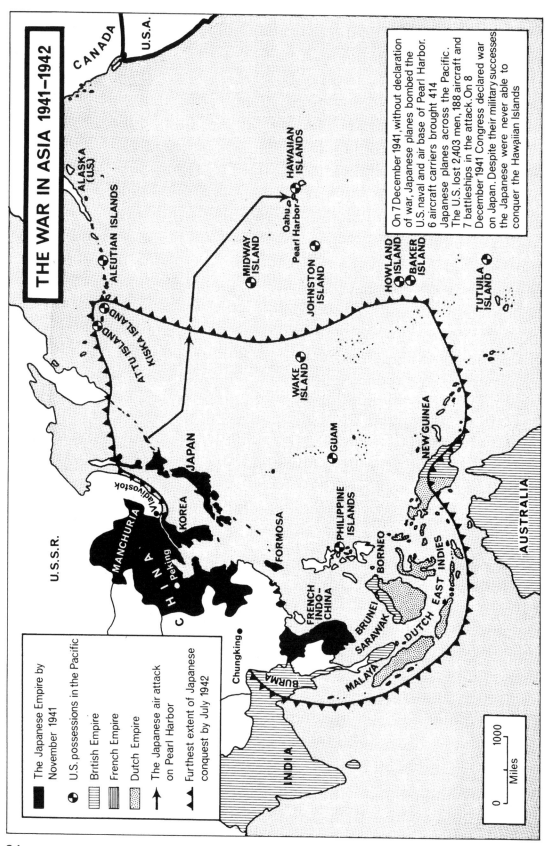

THE WAR IN ASIA 1941–1942

CANADA
U.S.A.

ALASKA (U.S.)

ALEUTIAN ISLANDS

ATTU ISLAND
KISKA ISLAND

MIDWAY ISLAND

Oahu
Pearl Harbor
HAWAIIAN ISLANDS

JOHNSTON ISLAND

HOWLAND ISLAND
BAKER ISLAND

TUTUILA ISLAND

WAKE ISLAND

GUAM

NEW GUINEA

AUSTRALIA

U.S.S.R.

Vladivostok

MANCHURIA

KOREA

JAPAN

Peking

CHINA

FORMOSA

PHILIPPINE ISLANDS

BORNEO
BRUNEI
SARAWAK

DUTCH EAST INDIES

FRENCH INDO-CHINA

MALAYA

Chungking

BURMA

INDIA

On 7 December 1941, without declaration of war, Japanese planes bombed the U.S. naval and air base of Pearl Harbor. 6 aircraft carriers brought 414 Japanese planes across the Pacific. The U.S. lost 2,403 men, 188 aircraft and 7 battleships in the attack. On 8 December 1941 Congress declared war on Japan. Despite their military successes the Japanese were never able to conquer the Hawaiian Islands

Legend:
- The Japanese Empire by November 1941
- U.S. possessions in the Pacific
- British Empire
- French Empire
- Dutch Empire
- The Japanese air attack on Pearl Harbor
- Furthest extent of Japanese conquest by July 1942

0   1000
Miles

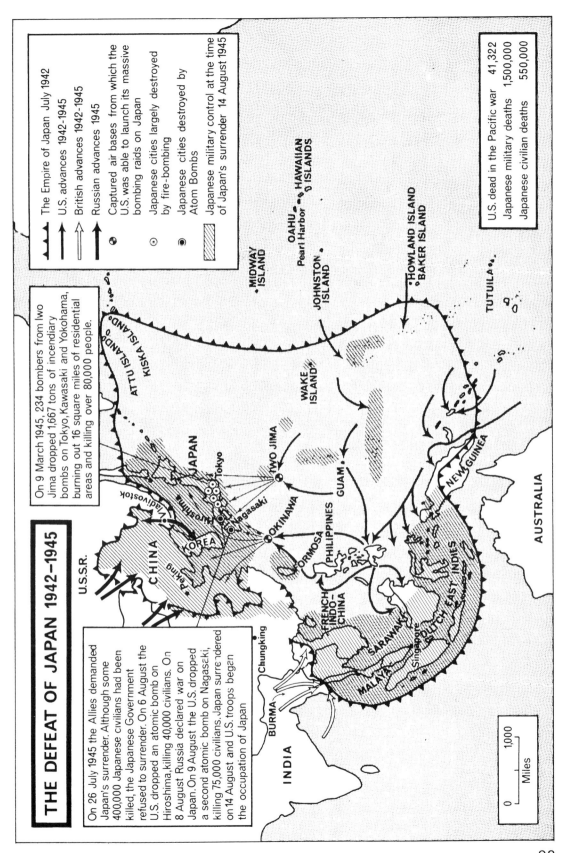

THE DEFEAT OF JAPAN 1942–1945

The Empire of Japan July 1942

→ U.S. advances 1942–1945

⇨ British advances 1942–1945

➡ Russian advances

◐ Captured air bases from which the U.S. was able to launch its massive bombing raids on Japan

⊙ Japanese cities largely destroyed by fire-bombing

● Japanese cities destroyed by Atom Bombs

▨ Japanese military control at the time of Japan's surrender 14 August 1945

U.S. dead in the Pacific war	41,322
Japanese military deaths	1,500,000
Japanese civilian deaths	550,000

On 9 March 1945, 234 bombers from Iwo Jima dropped 1,667 tons of incendiary bombs on Tokyo, Kawasaki and Yokohama, burning out 16 square miles of residential areas and killing over 80,000 people.

On 26 July 1945 the Allies demanded Japan's surrender. Although some 400,000 Japanese civilians had been killed, the Japanese Government refused to surrender. On 6 August the U.S. dropped an atomic bomb on Hiroshima, killing 40,000 civilians. On 8 August Russia declared war on Japan. On 9 August the U.S. dropped a second atomic bomb on Nagasaki, killing 75,000 civilians. Japan surrendered on 14 August and U.S. troops began the occupation of Japan

U.S.S.R.

ATTU ISLAND

KISKA ISLAND

MIDWAY ISLAND

OAHU HAWAIIAN
Pearl Harbor ISLANDS

JOHNSTON ISLAND

HOWLAND ISLAND
BAKER ISLAND

TUTUILA

WAKE ISLAND

JAPAN

Tokyo

Vladivostok

Hiroshima

Nagasaki

IWO JIMA

GUAM

KOREA

CHINA

Peking

OKINAWA

FORMOSA

PHILIPPINES

NEW GUINEA

FRENCH INDO-CHINA

SARAWAK

DUTCH EAST INDIES

MALAYA

Singapore

Chungking

BURMA

INDIA

AUSTRALIA

0   1,000

Miles

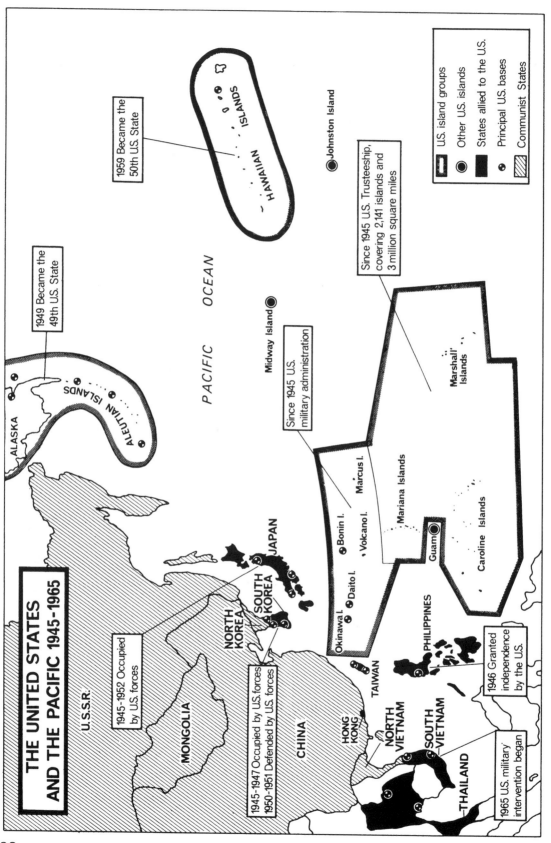

THE UNITED STATES
AND THE PACIFIC 1945-1965

U.S.S.R.

MONGOLIA

CHINA

ALASKA

ALEUTIAN ISLANDS

1949 Became the
49th U.S. State

PACIFIC OCEAN

HAWAIIAN ISLANDS

1959 Became the
50th U.S. State

Johnston Island

Midway Island

Since 1945 U.S. Trusteeship,
covering 2,141 islands and
3 million square miles

Since 1945 U.S.
military administration

Marshall
Islands

Marcus I.

Bonin I.

Volcano I.

Mariana Islands

Daito I.

Okinawa I.

Caroline Islands

Guam

JAPAN

NORTH
KOREA

SOUTH
KOREA

1945-1952 Occupied
by U.S. forces

1945-1947 Occupied by U.S. forces
1950-1951 Defended by U.S. forces

PHILIPPINES

1946 Granted
independence
by the U.S.

TAIWAN

HONG
KONG

NORTH
VIETNAM

SOUTH
VIETNAM

THAILAND

1965 U.S. military
intervention began

U.S. island groups

Other U.S. islands

States allied to the U.S.

Principal U.S. bases

Communist States

93

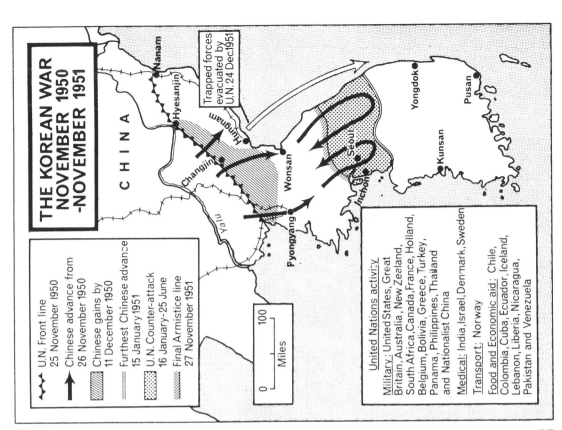

THE KOREAN WAR NOVEMBER 1950 -NOVEMBER 1951

CHINA

Nanam
Hyesanjin
Hungnam
Changjin
Yalu
Wonsan
Pyongyang
Seoul
Inchon
Yongdok
Kunsan
Pusan

Trapped forces evacuated by U.N. 24 Dec.1951

Legend:
- U.N. Front line 25 November 1950
- Chinese advance from 26 November 1950
- Chinese gains by 11 December 1950
- Furthest Chinese advance 15 January 1951
- U.N. Counter-attack 16 January-25 June
- Final Armistice line 27 November 1951

Miles 0 — 100

United Nations activity:
Military: United States, Great Britain, Australia, New Zealand, South Africa, Canada, France, Holland, Belgium, Bolivia, Greece, Turkey, Panama, Philippines, Thailand and Nationalist China

Medical: India, Israel, Denmark, Sweden

Transport: Norway

Food and Economic aid: Chile, Colombia, Cuba, Ecuador, Iceland, Lebanon, Liberia, Nicaragua, Pakistan and Venezuela

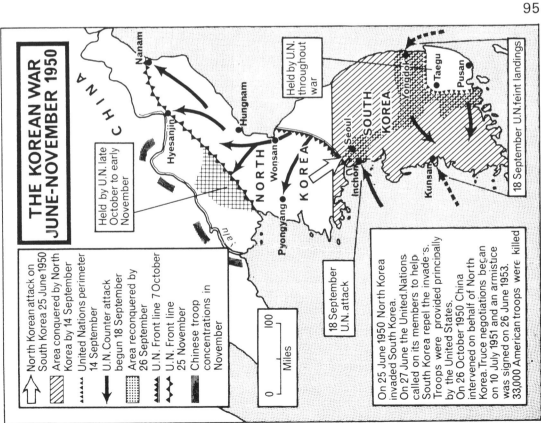

THE KOREAN WAR JUNE-NOVEMBER 1950

CHINA

Nanam
Hyesanjin
Hungnam
Wonsan
Pyongyang
Seoul
Inchon
Taegu
Yongdok
Pusan
Kunsan

NORTH KOREA
SOUTH KOREA

Yalu

Held by U.N. late October to early November

Held by U.N. throughout war

18 September U.N. feint landings

18 September U.N. attack

Legend:
- North Korean attack on South Korea 25 June 1950
- Area conquered by North Korea by 14 September
- United Nations perimeter 14 September
- U.N. Counter attack begun 18 September
- Area reconquered by 26 September
- U.N. Front line 7 October
- U.N. Front line 25 November
- Chinese troop concentrations in November

Miles 0 — 100

On 25 June 1950 North Korea invaded South Korea.
On 27 June the United Nations called on its members to help South Korea repel the invaders. Troops were provided principally by the United States.
On 26 October 1950 China intervened on behalf of North Korea. Truce negotiations began on 10 July 1951 and an armistice was signed on 26 June 1953. 33,000 American troops were killed

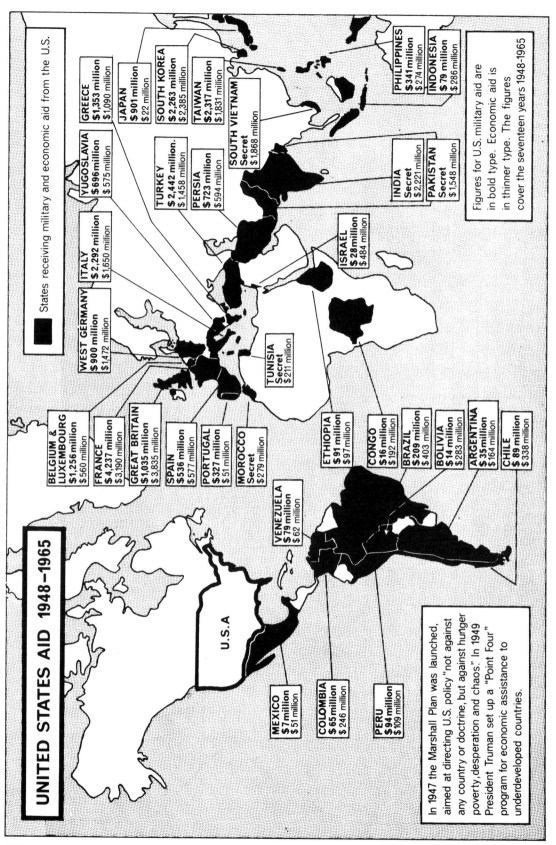

UNITED STATES AID 1948–1965

States receiving military and economic aid from the U.S.

GREECE
$1,353 million
$1,090 million

JAPAN
$901 million
$22 million

SOUTH KOREA
$2,263 million
$2,385 million

TAIWAN
$2,317 million
$1,831 million

SOUTH VIETNAM
Secret
$1,868 million

PHILIPPINES
$341 million
$274 million

INDONESIA
$79 million
$286 million

YUGOSLAVIA
$696 million
$575 million

TURKEY
$2,442 million.
$1,458 million

PERSIA
$723 million
$594 million

INDIA
Secret
$2,221 million

PAKISTAN
Secret
$1,548 million

Figures for U.S. military aid are in bold type. Economic aid is in thinner type. The figures cover the seventeen years 1948-1965

ITALY
$2,292 million
$1,650 million

ISRAEL
$28 million
$484 million

WEST GERMANY
$900 million
$1,472 million

TUNISIA
Secret
$211 million

BELGIUM &
LUXEMBOURG
$1,256 million
$560 million

FRANCE
$4,237 million
$3,190 million

GREAT BRITAIN
$1,035 million
$3,835 million

SPAIN
$536 million
$577 million

PORTUGAL
$327 million
$51 million

MOROCCO
Secret
$279 million

ETHIOPIA
$91 million
$97 million

CONGO
$16 million
$192 million

BRAZIL
$209 million
$403 million

BOLIVIA
$14 million
$283 million

ARGENTINA
$35 million
$164 million

CHILE
$89 million
$338 million

VENEZUELA
$79 million
$62 million

U.S.A

MEXICO
$7 million
$51 million

COLOMBIA
$65 million
$246 million

PERU
$94 million
$109 million

In 1947 the Marshall Plan was launched, aimed at directing U.S. policy "not against any country or doctrine, but against hunger poverty, desperation and chaos." In 1949 President Truman set up a "Point Four" program for economic assistance to underdeveloped countries.

96

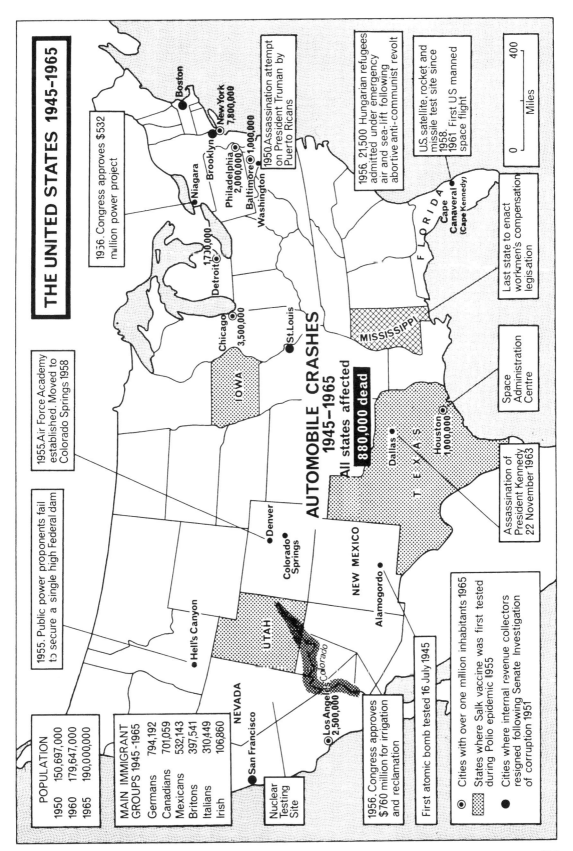

THE UNITED STATES 1945-1965

1956. Congress approves $532 million power project

1956. 21,500 Hungarian refugees admitted under emergency air and sea-lift following abortive anti-communist revolt

U.S. satellite, rocket and missile test site since 1958.
1961 First US manned space flight

Boston

New York 7,800,000

Brooklyn

Niagara

Philadelphia 2,000,000

Baltimore 1,000,000

Washington

1950.Assassination attempt on President Truman by Puerto Ricans

F L O R I D A

Cape Canaveral (Cape Kennedy)

Last state to enact workmen's compensation legislation

Detroit 1,700,000

Chicago 3,500,000

St.Louis

I O W A

MISSISSIPPI

Space Administration Centre

1955.Air Force Academy established. Moved to Colorado Springs 1958

AUTOMOBILE CRASHES 1945–1965
All states affected
880,000 dead

Dallas

Houston 1,000,000

T E X A S

Assassination of President Kennedy 22 November 1963

1955. Public power proponents fail to secure a single high Federal dam

Denver

Colorado Springs

NEW MEXICO

Alamogordo

Hell's Canyon

UTAH

Colorado

NEVADA

Cities with over one million inhabitants 1965

States where Salk vaccine was first tested during Polio epidemic 1955

Cities where internal revenue collectors resigned following Senate Investigation of corruption 1951

First atomic bomb tested 16 July 1945

POPULATION	
1950	150,697,000
1960	179,647,000
1965	190,000,000

MAIN IMMIGRANT GROUPS 1945-1965	
Germans	794,192
Canadians	701,059
Mexicans	532,143
Britons	397,541
Italians	310,449
Irish	106,860

San Francisco

Los Angeles 2,500,000

Nuclear Testing Site

1956. Congress approves $760 million for irrigation and reclamation

0   400
Miles

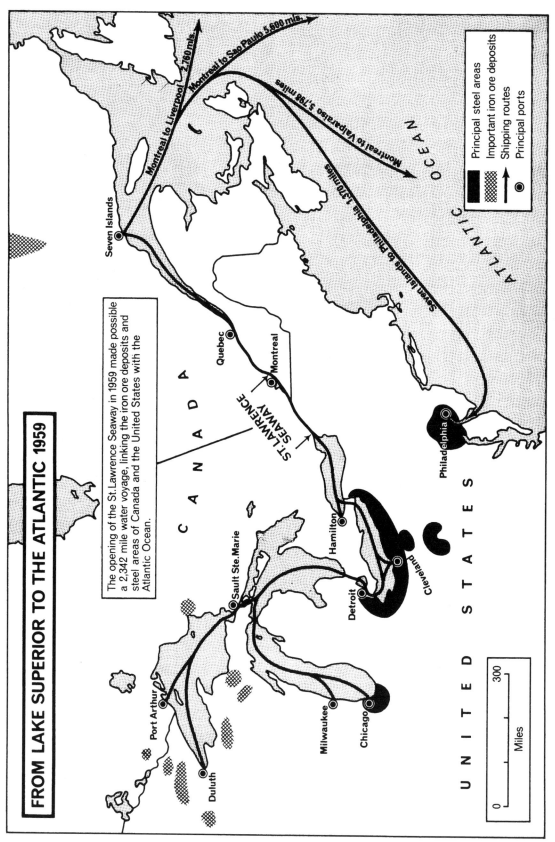

FROM LAKE SUPERIOR TO THE ATLANTIC 1959

The opening of the St. Lawrence Seaway in 1959 made possible a 2,342 mile water voyage, linking the iron ore deposits and steel areas of Canada and the United States with the Atlantic Ocean.

Principal steel areas
Important iron ore deposits
Shipping routes
Principal ports

ATLANTIC OCEAN

CANADA

UNITED STATES

Seven Islands

Montreal to Liverpool 2,760 mls.

Montreal to Sao Paulo 5,600 mls.

Montreal to Valparaiso 5,798 miles

Seven Islands to Philadelphia 1,370 miles

Quebec

Montreal

ST. LAWRENCE SEAWAY

Sault Ste. Marie

Hamilton

Cleveland

Detroit

Philadelphia

Port Arthur

Duluth

Milwaukee

Chicago

0   300
Miles

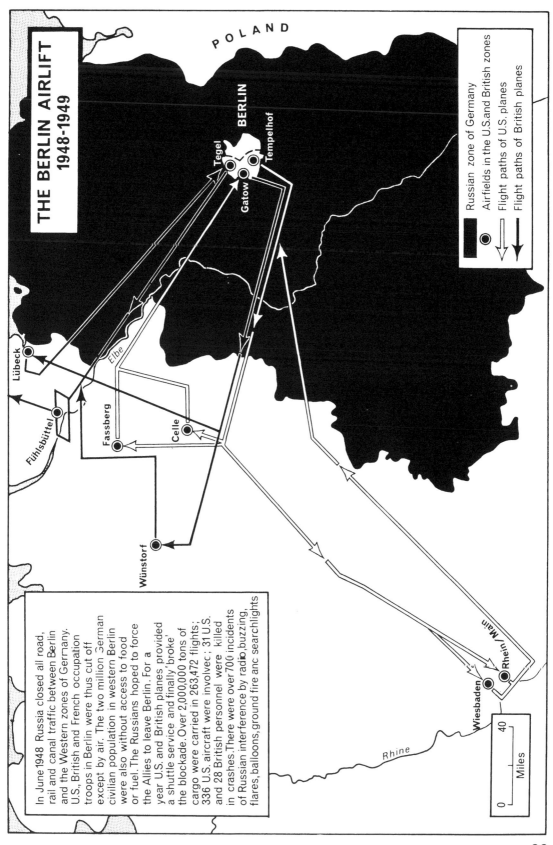

THE BERLIN AIRLIFT 1948-1949

POLAND

BERLIN

Tegel
Tempelhof
Gatow

Lübeck

Elbe

Fühlsbüttel

Fassberg

Celle

Wünstorf

Main

Rhine

Rhein/Main

Wiesbaden

Russian zone of Germany

Airfields in the U.S.and British zones

Flight paths of U.S. planes

Flight paths of British planes

In June 1948 Russia closed all road, rail and canal traffic between Berlin and the Western zones of Germany. U.S., British and French occupation troops in Berlin were thus cut off except by air. The two million German civilian population in western Berlin were also without access to food or fuel. The Russians hoped to force the Allies to leave Berlin. For a year U.S. and British planes provided a shuttle service and finally 'broke' the blockade. Over 2,000,000 tons of cargo were carried in 263,472 flights; 336 U.S. aircraft were involved; 31 U.S. and 28 British personnel were killed in crashes. There were over 700 incidents of Russian interference by radio, buzzing, flares, balloons, ground fire and searchlights.

0   40
Miles

99

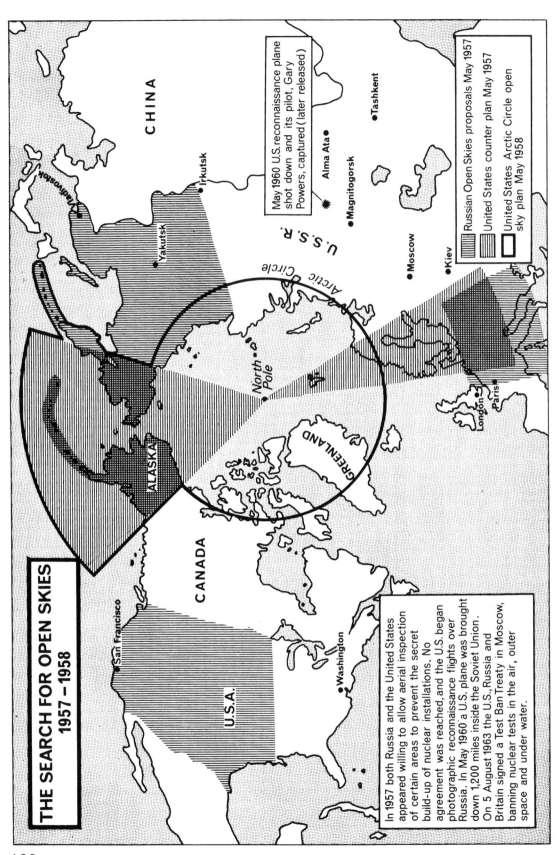

THE SEARCH FOR OPEN SKIES
1957 – 1958

CHINA

May 1960 U.S. reconnaissance plane shot down and its pilot, Gary Powers, captured (later released)

U.S.S.R.

● Irkutsk

● Alma Ata

✳ Magnitogorsk
● Tashkent

● Yakutsk

● Moscow

● Kiev

Vladivostok

Arctic Circle

North Pole

GREENLAND

London ●
Paris ●

ALASKA

CANADA

● San Francisco

U.S.A.

● Washington

Russian Open Skies proposals May 1957

United States counter plan May 1957

United States Arctic Circle open sky plan May 1958

In 1957 both Russia and the United States appeared willing to allow aerial inspection of certain areas to prevent the secret build-up of nuclear installations. No agreement was reached, and the U.S. began photographic reconnaissance flights over Russia. In May 1960 a U.S. plane was brought down 1,200 miles inside the Soviet Union. On 5 August 1963 the U.S., Russia and Britain signed a Test Ban Treaty in Moscow, banning nuclear tests in the air, outer space and under water.

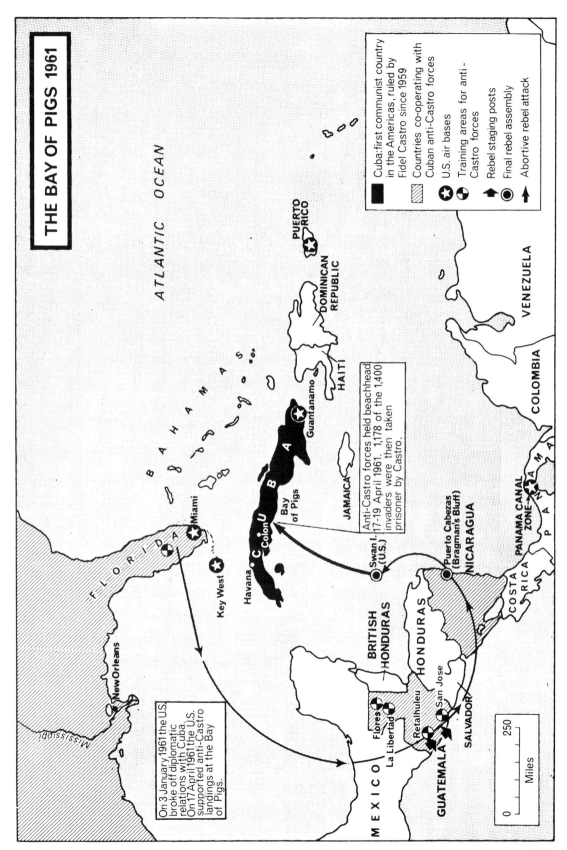

THE BAY OF PIGS 1961

ATLANTIC OCEAN

BAHAMAS

New Orleans

Mississippi

FLORIDA

Miami

Key West

Havana

C U B A

Colon

Bay of Pigs

Guantanamo

JAMAICA

HAITI

DOMINICAN REPUBLIC

PUERTO RICO

MEXICO

GUATEMALA

Flores

La Libertad

Retalhuleu

San Jose

SALVADOR

BRITISH HONDURAS

HONDURAS

Swan I. (U.S.)

Puerto Cabezas (Bragman's Bluff)

NICARAGUA

COSTA RICA

PANAMA CANAL ZONE

PANAMA

COLOMBIA

VENEZUELA

On 3 January 1961 the U.S. broke off diplomatic relations with Cuba. On 17 April 1961 the U.S. supported anti-Castro landings at the Bay of Pigs.

Anti-Castro forces held beachhead 17-19 April 1961. 1,178 of the 1,400 invaders were then taken prisoner by Castro.

■	Cuba: first communist country in the Americas, ruled by Fidel Castro since 1959
▨	Countries co-operating with Cuban anti-Castro forces
✪	U.S. air bases
◓◒	Training areas for anti-Castro forces
➤	Rebel staging posts
◉	Final rebel assembly
➤	Abortive rebel attack

0   250
Miles

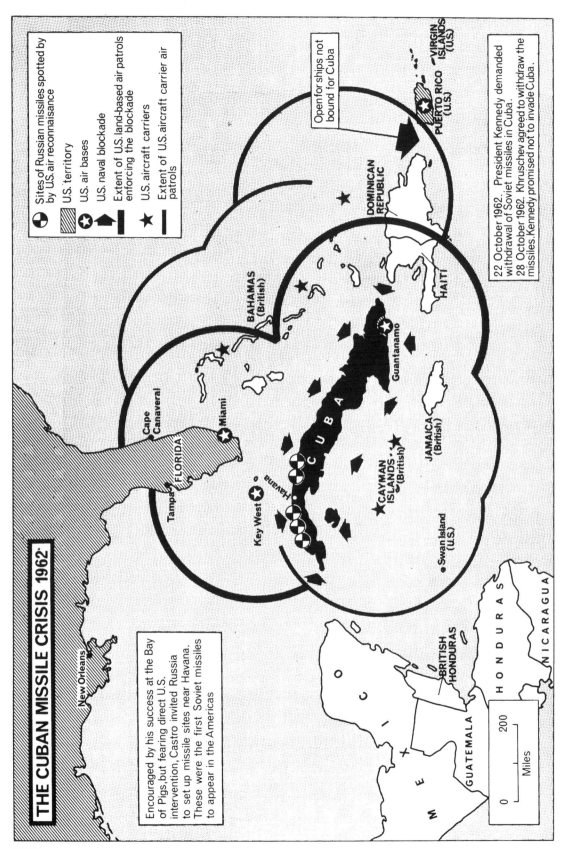

THE CUBAN MISSILE CRISIS 1962

Legend:
- Sites of Russian missiles spotted by U.S. air reconnaissance
- U.S. territory
- U.S. air bases
- U.S. naval blockade
- Extent of U.S. land-based air patrols enforcing the blockade
- U.S. aircraft carriers
- Extent of U.S. aircraft carrier air patrols

Encouraged by his success at the Bay of Pigs, but fearing direct U.S. intervention, Castro invited Russia to set up missile sites near Havana. These were the first Soviet missiles to appear in the Americas

Open for ships not bound for Cuba

22 October 1962. President Kennedy demanded withdrawal of Soviet missiles in Cuba.
28 October 1962. Khruschev agreed to withdraw the missiles. Kennedy promised not to invade Cuba.

New Orleans

FLORIDA
Tampa
Cape Canaveral
Miami
Key West

Havana
C U B A
Guantanamo

BAHAMAS (British)

CAYMAN ISLANDS (British)

JAMAICA (British)

Swan Island (U.S.)

HAITI
DOMINICAN REPUBLIC

PUERTO RICO (U.S.)
VIRGIN ISLANDS (U.S.)

M E X I C O
GUATEMALA
BRITISH HONDURAS
HONDURAS
NICARAGUA

0   200
Miles

102

INDO-CHINA 1945-1954

CHINA

Following the defeat of Japan in 1945, the Vietminh rebels opposed the return of French rule to Indo-China and demanded independence. The Vietminh, who were communist led, attacked the French. The U.S. paid France 78% of the cost of the war, 1953-1954. On 7 May 1954 French troops, besieged at Dien Bien Phu, surrendered. An armistice was signed on 21 July. "North" Vietnam went to the Vietminh and "South" Vietnam to a pro-French and pro-U.S. Government, following the Geneva Conference, April-July 1954.

Mekong

Red

TONKIN

Dien Bien Phu

Hanoi

NORTH VIETNAM

Haiphong

BURMA

Mekong

Gulf
of
Tonkin

HAINAN
(China)

Luang
Prabang

Vientiane

L A O S

Vinh

A N N A M

S I A M

(THAILAND)

Hué

Danang

Quangngai

Bangkok

Mekong

CAMBODIA

SOUTH VIETNAM

Binh Dinh

Pnompenh

Dalat

Phanrang

COCHIN CHINA

Saigon

	Boundary of French Indo-China
	Controlled by Vietminh : 1946-1950
	Gained by Vietminh : 1952-1954
◆◆◆◆	Vietnam as divided into North and South by the Geneva Conference of 1954

0   150
Miles

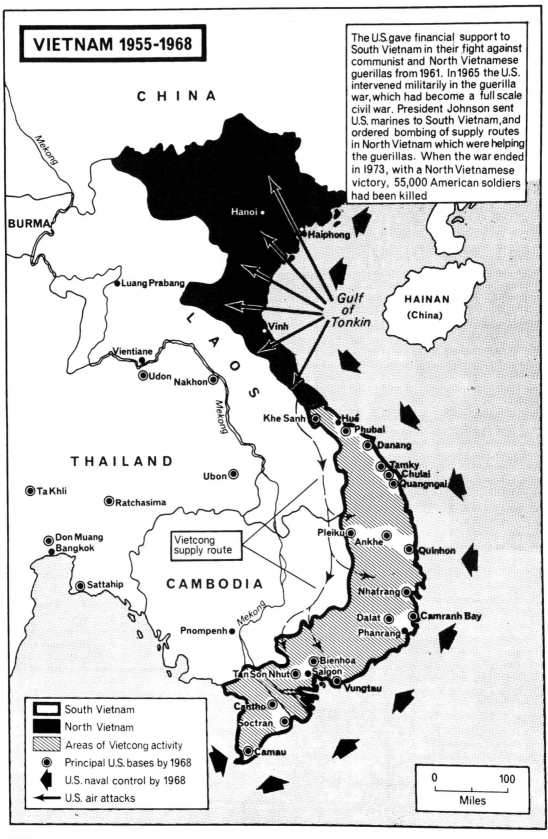

VIETNAM 1955-1968

CHINA

The U.S. gave financial support to South Vietnam in their fight against communist and North Vietnamese guerillas from 1961. In 1965 the U.S. intervened militarily in the guerilla war, which had become a full scale civil war. President Johnson sent U.S. marines to South Vietnam, and ordered bombing of supply routes in North Vietnam which were helping the guerillas. When the war ended in 1973, with a North Vietnamese victory, 55,000 American soldiers had been killed

Mekong

BURMA

Hanoi

Haiphong

Luang Prabang

HAINAN (China)

L A O S

Vientiane

Vinh

Gulf of Tonkin

Udon Nakhon

THAILAND

Mekong

Ubon

Khe Sanh Hué
Phubai
Danang
Tamky
Chulai
Quangngai

Ta Khli

Ratchasima

Pleiku Ankhe Quinhon

Don Muang
Bangkok

Vietcong supply route

C A M B O D I A

Nhatrang

Sattahip

Dalat Camranh Bay
Phanrang

Mekong

Pnompenh

Bienhoa
Tan Son Nhut Saigon
Vungtau

Cantho
Soctran

Camau

	South Vietnam
	North Vietnam
	Areas of Vietcong activity
⊚	Principal U.S. bases by 1968
◢	U.S. naval control by 1968
←	U.S. air attacks

0   100

Miles

104

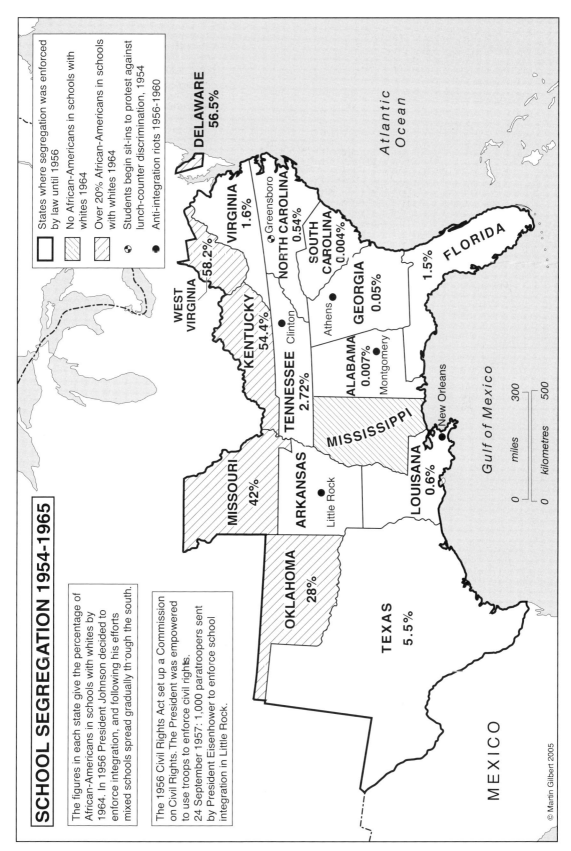

SCHOOL SEGREGATION 1954-1965

The figures in each state give the percentage of African-Americans in schools with whites by 1964. In 1956 President Johnson decided to enforce integration, and following his efforts mixed schools spread gradually through the south.

The 1956 Civil Rights Act set up a Commission on Civil Rights. The President was empowered to use troops to enforce civil rights.
24 September 1957: 1,000 paratroopers sent by President Eisenhower to enforce school integration in Little Rock.

States where segregation was enforced by law until 1956

No African-Americans in schools with whites 1964

Over 20% African-Americans in schools with whites 1964

Students begin sit-ins to protest against lunch-counter discrimination, 1954

Anti-integration riots 1956-1960

DELAWARE
56.5%

VIRGINIA
1.6%

Greensboro

NORTH CAROLINA
0.54%

SOUTH
CAROLINA
0.004%

FLORIDA
1.5%

WEST
VIRGINIA
58.2%

KENTUCKY
54.4%

Clinton

GEORGIA
0.05%

Athens

ALABAMA
0.007%

Montgomery

TENNESSEE
2.72%

MISSOURI
42%

ARKANSAS

Little Rock

MISSISSIPPI

LOUISANA
0.6%

New Orleans

OKLAHOMA
28%

TEXAS
5.5%

MEXICO

Atlantic
Ocean

Gulf of Mexico

0   300
miles

0   500
kilometres

© Martin Gilbert 2005

105

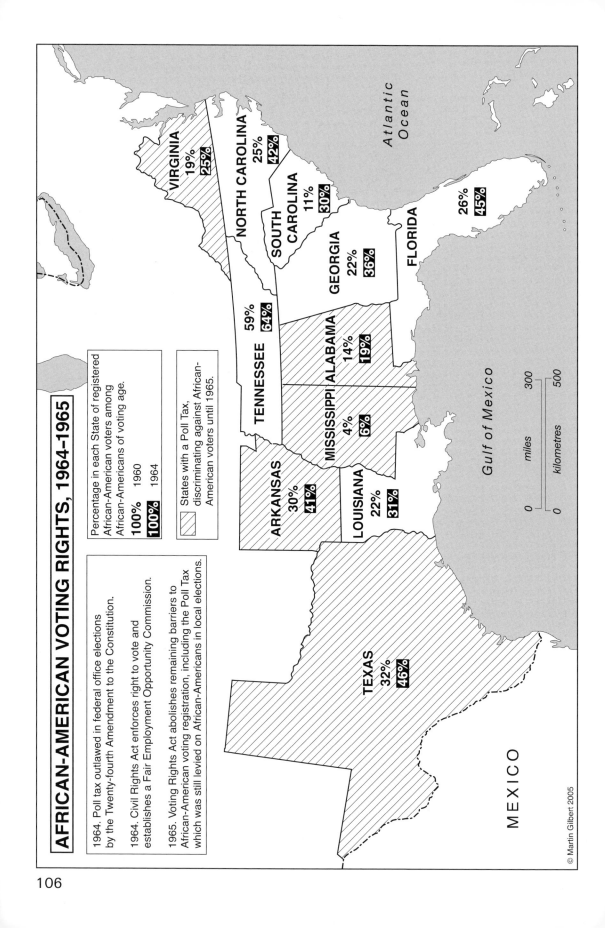

AFRICAN-AMERICAN VOTING RIGHTS, 1964–1965

1964. Poll tax outlawed in federal office elections by the Twenty-fourth Amendment to the Constitution.

1964. Civil Rights Act enforces right to vote and establishes a Fair Employment Opportunity Commission.

1965. Voting Rights Act abolishes remaining barriers to African-American voting registration, including the Poll Tax which was still levied on African-Americans in local elections.

Percentage in each State of registered African-American voters among African-Americans of voting age.

100% 1960
100% 1964

States with a Poll Tax, discriminating against African-American voters until 1965.

VIRGINIA
19%
25%

NORTH CAROLINA
25%
42%

SOUTH CAROLINA
11%
30%

GEORGIA
22%
36%

FLORIDA
26%
45%

TENNESSEE
59%
64%

ALABAMA
14%
19%

MISSISSIPPI
4%
6%

ARKANSAS
30%
41%

LOUISIANA
22%
31%

TEXAS
32%
46%

Atlantic Ocean

Gulf of Mexico

MEXICO

0   miles   300
0   kilometres   500

© Martin Gilbert 2005

106

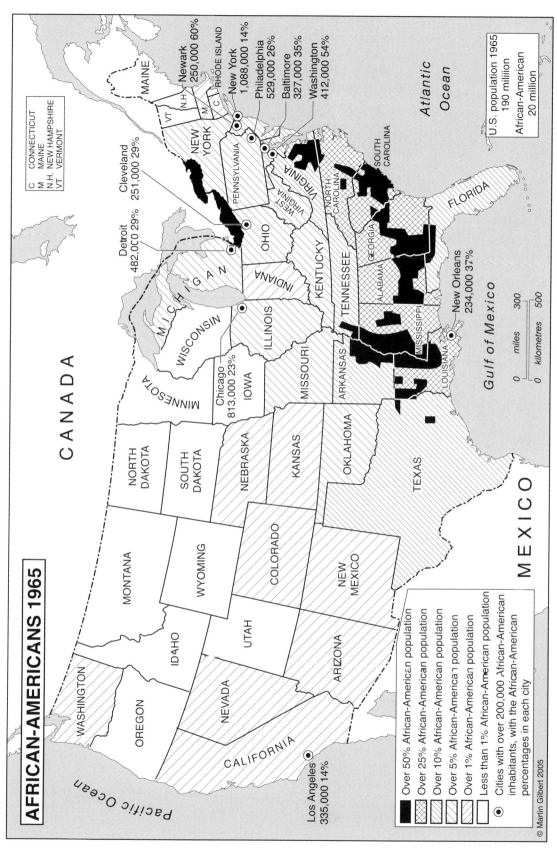

AFRICAN-AMERICANS 1965

CANADA

MEXICO

Pacific Ocean

Atlantic Ocean

Gulf of Mexico

C CONNECTICUT
M MAINE
N.H. NEW HAMPSHIRE
VT VERMONT

U.S. population 1965
190 million
African-American
20 million

Newark 250,000 60%
New York 1,088,000 14%
Philadelphia 529,000 26%
Baltimore 327,000 35%
Washington 412,000 54%

Cleveland 251,000 29%
Detroit 482,000 29%
Chicago 813,000 23%
Los Angeles 335,000 14%
New Orleans 234,000 37%

RHODE ISLAND

MAINE
N.H.
VT
NEW YORK
PENNSYLVANIA
OHIO
MICHIGAN
WISCONSIN
MINNESOTA
ILLINOIS
IOWA
INDIANA
WEST VIRGINIA
VIRGINIA
KENTUCKY
NORTH CAROLINA
SOUTH CAROLINA
TENNESSEE
GEORGIA
ALABAMA
MISSISSIPPI
ARKANSAS
LOUISIANA
MISSOURI
OKLAHOMA
TEXAS
FLORIDA
NORTH DAKOTA
SOUTH DAKOTA
NEBRASKA
KANSAS
COLORADO
NEW MEXICO
WYOMING
MONTANA
UTAH
IDAHO
NEVADA
ARIZONA
CALIFORNIA
WASHINGTON
OREGON

miles 0 300
kilometres 0 500

Over 50% African-American population
Over 25% African-American population
Over 10% African-American population
Over 5% African-American population
Over 1% African-American population
Less than 1% African-American population
⊙ Cities with over 200,000 African-American inhabitants, with the African-American percentages in each city

© Martin Gilbert 2005

107

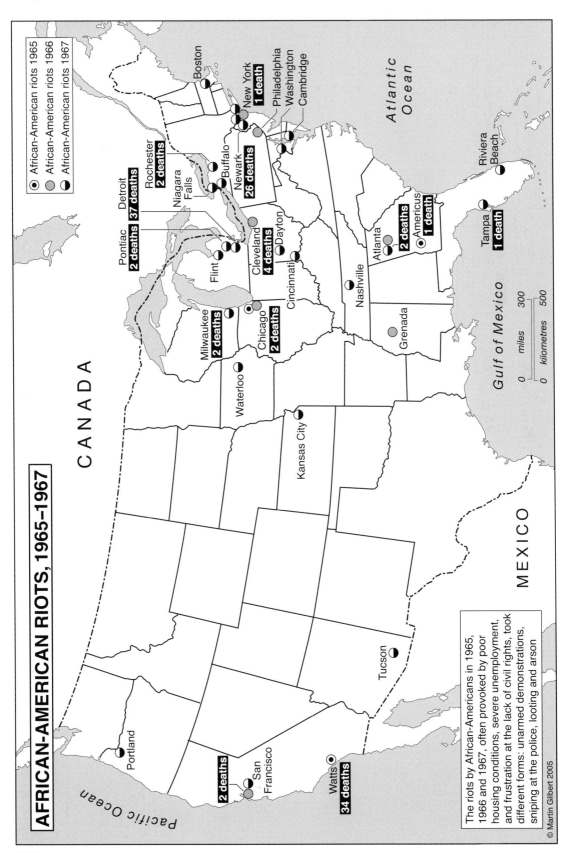

AFRICAN-AMERICAN RIOTS, 1965–1967

African-American riots 1965
African-American riots 1966
African-American riots 1967

CANADA

Pacific Ocean

Atlantic Ocean

Boston

New York
1 death

Philadelphia
Washington
Cambridge

Buffalo

Rochester
2 deaths

Newark
26 deaths

Detroit
37 deaths

Niagara
Falls

Pontiac
2 deaths

Flint

Dayton

Cleveland
4 deaths

Cincinnati

Milwaukee
2 deaths

Chicago
2 deaths

Waterloo

Nashville

Atlanta
2 deaths

Americus
1 death

Tampa
1 death

Riviera
Beach

Grenada

Kansas City

Tucson

Portland

San
Francisco
2 deaths

Watts
34 deaths

Gulf of Mexico

MEXICO

0   miles   300

0   kilometres   500

The riots by African-Americans in 1965,
1966 and 1967, often provoked by poor
housing conditions, severe unemployment,
and frustration at the lack of civil rights, took
different forms: unarmed demonstrations,
sniping at the police, looting and arson

© Martin Gilbert 2005

108

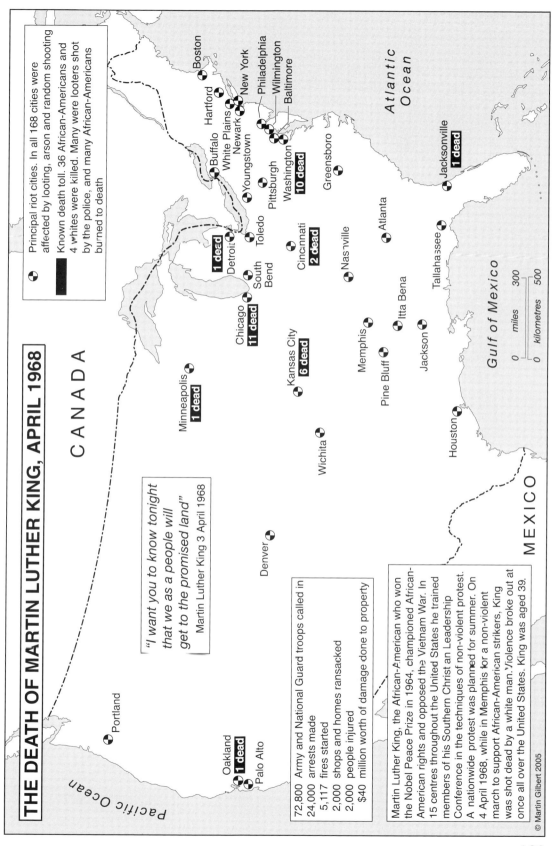

THE DEATH OF MARTIN LUTHER KING, APRIL 1968

CANADA

Pacific Ocean

Atlantic Ocean

Gulf of Mexico

MEXICO

- Principal riot cities. In all 168 cities were affected by looting, arson and random shooting
- Known death toll. 36 African-Americans and 4 whites were killed. Many were looters shot by the police, and many African-Americans burned to death

"I want you to know tonight that we as a people will get to the promised land"
Martin Luther King 3 April 1968

72,800   Army and National Guard troops called in
24,000   arrests made
5,117   fires started
2,000   shops and homes ransacked
2,000   people injured
$40   million worth of damage done to property

Martin Luther King, the African-American who won the Nobel Peace Prize in 1964, championed African-American rights and opposed the Vietnam War. In 15 centres throughout the United States he trained members of his Southern Christ an Leadership Conference in the techniques of non-violent protest. A nationwide protest was planned for summer. On 4 April 1968, while in Memphis for a non-violent march to support African-American strikers, King was shot dead by a white man. Violence broke out at once all over the United States. King was aged 39.

Portland

Oakland **1 dead**
Palo Alto

Denver

Minneapolis **1 dead**

Wichita

Kansas City **6 dead**

Chicago **11 dead**
South Bend

Detroit **1 dead**
Toledo

Cincinnati **2 dead**

Nashville

Pine Bluff

Jackson

Memphis

Itta Bena

Atlanta

Tallahassee

Houston

Buffalo
White Plains
Youngstown
Pittsburgh

Boston
Hartford
New York
Newark
Philadelphia
Wilmington
Baltimore
Washington **10 dead**

Greensboro

Jacksonville **1 dead**

0   miles   300
0   kilometres   500

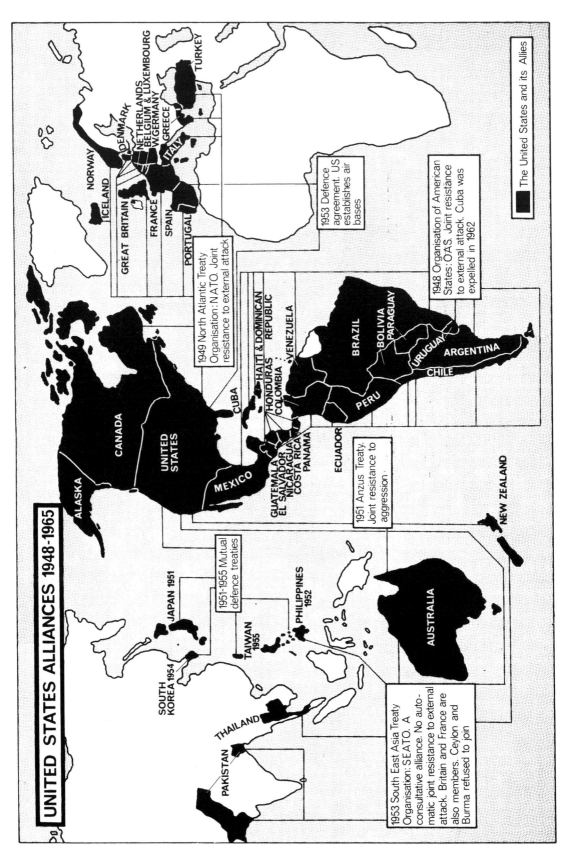

UNITED STATES ALLIANCES 1948-1965

The United States and its Allies

ALASKA

CANADA

UNITED STATES

MEXICO

GUATEMALA
EL SALVADOR
NICARAGUA
COSTA RICA
PANAMA

CUBA

HAITI & DOMINICAN REPUBLIC
HONDURAS
COLOMBIA
VENEZUELA

ECUADOR

PERU

BRAZIL
BOLIVIA
PARAGUAY
CHILE
URUGUAY
ARGENTINA

NORWAY
ICELAND
DENMARK
GREAT BRITAIN
FRANCE
SPAIN
PORTUGAL
NETHERLANDS
BELGIUM & LUXEMBOURG
W.GERMANY
ITALY
GREECE
TURKEY

JAPAN 1951
SOUTH KOREA 1954
TAIWAN 1955
PHILIPPINES 1952
THAILAND
PAKISTAN

AUSTRALIA

NEW ZEALAND

1949 North Atlantic Treaty Organisation: NATO. Joint resistance to external attack

1953 Defence agreement. US establishes air bases

1948 Organisation of American States: OAS. Joint resistance to external attack. Cuba was expelled in 1962

1951 Anzus Treaty. Joint resistance to aggression

1951-1955 Mutual defence treaties

1953 South East Asia Treaty Organisation: SEATO. A consultative alliance. No automatic joint resistance to external attack. Britain and France are also members. Ceylon and Burma refused to join

110

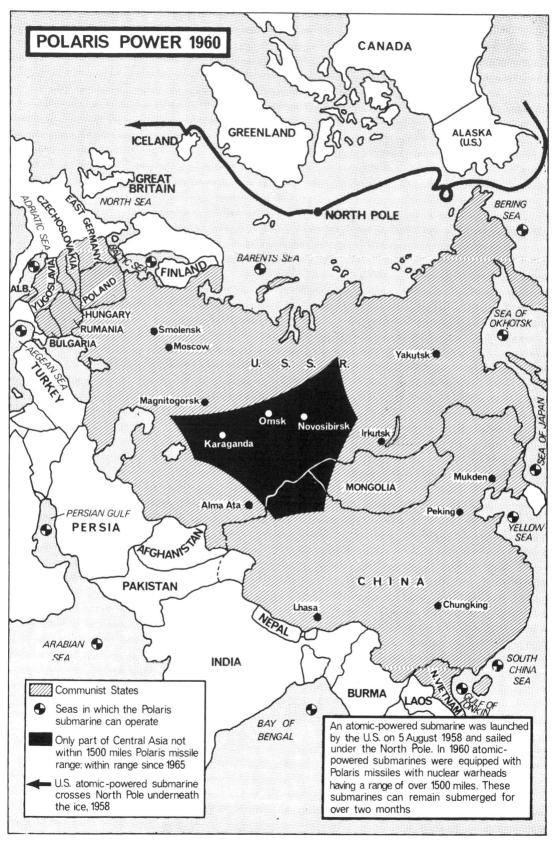

POLARIS POWER 1960

CANADA

GREENLAND

ICELAND

ALASKA (U.S.)

GREAT BRITAIN

NORTH SEA

NORTH POLE

BERING SEA

EAST GERMANY

BALTIC SEA

FINLAND

BARENTS SEA

SEA OF OKHOTSK

ADRIATIC SEA

CZECHOSLOVAKIA

YUGOSLAVIA

ALB.

POLAND

HUNGARY

RUMANIA

BULGARIA

AEGEAN SEA

TURKEY

Smolensk

Moscow

U. S. S. R.

Yakutsk

Magnitogorsk

Omsk

Novosibirsk

Irkutsk

SEA OF JAPAN

Karaganda

MONGOLIA

Mukden

PERSIAN GULF

PERSIA

Alma Ata

Peking

YELLOW SEA

AFGHANISTAN

PAKISTAN

C H I N A

NEPAL

Lhasa

Chungking

ARABIAN SEA

INDIA

BURMA

LAOS

N. VIETNAM

GULF OF TONKIN

SOUTH CHINA SEA

BAY OF BENGAL

Communist States

⊕ Seas in which the Polaris submarine can operate

■ Only part of Central Asia not within 1500 miles Polaris missile range: within range since 1965

← U.S. atomic-powered submarine crosses North Pole underneath the ice, 1958

An atomic-powered submarine was launched by the U.S. on 5 August 1958 and sailed under the North Pole. In 1960 atomic-powered submarines were equipped with Polaris missiles with nuclear warheads having a range of over 1500 miles. These submarines can remain submerged for over two months

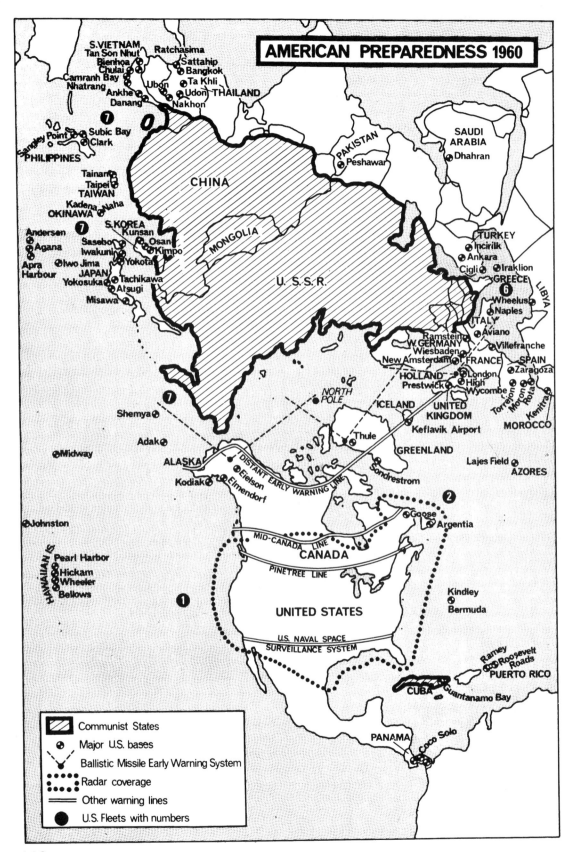

AMERICAN PREPAREDNESS 1960

S.VIETNAM
Tan Son Nhut • Ratchasima
Bienhoa • Sattahip
Chulai • Bangkok
Camranh Bay • Ta Khli
Nhatrang • Ubon THAILAND
Ankhe • Udon
Danang • Nakhon

Sangley Point • Subic Bay
• Clark
PHILIPPINES

Tainan
Taipei
TAIWAN
Kadena • Naha
OKINAWA

Andersen
Agana

Apra • Iwo Jima
Harbour
Yokosuka • Tachikawa
Atsugi
Misawa

S.KOREA • Kunsan
Sasebo • Osan
Iwakuni • Kimpo
Yokota

CHINA

MONGOLIA

U.S.S.R.

PAKISTAN
• Peshawar

SAUDI
ARABIA
• Dhahran

TURKEY
Incirlik
• Ankara
Cigli • Iraklion
GREECE
Wheelus
• Naples
ITALY
Ramstein • Aviano
W.GERMANY • Villefranche
Wiesbaden
New Amsterdam FRANCE
HOLLAND • London SPAIN
Prestwick • High • Zaragoza
Wycombe
Torrejon Moron Rota
ICELAND UNITED
KINGDOM MOROCCO
Kentira
LIBYA

NORTH
POLE

Shemya

Adak

Midway

ALASKA
Eielson
Kodiak • Elmendorf

DISTANT EARLY WARNING LINE

Thule
Keflavik Airport

GREENLAND
Sondrestrom

Lajes Field
AZORES

Johnston

HAWAIIAN IS.
Pearl Harbor
Hickam
Wheeler
Bellows

MID-CANADA LINE
CANADA
PINETREE LINE

UNITED STATES

U.S. NAVAL SPACE
SURVEILLANCE SYSTEM

Goose
Argentia

Kindley
Bermuda

Ramey • Roosevelt
Roads
PUERTO RICO
CUBA • Guantanamo Bay

PANAMA Coco Solo

Legend

- ▨ Communist States
- ⊕ Major U.S. bases
- ⋎ Ballistic Missile Early Warning System
- •••• Radar coverage
- ═ Other warning lines
- ● U.S. Fleets with numbers

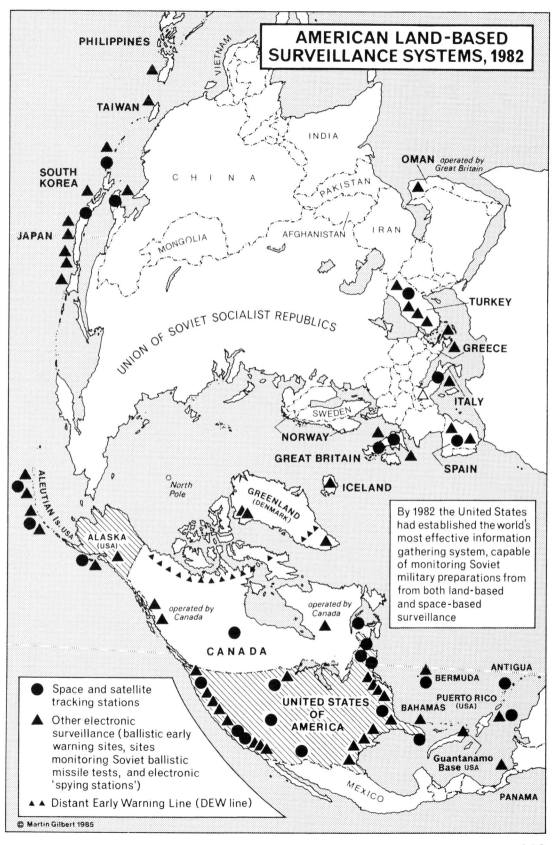

AMERICAN LAND-BASED SURVEILLANCE SYSTEMS, 1982

PHILIPPINES

VIETNAM

TAIWAN

INDIA

CHINA

OMAN *operated by Great Britain*

SOUTH KOREA

PAKISTAN

JAPAN

MONGOLIA

AFGHANISTAN

IRAN

TURKEY

GREECE

UNION OF SOVIET SOCIALIST REPUBLICS

ITALY

SWEDEN

NORWAY

GREAT BRITAIN

SPAIN

ALEUTIAN Is. USA

North Pole

GREENLAND (DENMARK)

ICELAND

ALASKA (USA)

By 1982 the United States had established the world's most effective information gathering system, capable of monitoring Soviet military preparations from from both land-based and space-based surveillance

operated by Canada

operated by Canada

CANADA

ANTIGUA

BERMUDA

PUERTO RICO (USA)

BAHAMAS

UNITED STATES OF AMERICA

● Space and satellite tracking stations

▲ Other electronic surveillance (ballistic early warning sites, sites monitoring Soviet ballistic missile tests, and electronic 'spying stations')

▲ ▲ Distant Early Warning Line (DEW line)

Guantanamo Base USA

MEXICO

PANAMA

© Martin Gilbert 1985

113

THE UNITED STATES AND THE SOVIET UNION IN OUTER SPACE

Between 1957 and 1981 a total of 2,725 satellites were launched, most of them by the United States and the Soviet Union. Some of the principal satellites in orbit in 1981 are shown here. In March 1981 the US National Aeronautics and Space Administration (NASA) launched its Columbia Orbiter, the first re-usable space vehicle (44 missions planned by the end of 1985, nine of them military)

SATELLITES

Early Warning
USA   22
USSR 25

Communications
USA   118
USSR   366
NATO   5
UK   4
France   2

Photographic reconnaisance
USA   235
USSR   538
China   3

Electronic reconnaisance
USA   790
USSR   125

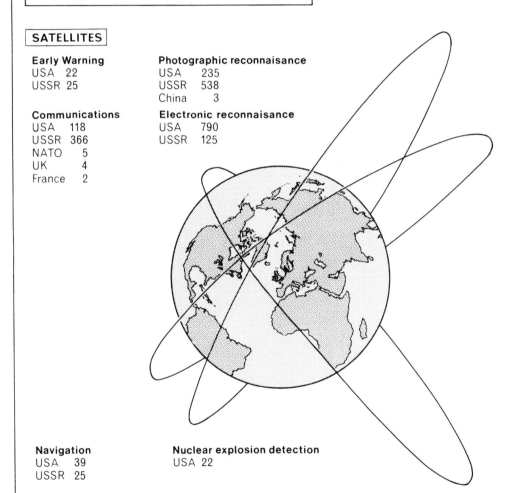

Navigation
USA   39
USSR 25

Nuclear explosion detection
USA 22

Ocean surveillance
USA   18
USSR 32

Interception - destruction
USSR 33

In January 1985, at Geneva, the United States and the Soviet Union agreed to begin talks aimed at an agreement over the restriction of warfare in outer space. The United States was involved in the development of anti-satellite missiles and anti-missile lasers, and the Soviet Union in anti-satellite satellites

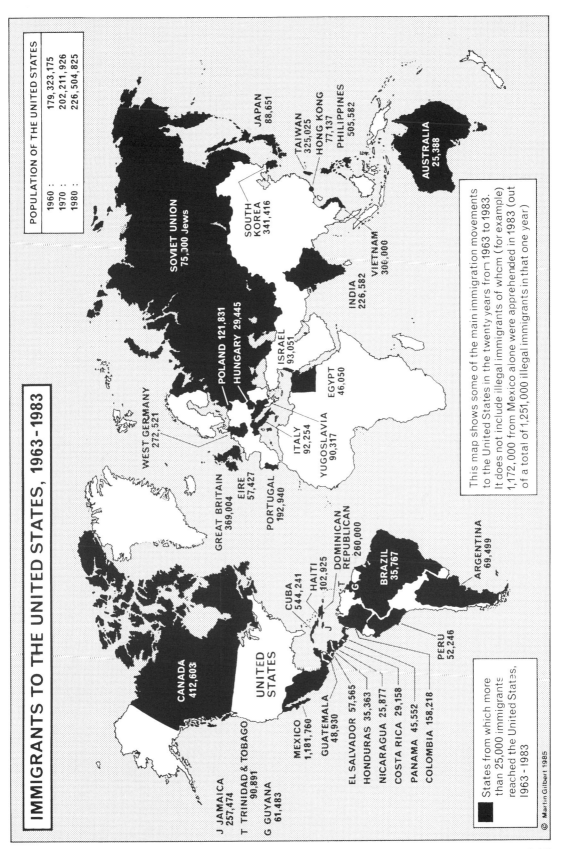

IMMIGRANTS TO THE UNITED STATES, 1963–1983

POPULATION OF THE UNITED STATES

1960 :	179,323,175
1970 :	202,211,926
1980 :	226,504,825

JAPAN 88,651

TAIWAN 325,025

HONG KONG 77,137

PHILIPPINES 505,582

AUSTRALIA 25,388

SOVIET UNION 75,000 Jews

SOUTH KOREA 341,416

VIETNAM 306,000

INDIA 226,582

POLAND 121,831

HUNGARY 29,445

ISRAEL 93,051

EGYPT 46,050

WEST GERMANY 272,521

ITALY 92,254

YUGOSLAVIA 90,317

GREAT BRITAIN 369,004

EIRE 57,427

PORTUGAL 192,940

DOMINICAN REPUBLIC 260,000

ARGENTINA 69,499

BRAZIL 35,767

CUBA 544,241

HAITI 102,925

PERU 52,246

CANADA 412,603

UNITED STATES

MEXICO 1,181,760

GUATEMALA 48,930

EL SALVADOR 57,565

HONDURAS 35,363

NICARAGUA 25,877

COSTA RICA 29,158

PANAMA 45,552

COLOMBIA 158,218

J JAMAICA 257,474

T TRINIDAD & TOBAGO 90,891

G GUYANA 61,483

This map shows some of the main immigration movements to the United States in the twenty years from 1963 to 1983. It does not include illegal immigrants of whcm (for example) 1,172,000 from Mexico alone were apprehended in 1983 (out of a total of 1,251,000 illegal immigrants in that one year)

States from which more than 25,000 immigrants reached the United States, 1963–1983

© Martin Gilbert 1985

115

THE UNITED STATES IN THE PACIFIC, 1823-1993

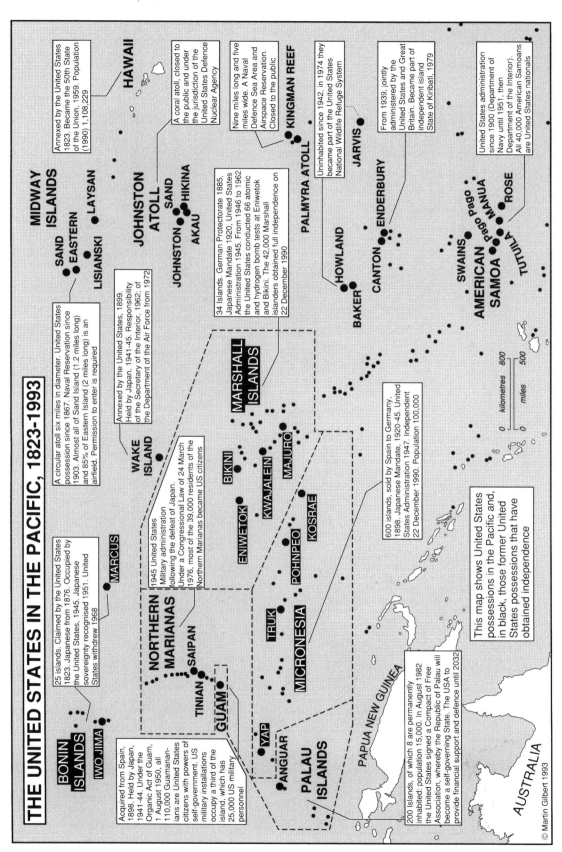

BONIN ISLANDS

IWO JIMA

25 islands. Claimed by the United States 1823. Japanese from 1876. Occupied by the United States. 1945. Japanese sovereignty recognised 1951. United States withdrew 1968

MARCUS

Acquired from Spain, 1898. Held by Japan, 1941-44. Under the Organic Act of Guam, 1 August 1950, all 110,000 Guamananians are United States citizens with powers of self-government. US military installations occupy a third of the island, which has 25,000 US military personnel

NORTHERN MARIANAS

SAIPAN

TINIAN

GUAM

1945 United States Military administration following the defeat of Japan. Under a Congressional Law of 24 March 1976, most of the 39,000 residents of the Northern Marianas became US citizens

YAP

ANGUAR

PALAU ISLANDS

200 Islands, of which 8 are permanently inhabited: population 15,000. In August 1982 the United States signed a Compact of Free Association, whereby the Republic of Palau will become a self-governing State. The USA to provide financial support and defence until 2032

TRUK

MICRONESIA

POHNPEO

KOSRAE

ENIWETOK

BIKINI

KWAJALEIN

MAJURO

MARSHALL ISLANDS

600 islands, sold by Spain to Germany, 1898. Japanese Mandate, 1920-45. United States Administration 1947. Independent 22 December 1990. Population 100,000

34 Islands. German Protectorate 1885, Japanese Mandate 1920, United States Administration 1945. From 1946 to 1962 the United States conducted 66 atomic and hydrogen bomb tests at Eniwetok and Bikini. The 42,000 Marshall islanders obtained full independence on 22 December 1990

WAKE ISLAND

Annexed by the United States, 1899. Held by Japan, 1941-45. Responsibility of the Secretary of the Interior, 1962; of the Department of the Air Force from 1972

A circular atoll six miles in diameter. United States possession since 1867. Naval Reservation since 1903. Almost all of Sand Island (1.2 miles long) and 85% of Eastern Island (2 miles long) is an airfield. Permission to enter is required

MIDWAY ISLANDS

SAND

EASTERN

LISIANSKI ● LAYSAN

HAWAII

Annexed by the United States 1823. Became the 50th State of the Union, 1959. Population (1990) 1,108,229

JOHNSTON ATOLL

JOHNSTON

AKAU

SAND

HIKINA

A coral atoll, closed to the public and under the jurisdiction of the United States Defence Nuclear Agency

Nine miles long and five miles wide. A Naval Defence Sea Area and Airspace Reservation. Closed to the public

KINGMAN REEF

PALMYRA ATOLL

Uninhabited since 1942, in 1974 they became part of the United States National Wildlife Refuge System

JARVIS

ENDERBURY

CANTON

From 1939, jointly administered by the United States and Great Britain. Became part of independent island State of Kiribati, 1979

HOWLAND

BAKER

SWAINS

pago ● pago

AMERICAN SAMOA

MANUA

ROSE

TUTUILA

United States administration since 1900 (Department of Navy until 1951, then Department of the Interior). All 40,000 American Samoans are United States nationals

This map shows United States possessions in the Pacific and, in black, those former United States possessions that have obtained independence

PAPUA NEW GUINEA

AUSTRALIA

0   800 kilometres
0 500 miles

© Martin Gilbert 1993

GREAT POWER CONFRONTATION AND CONCILIATION, 1972-1986

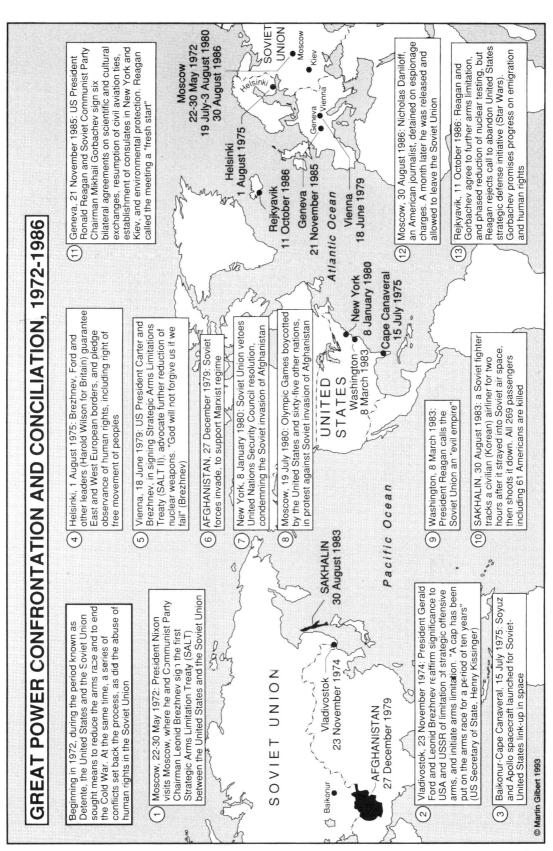

Beginning in 1972, during the period known as Detente, the United States and the Soviet Union sought means to reduce the arms race and to end the Cold War. At the same time, a series of conflicts set back the process, as did the abuse of human rights in the Soviet Union

(1) Moscow, 22-30 May 1972: President Nixon visits Moscow, where he and Communist Party Chairman Leonid Brezhnev sign the first Strategic Arms Limitation Treaty (SALT) between the United States and the Soviet Union

(2) Vladivostok, 23 November 1974: President Gerald Ford and Leonid Brezhnev reaffirm significance to USA and USSR of limitation of strategic offensive arms, and initiate arms limitation. "A cap has been put on the arms race for a period of ten years" (US Secretary of State, Henry Kissinger)

(3) Baikonur-Cape Canaveral, 15 July 1975: Soyuz and Apollo spacecraft launched for Soviet-United States link-up in space

(4) Helsinki, 1 August 1975: Brezhnev, Ford and other leaders (Harold Wilson for Britain) guarantee East and West European borders, and pledge observance of human rights, including right of free movement of peoples

(5) Vienna, 18 June 1979: US President Carter and Brezhnev, in signing Strategic Arms Limitations Treaty (SALT II), advocate further reduction of nuclear weapons. "God will not forgive us if we fail" (Brezhnev)

(6) AFGHANISTAN, 27 December 1979: Soviet forces invade, to support Marxist regime

(7) New York, 8 January 1980: Soviet Union vetoes United Nations Security Council resolution, condemning the Soviet invasion of Afghanistan

(8) Moscow, 19 July 1980: Olympic Games boycotted by the United States and sixty-five other nations, in protest against Soviet invasion of Afghanistan

(9) Washington, 8 March 1983: President Reagan calls the Soviet Union an "evil empire"

(10) SAKHALIN, 30 August 1983: a Soviet fighter tracks a civilian (Korean) airliner for two hours after it strayed into Soviet air space, then shoots it down. All 269 passengers including 61 Americans are killed

(11) Geneva, 21 November 1985: US President Ronald Reagan and Soviet Communist Party Chairman Mikhail Gorbachev sign six bilateral agreements on scientific and cultural exchanges, resumption of civil aviation ties, establishment of consulates in New York and Kiev, and environmental protection. Reagan called the meeting a "fresh start"

(12) Moscow, 30 August 1986: Nicholas Daniloff, an American journalist, detained on espionage charges. A month later he was released and allowed to leave the Soviet Union

(13) Rejkyavik, 11 October 1986: Reagan and Gorbachev agree to further arms limitation, and phased reduction of nuclear testing, but Reagan rejects call to abandon United States strategic defense initiative (Star Wars). Gorbachev promises progress on emigration and human rights

© Martin Gilbert 1993

THE COLD WAR AND ARMS SUPPLIES, 1984-1988

One aspect of the Cold War was the build-up throughout the world of Soviet and American spheres of influence. In every region of the globe nations took sides in the ideological divide and were armed by their respective patrons. Local conflicts and confrontations were often thus exacerbated or sustained, as between East and West Europe, North and South Korea, India and Pakistan, and Israel and its Arab neighbours. This map shows respective arms supplies in the last five years of United States - Soviet confrontation

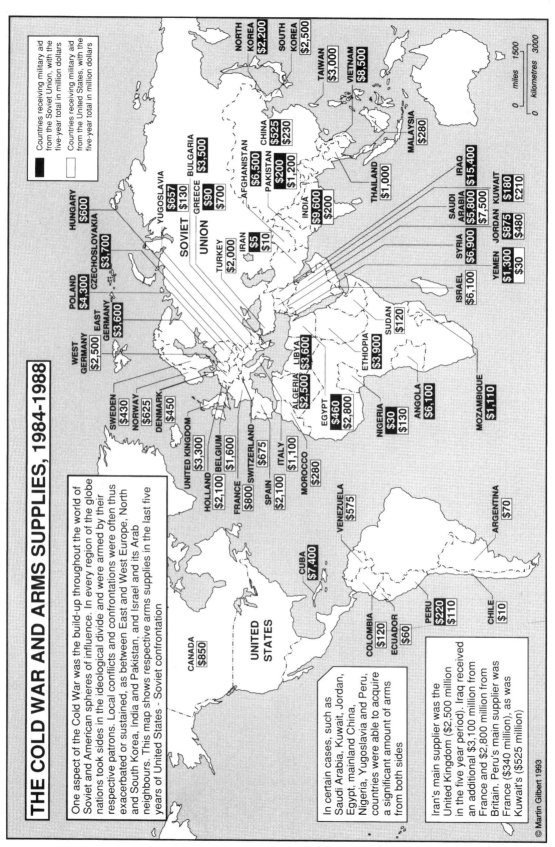

In certain cases, such as Saudi Arabia, Kuwait, Jordan, Egypt, mainland China, Nigeria, Yugoslavia and Peru, countries were able to acquire a significant amount of arms from both sides

Iran's main supplier was the United Kingdom ($2,500 million in the five year period). Iraq received an additional $3,100 million from France and $2,800 million from Britain. Peru's main supplier was France ($340 million), as was Kuwait's ($525 million).

Countries receiving military aid from the Soviet Union, with the five-year total in million dollars

Countries receiving military aid from the United States, with the five-year total in million dollars

CANADA $850

UNITED STATES

CUBA $7,400

VENEZUELA $575

COLOMBIA $120

ECUADOR $60

PERU $220 $110

CHILE $10

ARGENTINA $70

SWEDEN $430

NORWAY $625

DENMARK $450

WEST GERMANY $2,500

EAST GERMANY $3,600

POLAND $4,300

CZECHOSLOVAKIA $3,700

HUNGARY $600

YUGOSLAVIA $657 $130

BULGARIA $3,500

SOVIET UNION

GREECE $90 $700

TURKEY $2,000

UNITED KINGDOM $3,300

HOLLAND $2,100

BELGIUM $1,600

FRANCE $800

SWITZERLAND $675

SPAIN $2,100

ITALY $1,100

MOROCCO $280

ALGERIA $2,500

LIBYA $3,600

EGYPT $460 $2,800

NIGERIA $30 $130

ANGOLA $6,100

MOZAMBIQUE $1,110

SUDAN $120

ETHIOPIA $3,900

IRAN $5 $10

AFGHANISTAN $6,500

PAKISTAN $200 $1,200

INDIA $9,600 $200

CHINA $525 $230

THAILAND $1,000

MALAYSIA $280

ISRAEL $6,100

SYRIA $6,900

YEMEN $1,300 $30

JORDAN $875 $480

KUWAIT $180 £210

SAUDI ARABIA $5,800 $7,500

IRAQ $15,400

NORTH KOREA $2,200

SOUTH KOREA $2,500

TAIWAN $3,000

VIETNAM $8,500

0   miles   1500
0   kilometres   3000

© Martin Gilbert 1993

118

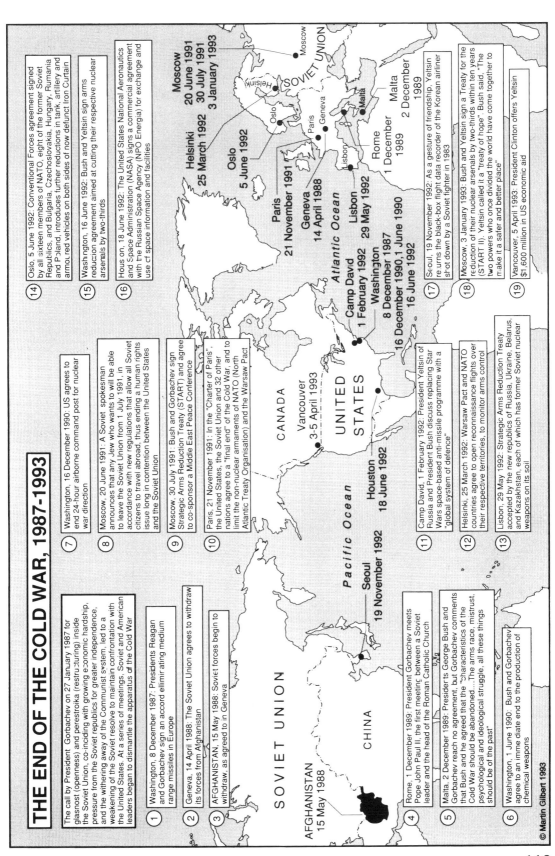

THE END OF THE COLD WAR, 1987-1993

The call by President Gorbachev on 27 January 1987 for glasnost (openness) and perestroika (restructuring) inside the Soviet Union, co-inciding with growing economic hardship, pressure from the Soviet republics for greater independence, and the withering away of the Communist system, led to a weakening of the Soviet resolve to maintain confrontation with the United States. At a series of meetings, Soviet and American leaders began to dismantle the apparatus of the Cold War

(1) Washington, 8 December 1987: Presidents Reagan and Gorbachev sign an accord eliminating medium range missiles in Europe

(2) Geneva, 14 April 1988: The Soviet Union agrees to withdraw its forces from Afghanistan

(3) AFGHANISTAN, 15 May 1988: Soviet forces begin to withdraw, as agreed to in Geneva

(4) Rome, 1 December 1989: President Gorbachev meets Pope John Paul II, the first meeting between a Soviet leader and the head of the Roman Catholic Church

(5) Malta, 2 December 1989: Presidents George Bush and Gorbachev reach no agreement, but Gorbachev comments that Bush and he agreed that the "characteristics of the Cold War should be abandoned....The arms race, mistrust, psychological and ideological struggle, all these things should be of the past"

(6) Washington, 1 June 1990: Bush and Gorbachev agree to an immediate end to the production of chemical weapons

(7) Washington, 16 December 1990: US agrees to end 24-hour airborne command post for nuclear war direction

(8) Moscow, 20 June 1991: A Soviet spokesman announces that any Jew who wants to will be able to leave the Soviet Union from 1 July 1991, in accordance with new regulations that allow all Soviet citizens to travel abroad, thus ending a human rights issue long in contention between the United States and the Soviet Union

(9) Moscow, 30 July 1991: Bush and Gorbachev sign Strategic Arms Reduction Treaty (START) and agree to co-sponsor a Middle East Peace Conference

(10) Paris, 21 November 1991: In the "Charter of Paris", the United States, the Soviet Union and 32 other nations agree to a "final end" of the Cold War, and to limit the non-nuclear armaments of NATO (North Atlantic Treaty Organisation) and the Warsaw Pact

(11) Camp David, 1 February 1992: President Yeltsin of Russia and President Bush discuss replacing Star Wars space-based anti-missile programme with a "global system of defence"

(12) Helsinki, 25 March 1992: Warsaw Pact and NATO countries agree to open reconnaissance flights over their respective territories, to monitor arms control

(13) Lisbon, 29 May 1992: Strategic Arms Reduction Treaty accepted by the new republics of Russia, Ukraine, Belarus, and Kazakhstan, each of which has former Soviet nuclear weapons on its soil

(14) Oslo, 5 June 1992: Conventional Forces agreement signed by all sixteen members of NATO, eight of the former Soviet Republics, and Bulgaria, Czechoslovakia, Hungary, Rumania and Poland, introduces further reductions in tank, artillery and armoured vehicles on both sides of now defunct Iron Curtain

(15) Washington, 16 June 1992: Bush and Yeltsin sign arms reduction agreement aimed at cutting their respective nuclear arsenals by two-thirds

(16) Houston, 18 June 1992: The United States National Aeronautics and Space Administration (NASA) signs a commercial agreement with the Russian Space Agency (NPO Energia) for exchange and use of space information and facilities

(17) Seoul, 19 November 1992: As a gesture of friendship, Yeltsin returns the black-box flight data recorder of the Korean airliner shot down by a Soviet fighter in 1983

(18) Seoul, 3 January 1993: Bush and Yeltsin sign a Treaty for the reduction of their nuclear arsenals by two-thirds within ten years (START II). Yeltsin called it a "treaty of hope". Bush said, "The two powers who once divided the world have come together to make it a safer and better place"

(19) Vancouver, 5 April 1993: President Clinton offers Yeltsin $1,600 million in US economic aid

CANADA

UNITED STATES

Vancouver
3-5 April 1993

Houston
18 June 1992

Pacific Ocean

Seoul
19 November 1992

Atlantic Ocean

Camp David
1 February 1992

Washington
8 December 1987
16 December 1990, 1 June 1990
16 June 1992

Lisbon
29 May 1992

Geneva
14 April 1988

Paris
21 November 1991

Oslo
5 June 1992

Helsinki
25 March 1992

Moscow
20 June 1991
30 July 1991
3 January 1993

SOVIET UNION

Helsinki

Oslo

Paris

Geneva

Lisbon

Malta
2 December 1989

Rome
1 December 1989

Moscow

SOVIET UNION

CHINA

AFGHANISTAN
15 May 1988

© Martin Gilbert 1993

119

MILITARY, ECONOMIC AND HUMANITARIAN MISSIONS, 1975-1993

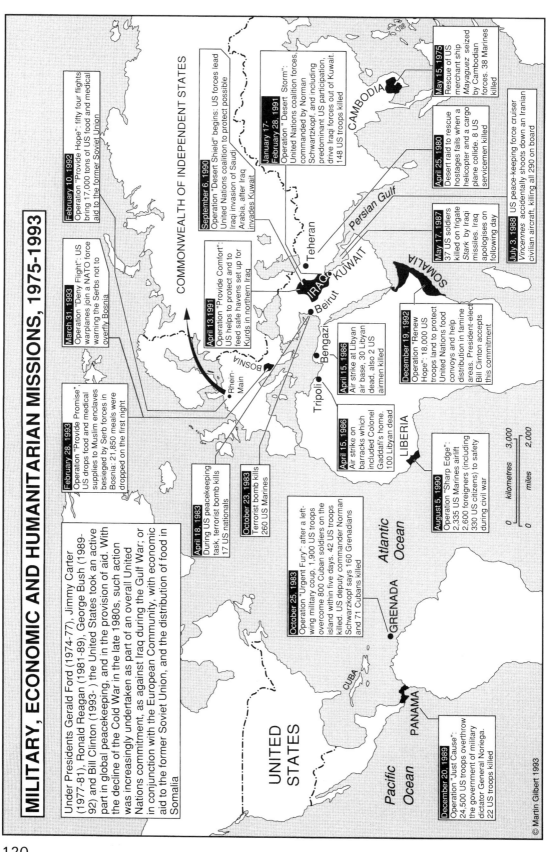

Under Presidents Gerald Ford (1974-77), Jimmy Carter (1977-81), Ronald Reagan (1981-89), George Bush (1989-92) and Bill Clinton (1993-) the United States took an active part in global peacekeeping, and in the provision of aid. With the decline of the Cold War in the late 1980s, such action was increasingly undertaken as part of an overall United Nations commitment, as against Iraq during the Gulf War; or in conjunction with the European Community, with economic aid to the former Soviet Union, and the distribution of food in Somalia

COMMONWEALTH OF INDEPENDENT STATES

February 10, 1992
Operation "Provide Hope": fifty four flights bring 17,000 tons of US food and medical aid to the former Soviet Union

March 31, 1993
Operation "Deny Flight": US warplanes join a NATO force warning the Serbs not to overfly Bosnia

September 6, 1990
Operation "Desert Shield" begins: US forces lead United Nations coalition to protect possible Iraqi invasion of Saudi Arabia, after Iraq invades Kuwait

January 17-February 28, 1991
Operation "Desert Storm": United Nations coalition forces, commanded by Norman Schwartzkopf, and including predominant US participation, drive Iraqi forces out of Kuwait. 148 US troops killed

May 15, 1975
Rescue of US merchant ship Mayaguez seized by Cambodian forces. 38 Marines killed

April 25, 1980
Desert raid to rescue hostages fails when a helicopter and a cargo plane collide. 8 US servicemen killed

April 13, 1991
Operation "Provide Comfort": US helps to protect and to feed safe havens set up for Kurds in northern Iraq

May 17, 1987
37 US soldiers killed on frigate Stark by Iraqi missiles. Iraq apologises on following day

July 3, 1988 US peace-keeping force cruiser Vincennes accidentally shoots down an Iranian civilian aircraft, killing all 290 on board

February 28, 1993
Operation "Provide Promise": US drops food and medical supplies to Muslim enclaves besieged by Serb forces in Bosnia: 21,850 meals were dropped on the first night

April 18, 1983
During US peacekeeping task, terrorist bomb kills 17 US nationals

October 23, 1983
Terrorist bomb kills 260 US Marines

April 15, 1986
Air strike at Libyan air base, 30 Libyan dead, also 2 US airmen killed

April 15, 1986
Air strike on barracks which included Colonel Gaddafi's home. 100 Libyan dead

December 19, 1992
Operation "Renew Hope": 18,000 US troops land to protect United Nations food convoys and help distribution in famine areas. President-elect Bill Clinton accepts this commitment

August 5, 1990
Operation "Sharp Edge": 2,335 US Marines airlift 2,600 foreigners (including 330 US citizens) to safety during civil war

October 25, 1983
Operation "Urgent Fury": after a left-wing military coup, 1,900 US troops overcome 800 Cuban soldiers on the island within five days. 42 US troops killed. US deputy commander Norman Schwarzkopf says 160 Grenadians and 71 Cubans killed

December 20, 1989
Operation "Just Cause": 24,500 US troops overthrow the government of military dictator General Noriega. 22 US troops killed

CAMBODIA

Teheran

Persian Gulf

IRAQ

KUWAIT

Beirut

SOMALIA

Tripoli

Bengazi

BOSNIA

Rhein-Main

LIBERIA

GRENADA

CUBA

PANAMA

UNITED STATES

Pacific Ocean

Atlantic Ocean

0   3,000
kilometres
0   2,000
miles

© Martin Gilbert 1993

120

MAJOR NATURAL AND ACCIDENTAL DISASTERS, 1972-1993

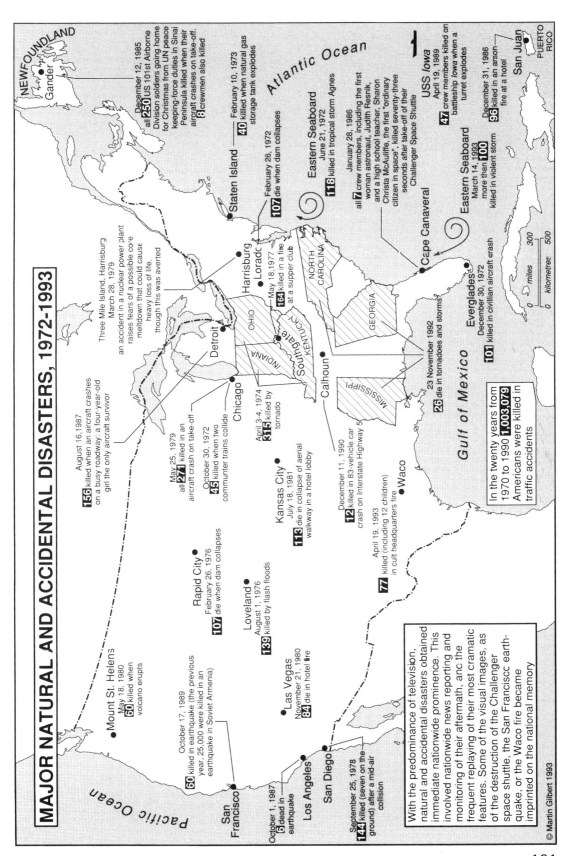

NEWFOUNDLAND
Gander

December 12, 1985 all **250** US 101st Airborne Division soldiers going home for Christmas from UN peace keeping-force duties in Sinai Peninsula killed when their aircraft crashes on take-off. **8** crewmen also killed

Atlantic Ocean

February 10, 1973 **40** killed when natural gas storage tank explodes

Staten Island

February 26, 1972 **107** die when dam collapses

Eastern Seaboard June 21, 1972 **118** killed in tropical storm Agnes

January 28, 1986 all **7** crew members, including the first woman astronaut, Judith Resnik, and a high school teacher, Sharon Christa McAuliffe, the first "ordinary citizen in space", killed seventy-three seconds after take-off of their Challenger Space Shuttle

USS *Iowa* April 19, 1989 **47** crew members killed on battleship *Iowa* when a turret explodes

December 31, 1986 **96** killed in an arson fire at a hotel

San Juan

PUERTO RICO

Cape Canaveral

Eastern Seaboard March 14, 1993 more than **100** killed in violent storm

Three Mile Island, Harrisburg March 28, 1979 an accident in a nuclear power plant raises fears of a possible core meltdown that could cause heavy loss of life, though this was averted

Harrisburg

Lorado

May 18, 1977 **164** killed in a fire at a supper club

NORTH CAROLINA

GEORGIA

23 November 1992 **26** die in tornadoes and storms

Everglades December 30, 1972 **101** killed in civilian aircraft crash

OHIO

INDIANA

Detroit

KENTUCKY

Southgate

Calhoun

MISSISSIPPI

August 16, 1987 **156** killed when an aircraft crashes on a busy roadway: a four-year-old girl the only aircraft survivor

May 25, 1979 all **271** killed in an aircraft crash on take-off

October 30, 1972 **45** killed when two commuter trains collide

Chicago

April 3-4, 1974 **315** killed by tornado

Kansas City July 18, 1981 **113** die in collapse of aerial walkway in a hotel lobby

December 11, 1990 **12** killed in 83-vehicle car crash on Interstate Highway 5

April 19, 1993 **77** killed (including 12 children) in cult headquarters fire

Waco

Gulf of Mexico

In the twenty years from 1970 to 1990 **1,003,079** Americans were killed in traffic accidents

0   miles   300
0 kilometres 500

Rapid City February 26, 1976 **107** die when dam collapses

Mount St. Helens May 18, 1980 **60** killed when volcano erupts

October 17, 1989 **60** killed in earthquake (the previous year, 25,000 were killed in an earthquake in Soviet Armenia)

Loveland August 1, 1976 **139** killed by flash floods

Las Vegas November 21, 1980 **84** die in hotel fire

San Francisco

October 1, 1987 **6** dead in earthquake

Los Angeles

San Diego

September 25, 1978 **144** killed (seven on the ground) after a mid-air collision

Pacific Ocean

With the predominance of television, natural and accidental disasters obtained immediate nationwide prominence. This involved nationwide news reporting and monitoring of their aftermath, and the frequent replaying of their most dramatic features. Some of the visual images, as of the destruction of the Challenger space shuttle, the San Francisco earthquake, or the Waco fire became imprinted on the national memory

© Martin Gilbert 1993

121

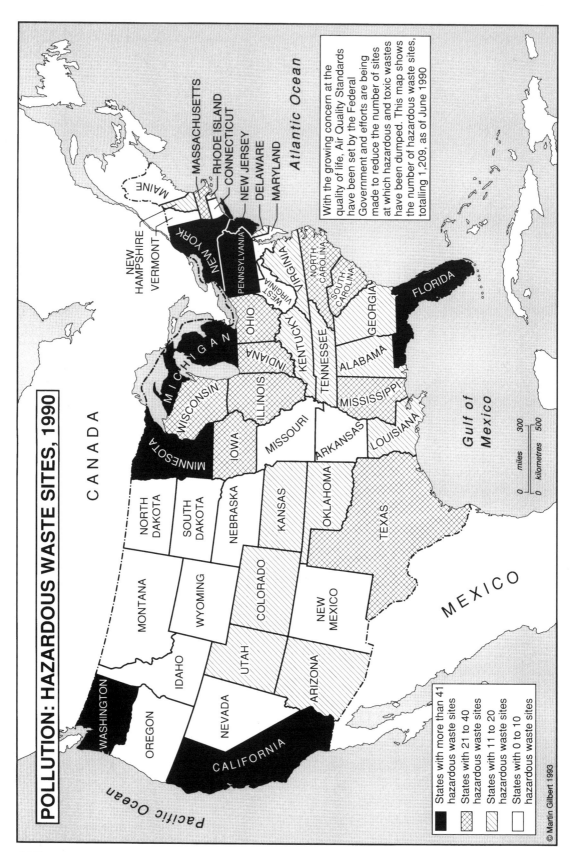

POLLUTION: HAZARDOUS WASTE SITES, 1990

With the growing concern at the quality of life, Air Quality Standards have been set by the Federal Government and efforts are being made to reduce the number of sites at which hazardous and toxic wastes have been dumped. This map shows the number of hazardous waste sites, totalling 1,209, as of June 1990

CANADA

Atlantic Ocean

Pacific Ocean

Gulf of Mexico

MEXICO

MASSACHUSETTS
RHODE ISLAND
CONNECTICUT
NEW JERSEY
DELAWARE
MARYLAND

NEW HAMPSHIRE
VERMONT
MAINE
NEW YORK
PENNSYLVANIA

MICHIGAN
WISCONSIN
MINNESOTA
NORTH DAKOTA
SOUTH DAKOTA
NEBRASKA
IOWA
ILLINOIS
INDIANA
OHIO
WEST VIRGINIA
VIRGINIA
NORTH CAROLINA
SOUTH CAROLINA
GEORGIA
FLORIDA
KENTUCKY
TENNESSEE
ALABAMA
MISSISSIPPI
MISSOURI
ARKANSAS
LOUISIANA
KANSAS
OKLAHOMA
TEXAS
COLORADO
NEW MEXICO
WYOMING
MONTANA
IDAHO
UTAH
ARIZONA
NEVADA
CALIFORNIA
OREGON
WASHINGTON

0   300   miles
0   500   kilometres

States with more than 41 hazardous waste sites

States with 21 to 40 hazardous waste sites

States with 11 to 20 hazardous waste sites

States with 0 to 10 hazardous waste sites

MURDER IN THE UNITED STATES, 1991

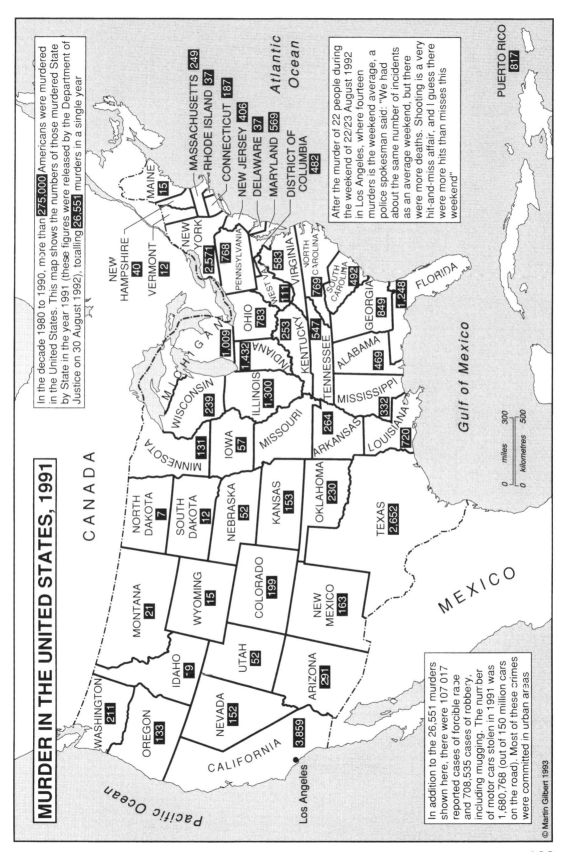

In the decade 1980 to 1990, more than 275,000 Americans were murdered in the United States. This map shows the numbers of those murdered State by State in the year 1991 (these figures were released by the Department of Justice on 30 August 1992), totalling 26,551 murders in a single year

After the murder of 22 people during the weekend of 22/23 August 1992 in Los Angeles, where fourteen murders is the weekend average, a police spokesman said: "We had about the same number of incidents as an average weekend, but there were more deaths. Shooting is a very hit-and-miss affair, and I guess there were more hits than misses this weekend"

In addition to the 26,551 murders shown here, there were 107 017 reported cases of forcible rape and 708,535 cases of robbery, including mugging. The number of motor cars stolen in 1991 was 1,680,768 (out of 150 million cars on the road). Most of these crimes were committed in urban areas

PACIFIC OCEAN

Atlantic Ocean

Gulf of Mexico

CANADA

MEXICO

PUERTO RICO 817

Los Angeles

State	Number
MAINE	15
NEW HAMPSHIRE	40
VERMONT	12
MASSACHUSETTS	249
RHODE ISLAND	37
CONNECTICUT	187
NEW JERSEY	406
DELAWARE	37
MARYLAND	569
DISTRICT OF COLUMBIA	482
NEW YORK	2,571
PENNSYLVANIA	768
WEST VIRGINIA	111
VIRGINIA	583
NORTH CAROLINA	769
SOUTH CAROLINA	492
GEORGIA	849
FLORIDA	1,248
OHIO	783
INDIANA	253
KENTUCKY	547
TENNESSEE	567
ALABAMA	469
MICHIGAN	1,009
WISCONSIN	239
ILLINOIS	1,300
MISSISSIPPI	332
IOWA	57
MISSOURI	264
ARKANSAS	264
LOUISIANA	720
MINNESOTA	131
NORTH DAKOTA	7
SOUTH DAKOTA	12
NEBRASKA	52
KANSAS	153
OKLAHOMA	230
TEXAS	2,652
MONTANA	21
WYOMING	15
COLORADO	199
NEW MEXICO	163
IDAHO	9
UTAH	52
ARIZONA	291
WASHINGTON	211
OREGON	133
NEVADA	152
CALIFORNIA	3,859

0 miles 300
0 kilometres 500

© Martin Gilbert 1993

123

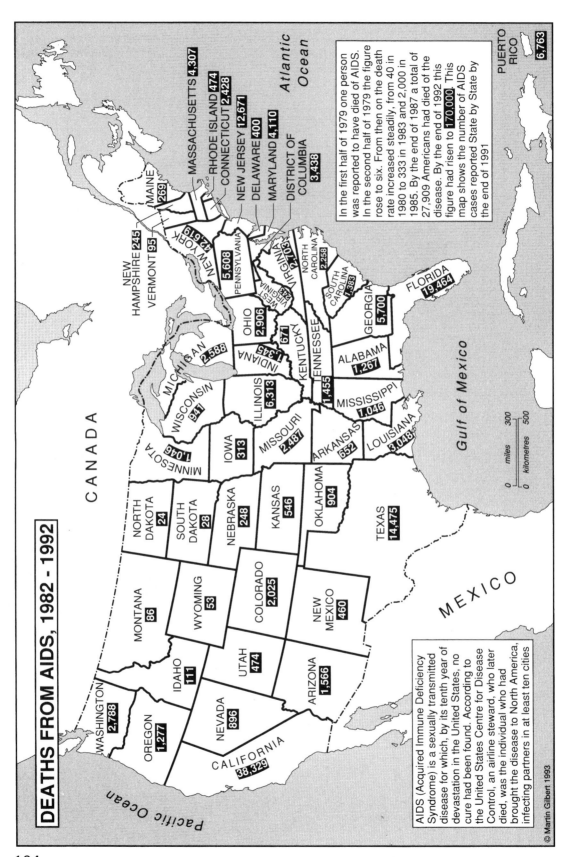

DEATHS FROM AIDS, 1982 - 1992

In the first half of 1979 one person was reported to have died of AIDS. In the second half of 1979 the figure rose to six. From then on the death rate increased steadily, from 40 in 1980 to 333 in 1983 and 2,000 in 1985. By the end of 1987 a total of 27,909 Americans had died of the disease. By the end of 1992 this figure had risen to 170,000. This map shows the number of AIDS cases reported State by State by the end of 1991

AIDS (Acquired Immune Deficiency Syndrome) is a sexually transmitted disease for which, by its tenth year of devastation in the United States, no cure had been found. According to the United States Centre for Disease Control, an airline steward, who later died, was the individual who had brought the disease to North America, infecting partners in at least ten cities

MASSACHUSETTS 4,307
RHODE ISLAND 474
CONNECTICUT 2,428
NEW JERSEY 12,671
DELAWARE 400
MARYLAND 4,110
DISTRICT OF COLUMBIA 3,438

MAINE 269
NEW HAMPSHIRE 215
VERMONT 95
NEW YORK 42,619
PENNSYLVANIA 5,608
WEST VIRGINIA 246
VIRGINIA 2,033
NORTH CAROLINA 2,258
SOUTH CAROLINA 1,883
GEORGIA 5,700
FLORIDA 19,464

OHIO 2,906
KENTUCKY 671
TENNESSEE 1,455
ALABAMA 1,267
MISSISSIPPI 1,046

MICHIGAN 2,588
INDIANA 1,845
ILLINOIS 6,313
WISCONSIN 941
IOWA 313
MISSOURI 2,487
ARKANSAS 552
LOUISIANA 3,048

MINNESOTA 1,046
NORTH DAKOTA 24
SOUTH DAKOTA 28
NEBRASKA 248
KANSAS 546
OKLAHOMA 904
TEXAS 14,475

MONTANA 86
WYOMING 53
COLORADO 2,025
NEW MEXICO 460

IDAHO 111
UTAH 474
ARIZONA 1,566

WASHINGTON 2,788
OREGON 1,277
NEVADA 896
CALIFORNIA 38,329

PUERTO RICO 6,763

Atlantic Ocean

Pacific Ocean

CANADA

MEXICO

Gulf of Mexico

0   miles   300
0   kilometres   500

© Martin Gilbert 1993

124

IMMIGRATION TO THE UNITED STATES, 1991

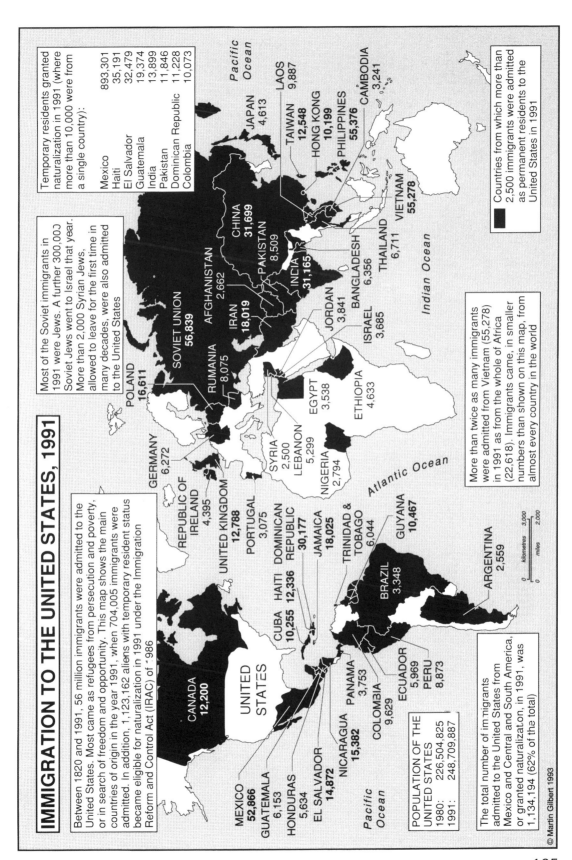

Between 1820 and 1991, 56 million immigrants were admitted to the United States. Most came as refugees from persecution and poverty, or in search of freedom and opportunity. This map shows the main countries of origin in the year 1991, when 704,005 immigrants were admitted. In addition, 1,123,162 aliens with temporary resident status became eligible for naturalization in 1991 under the Immigration Reform and Control Act (IRAC) of ˙986

Most of the Soviet immigrants in 1991 were Jews. A further 300,000 Soviet Jews went to Israel that year. More than 2,000 Syrian Jews, allowed to leave for the first time in many decades, were also admitted to the United States

Temporary residents granted naturalization in 1991 (where more than 10,000 were from a single country):

Mexico	893,301
Haiti	35,191
El Salvador	32,479
Guatemala	19,374
India	13,899
Pakistan	11,846
Dominican Republic	11,228
Colombia	10,073

■ Countries from which more than 2,500 immigrants were admitted as permanent residents to the United States in 1991

Pacific Ocean

JAPAN 4,613
LAOS 9,887
TAIWAN 12,548
HONG KONG 10,199
PHILIPPINES 55,376
CAMBODIA 3,241
CHINA 31,699
PAKISTAN 8,509
VIETNAM 55,278
AFGHANISTAN 2,662
INDIA 31,165
BANGLADESH 6,356
THAILAND 6,711
SOVIET UNION 56,839
IRAN 18,019
RUMANIA 8,075
JORDAN 3,841
ISRAEL 3,685
POLAND 16,611
GERMANY 6,272
SYRIA 2,500
LEBANON 5,299
EGYPT 3,538
ETHIOPIA 4,633
NIGERIA 2,794

Indian Ocean

REPUBLIC OF IRELAND 4,395
UNITED KINGDOM 12,788
PORTUGAL 3,075

Atlantic Ocean

More than twice as many immigrants were admitted from Vietnam (55,278) in 1991 as from the whole of Africa (22,618). Immigrants came, in smaller numbers than shown on this map, from almost every country in the world

CANADA 12,200

UNITED STATES

CUBA 10,255
HAITI 12,336
DOMINICAN REPUBLIC 30,177
JAMAICA 18,025
TRINIDAD & TOBAGO 6,044
GUYANA 10,467

MEXICO 52,866
GUATEMALA 6,153
HONDURAS 5,634
EL SALVADOR 14,872
NICARAGUA 15,382
PANAMA 3,753
COLOMBIA 9,629
ECUADOR 5,969
PERU 8,873
BRAZIL 3,348
ARGENTINA 2,559

Pacific Ocean

POPULATION OF THE UNITED STATES
1980:   226,504,825
1991:   248,709,887

The total number of immigrants admitted to the United States from Mexico and Central and South America, or granted naturalization, in 1991, was 1,134,194 (62% of the total)

0   kilometres   3,000
0   miles   2,000

© Martin Gilbert 1993

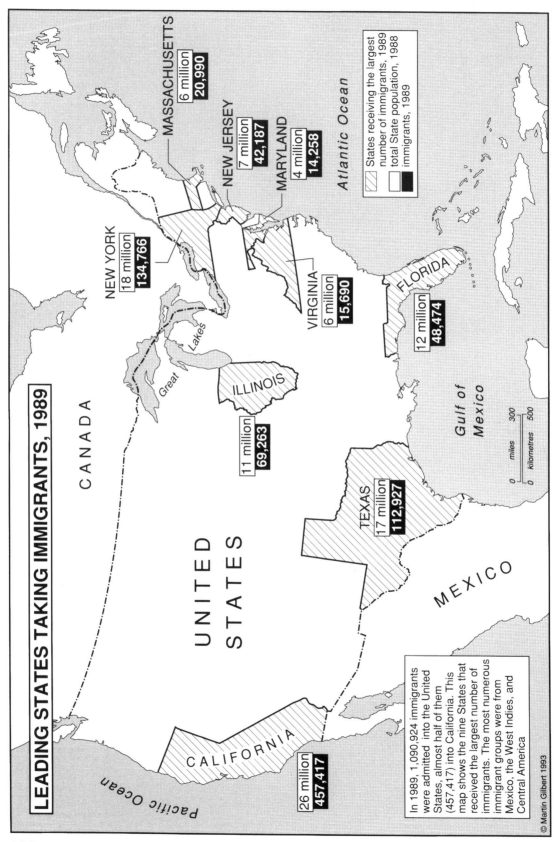

LEADING STATES TAKING IMMIGRANTS, 1989

CANADA

UNITED STATES

Pacific Ocean

Atlantic Ocean

Gulf of Mexico

MEXICO

Great Lakes

States receiving the largest number of immigrants, 1989

total State population, 1988

immigrants, 1989

MASSACHUSETTS
6 million
20,990

NEW JERSEY
7 million
42,187

MARYLAND
4 million
14,258

NEW YORK
18 million
134,766

VIRGINIA
6 million
15,690

FLORIDA
12 million
48,474

ILLINOIS
11 million
69,263

TEXAS
17 million
112,927

CALIFORNIA
26 million
457,417

0 miles 300
0 kilometres 500

In 1989, 1,090,924 immigrants were admitted into the United States, almost half of them (457,417) into California. This map shows the nine States that received the largest number of immigrants. The most numerous immigrant groups were from Mexico, the West Indies, and Central America

© Martin Gilbert 1993

NATIONAL ANCESTRY OF UNITED STATES CITIZENS

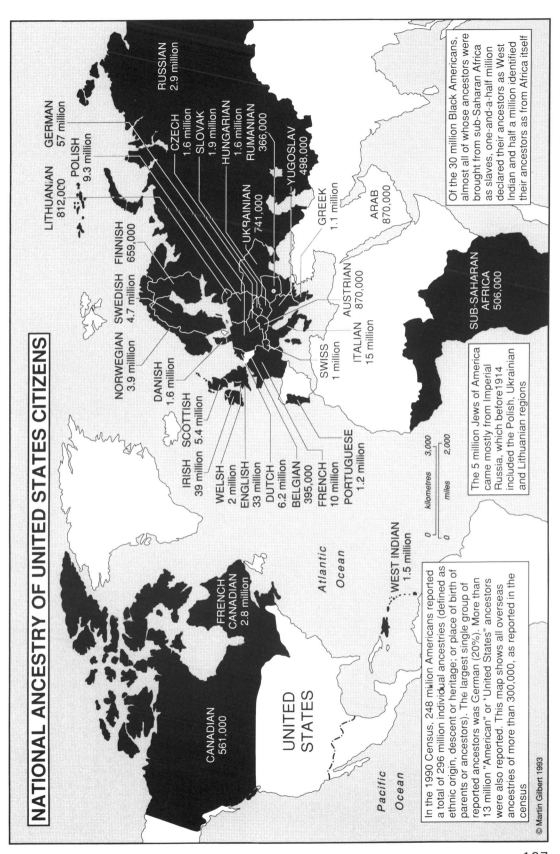

RUSSIAN 2.9 million

GERMAN 57 million

LITHUANIAN 812,000

POLISH 9.3 million

CZECH 1.6 million

SLOVAK 1.9 million

HUNGARIAN 1.6 million

RUMANIAN 366,000

YUGOSLAV 498,000

UKRAINIAN 741,000

GREEK 1.1 million

ARAB 870,000

FINNISH 659,000

SWEDISH 4.7 million

NORWEGIAN 3.9 million

AUSTRIAN 870,000

SUB-SAHARAN AFRICA 506,000

DANISH 1.6 million

SCOTTISH 5.4 million

IRISH 39 million

WELSH 2 million

ENGLISH 33 million

DUTCH 6.2 million

BELGIAN 395,000

FRENCH 10 million

PORTUGUESE 1.2 million

SWISS 1 million

ITALIAN 15 million

Of the 30 million Black Americans, almost all of whose ancestors were brought from sub-Saharan Africa as slaves, one-and-a-half million declared their ancestors as West Indian and half a million identified their ancestors as from Africa itself

The 5 million Jews of America came mostly from Imperial Russia, which before 1914 included the Polish, Ukrainian and Lithuanian regions

0   kilometres   3,000

0   miles   2,000

FRENCH CANADIAN 2.8 million

Atlantic Ocean

WEST INDIAN 1.5 million

CANADIAN 561,000

UNITED STATES

Pacific Ocean

In the 1990 Census, 248 million Americans reported a total of 296 million individual ancestries (defined as ethnic origin, descent or heritage; or place of birth of parents or ancestors). The largest single group of reported ancestors was German (20%). More than 13 million "American" or "United States" ancestors were also reported. This map shows all overseas ancestries of more than 300,000, as reported in the census

© Martin Gilbert 1993

127

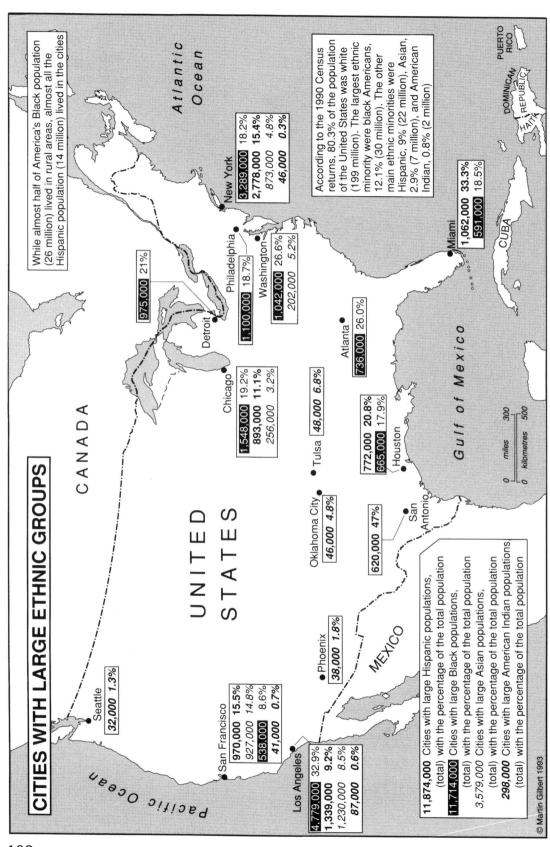

CITIES WITH LARGE ETHNIC GROUPS

CANADA

UNITED STATES

MEXICO

Atlantic Ocean

Pacific Ocean

Gulf of Mexico

While almost half of America's Black population (26 million) lived in rural areas, almost all the Hispanic population (14 million) lived in the cities

According to the 1990 Census returns, 80.3% of the population of the United States was white (199 million). The largest ethnic minority were black Americans, 12.1% (30 million). The other main ethnic minorities were Hispanic, 9% (22 million), Asian, 2.9% (7 million), and American Indian, 0.8% (2 million)

New York
3,289,000	18.2%
2,778,000	15.4%
873,000	4.8%
46,000	*0.3%*

Philadelphia
| 1,100,000 | 18.7% |

Washington
| 1,042,000 | 26.6% |
| 202,000 | 5.2% |

Detroit
| 975,000 | 21% |

Chicago
1,548,000	19.2%
893,000	11.1%
256,000	3.2%

Atlanta
| 736,000 | 26.0% |

Tulsa *48,000 6.8%*

Houston
| 772,000 | 20.8% |
| 665,000 | 17.9% |

Oklahoma City *46,000 4.8%*

San Antonio
| 620,000 | 47% |

Miami
| 1,062,000 | 33.3% |
| 591,000 | 18.5% |

Phoenix *38,000 1.8%*

Seattle *32,000 1.3%*

San Francisco
970,000	15.5%
927,000	14.8%
538,000	8.6%
41,000	*0.7%*

Los Angeles
4,779,000	32.9%
1,339,000	9.2%
1,230,000	8.5%
87,000	*0.6%*

CUBA

HAITI

DOMINICAN REPUBLIC

PUERTO RICO

0   miles   300
0 kilometres 500

11,874,000 Cities with large Hispanic populations, (total) with the percentage of the total population

11,714,000 Cities with large Black populations, (total) with the percentage of the total population

3,579,000 Cities with large Asian populations, (total) with the percentage of the total population

298,000 Cities with large American Indian populations, (total) with the percentage of the total population

© Martin Gilbert 1993

128

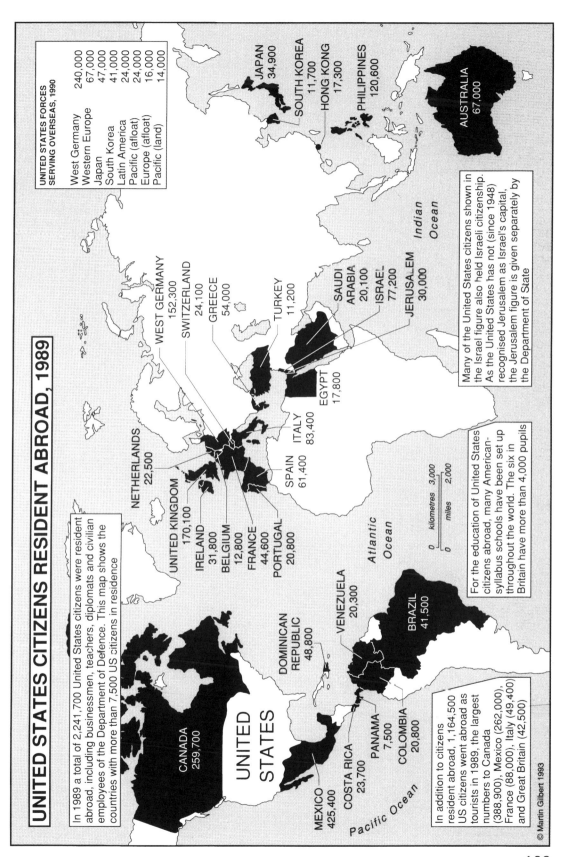

UNITED STATES CITIZENS RESIDENT ABROAD, 1989

In 1989 a total of 2,241,700 United States citizens were resident abroad, including businessmen, teachers, diplomats and civilian employees of the Department of Defence. This map shows the countries with more than 7,500 US citizens in residence

UNITED STATES FORCES
SERVING OVERSEAS, 1990

West Germany	240,000
Western Europe	67,000
Japan	47,000
South Korea	41,000
Latin America	24,000
Pacific (afloat)	24,000
Europe (afloat)	16,000
Pacific (land)	14,000

JAPAN 34,900

SOUTH KOREA 11,700

HONG KONG 17,300

PHILIPPINES 120,600

AUSTRALIA 67,000

Indian Ocean

Many of the United States citizens shown in the Israel figure also held Israeli citizenship. As the United States has not (since 1948) recognised Jerusalem as Israel's capital, the Jerusalem figure is given separately by the Department of State

WEST GERMANY 152,300

SWITZERLAND 24,100

GREECE 54,000

TURKEY 11,200

SAUDI ARABIA 20,100

ISRAEL 77,200

JERUSALEM 30,000

EGYPT 17,800

NETHERLANDS 22,500

ITALY 83,400

SPAIN 61,400

UNITED KINGDOM 170,100

IRELAND 31,800

BELGIUM 12,800

FRANCE 44,600

PORTUGAL 20,800

Atlantic Ocean

For the education of United States citizens abroad, many American-syllabus schools have been set up throughout the world. The six in Britain have more than 4,000 pupils

| 0 | kilometres | 3,000 |
| 0 | miles | 2,000 |

VENEZUELA 20,300

DOMINICAN REPUBLIC 48,800

BRAZIL 41,500

CANADA 259,700

UNITED STATES

MEXICO 425,400

COSTA RICA 23,700

PANAMA 7,500

COLOMBIA 20,800

Pacific Ocean

In addition to citizens resident abroad, 1,164,500 US citizens went abroad as tourists in 1989, the largest numbers to Canada (388,900), Mexico (262,000), France (88,000), Italy (49,400) and Great Britain (42,500)

THE VISA LOTTERY PROGRAM, 1990-1993

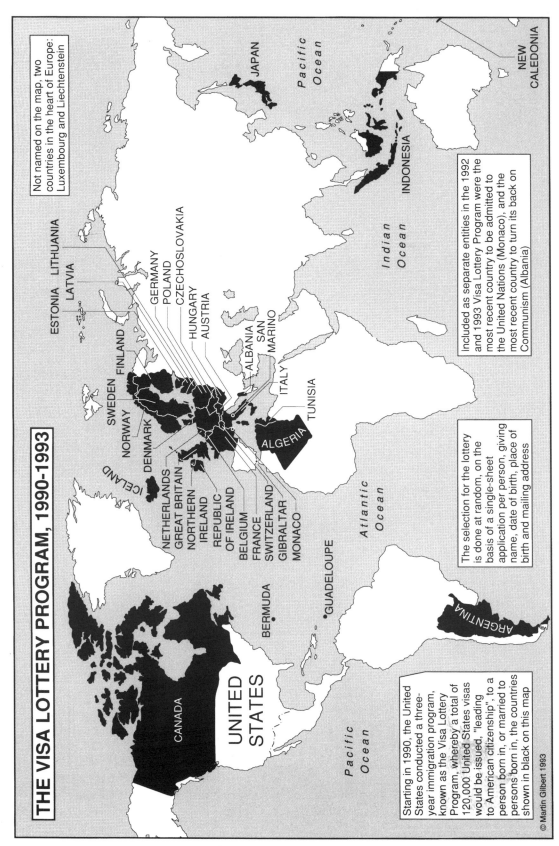

Not named on the map, two countries in the heart of Europe: Luxembourg and Liechtenstein

Included as separate entities in the 1992 and 1993 Visa Lottery Program were the most recent country to be admitted to the United Nations (Monaco), and the most recent country to turn its back on Communism (Albania)

The selection for the lottery is done at random, on the basis of a single-sheet application per person, giving name, date of birth, place of birth and mailing address

Starting in 1990, the United States conducted a three-year immigration program, known as the Visa Lottery Program, whereby a total of 120,000 United States visas would be issued, "leading to American citizenship", to a person born in, or married to persons born in, the countries shown in black on this map

JAPAN

NEW CALEDONIA

INDONESIA

Pacific Ocean

Indian Ocean

ESTONIA   LITHUANIA   LATVIA

GERMANY
POLAND
CZECHOSLOVAKIA
HUNGARY
AUSTRIA
ALBANIA
SAN MARINO

SWEDEN   FINLAND
NORWAY
DENMARK
ICELAND
NETHERLANDS
GREAT BRITAIN
NORTHERN IRELAND
REPUBLIC OF IRELAND
BELGIUM
FRANCE
SWITZERLAND
GIBRALTAR
MONACO

ITALY
TUNISIA

ALGERIA

Atlantic Ocean

BERMUDA

GUADELOUPE

ARGENTINA

CANADA

UNITED STATES

Pacific Ocean

130

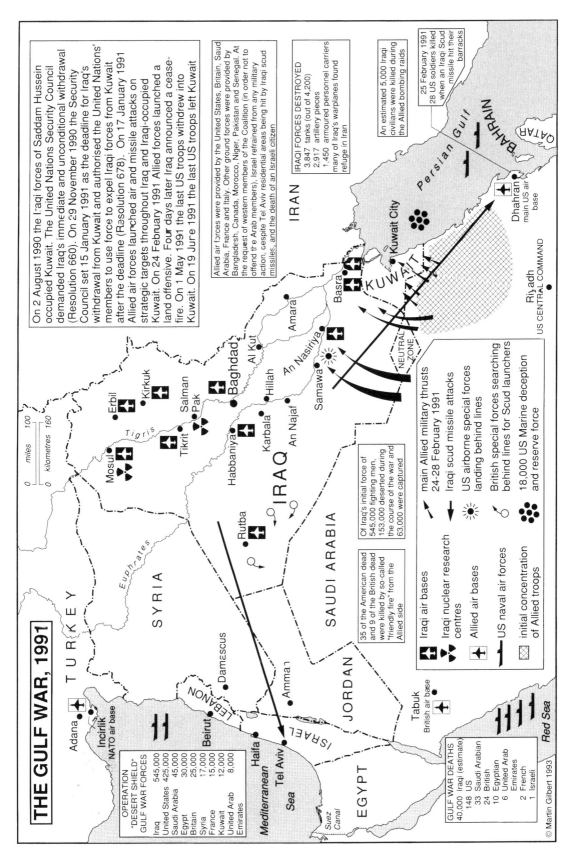

THE GULF WAR, 1991

On 2 August 1990 the Iraqi forces of Saddam Hussein occupied Kuwait. The United Nations Security Council demanded Iraq's immediate and unconditional withdrawal (Resolution 660). On 29 November 1990 the Security Council set 15 January 1991 as the deadline for Iraq's withdrawal from Kuwait and authorised the United Nations' members to use force to expel Iraqi forces from Kuwait after the deadline (Resolution 678). On 17 January 1991 Allied air forces launched air and missile attacks on strategic targets throughout Iraq and Iraqi-occupied Kuwait. On 24 February 1991 Allied forces launched a land offensive. Four days later Iraq announced a cease-fire. On 1 May 1991 the last US troops withdrew into Kuwait. On 19 June 1991 the last US troops left Kuwait.

Allied air forces were provided by the United States, Britain, Saudi Arabia, France and Italy. Other ground forces were provided by Bangladesh, Canada, Morocco, Niger, Pakistan and Senegal. At the request of western members of the Coalition (in order not to offend the Arab members), Israel refrained from any military action, despite Tel Aviv residential areas being hit by Iraqi scud missiles, and the death of an Israeli citizen

IRAQI FORCES DESTROYED
3,847 tanks (out of 4,200)
2,917 artillery pieces
1,450 armoured personnel carriers
many of Iraq's warplanes found refuge in Iran

25 February 1991
28 US soldiers killed when an Iraqi Scud missile hit their barracks

An estimated 5,000 Iraqi civilians were killed during the Allied bombing raids

Of Iraq's initial force of 545,000 fighting men, 153,000 deserted during the course of the war and 63,000 were captured

35 of the American dead and 9 of the British dead were killed by so-called "friendly fire" from the Allied side

| main Allied military thrusts 24–28 February 1991 |
| Iraqi scud missile attacks |
| US airborne special forces landing behind lines |
| British special forces searching behind lines for Scud launchers |
| 18,000 US Marine deception and reserve force |

| Iraqi air bases |
| Iraqi nuclear research centres |
| Allied air bases |
| US naval air forces |
| initial concentration of Allied troops |

OPERATION "DESERT SHIELD" GULF WAR FORCES
Iraq	545,000
United States	425,000
Saudi Arabia	45,000
Egypt	30,000
Britain	25,000
Syria	17,000
France	15,000
Kuwait	12,000
United Arab Emirates	8,000

GULF WAR DEATHS
Iraqi (estimate)	40,000
US	148
Saudi Arabian	33
British	24
Egyptian	10
United Arab Emirates	6
French	2
Israeli	1

TURKEY
Adana — NATO air base
Incirlik
Mosul
Erbil
Kirkuk
Tikrit
Salman Pak
Baghdad
Al Kut
Habbaniya
Hillah
Karbala
An Najaf
Samawa
An Nasiriya
Amara
Basra
Rutba
Tigris
Euphrates
SYRIA
Damascus
LEBANON
Beirut
Haifa
Tel Aviv
ISRAEL
Mediterranean Sea
Amman
JORDAN
EGYPT
Suez Canal
Red Sea
Tabuk — British air base
SAUDI ARABIA
Riyadh — US CENTRAL COMMAND
Dhahran — main US air base
KUWAIT
Kuwait City
NEUTRAL ZONE
Persian Gulf
BAHRAIN
QATAR
IRAN
IRAQ

0 miles 100
0 kilometres 160

© Martin Gilbert 1993

131

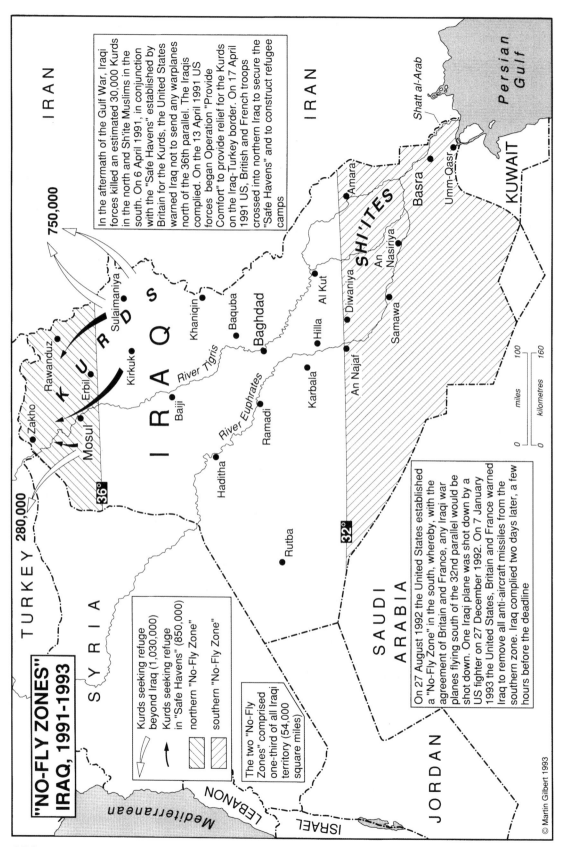

"NO-FLY ZONES" IRAQ, 1991-1993

750,000

TURKEY 280,000

In the aftermath of the Gulf War, Iraqi forces killed an estimated 30,000 Kurds in the north and Sh'ite Muslims in the south. On 6 April 1991, in conjunction with the "Safe Havens" established by Britain for the Kurds, the United States warned Iraq not to send any warplanes north of the 36th parallel. The Iraqis complied. On the 13 April 1991 US forces began Operation "Provide Comfort" to provide relief for the Kurds on the Iraq-Turkey border. On 17 April 1991 US, British and French troops crossed into northern Iraq to secure the "Safe Havens" and to construct refugee camps

On 27 August 1992 the United States established a "No-Fly Zone" in the south, whereby, with the agreement of Britain and France, any Iraqi war planes flying south of the 32nd parallel would be shot down. One Iraqi plane was shot down by a US fighter on 27 December 1992. On 7 January 1993 the United States, Britain and France warned Iraq to remove all anti-aircraft missiles from the southern zone. Iraq complied two days later, a few hours before the deadline

IRAN

IRAN

Persian Gulf

Shatt al-Arab

KUWAIT

Umm Qasr

Basra

Amara

An Nasiriya

SHI'ITES

Samawa

Diwaniya

Al Kut

An Najaf

Karbala

Hilla

Baghdad

Baquba

Khaniqin

Ramadi

Haditha

Rutba

Baiji

Kirkuk

Mosul

Zakho

Erbil

Rawanduz

Sulaimaniya

K U R D S

I R A Q

River Tigris

River Euphrates

36°

32°

S Y R I A

TURKEY

LEBANON

Mediterranean

ISRAEL

JORDAN

SAUDI ARABIA

Kurds seeking refuge beyond Iraq (1,030,000)

Kurds seeking refuge in "Safe Havens" (850,000)

northern "No-Fly Zone"

southern "No-Fly Zone"

The two "No-Fly Zones" comprised one-third of all Iraqi territory (54,000 square miles)

miles | 0 ... 100
kilometres | 0 ... 160

© Martin Gilbert 1993

132

UNITED STATES ARMS SALES, 1992

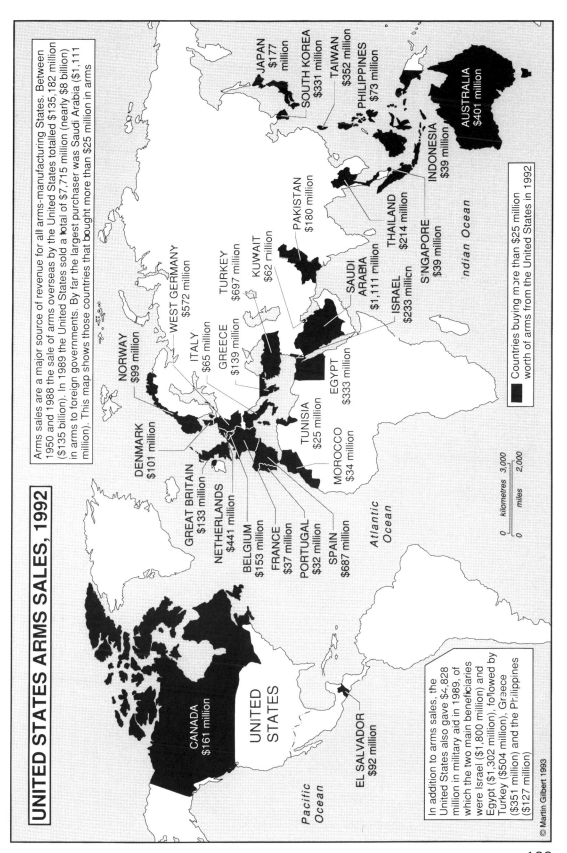

Arms sales are a major source of revenue for all arms-manufacturing States. Between 1950 and 1988 the sale of arms overseas by the United States totalled $135,182 million ($135 billion). In 1989 the United States totalled $7,715 million (nearly $8 billion) in arms to foreign governments. By far the largest purchaser was Saudi Arabia ($1,111 million). This map shows those countries that bought more than $25 million in arms

PACIFIC OCEAN

CANADA
$161 million

UNITED STATES

EL SALVADOR
$92 million

Atlantic Ocean

NORWAY $99 million

DENMARK $101 million

GREAT BRITAIN $133 million

NETHERLANDS $441 million

BELGIUM $153 million

FRANCE $37 million

PORTUGAL $32 million

SPAIN $687 million

WEST GERMANY $572 million

ITALY $65 million

GREECE $139 million

TURKEY $697 million

KUWAIT $62 million

TUNISIA $25 million

MOROCCO $34 million

EGYPT $333 million

SAUDI ARABIA $1,111 million

ISRAEL $233 million

PAKISTAN $180 million

SINGAPORE $39 million

THAILAND $214 million

INDONESIA $39 million

JAPAN $177 million

SOUTH KOREA $331 million

TAIWAN $352 million

PHILIPPINES $73 million

AUSTRALIA $401 million

Indian Ocean

0   kilometres   3,000
0   miles   2,000

Countries buying more than $25 million worth of arms from the United States in 1992

In addition to arms sales, the United States also gave $4,828 million in military aid in 1989, of which the two main beneficiaries were Israel ($1,800 million) and Egypt ($1,302 million), followed by Turkey ($504 million), Greece ($351 million) and the Philippines ($127 million)

© Martin Gilbert 1993

133

MAIN RECIPIENTS OF UNITED STATES ECONOMIC AID, 1992

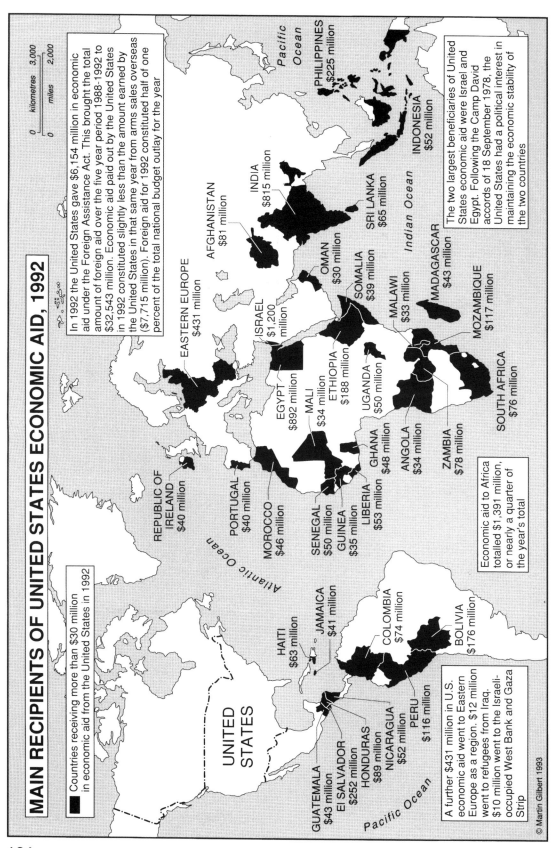

■ Countries receiving more than $30 million in economic aid from the United States in 1992

In 1992 the United States gave $6,154 million in economic aid under the Foreign Assistance Act. This brought the total amount of foreign aid over the five year period 1988-1992 to $32,543 million. Economic aid paid out by the United States in 1992 constituted slightly less than the amount earned by the United States in that same year from arms sales overseas ($7,715 million). Foreign aid for 1992 constituted half of one percent of the total national budget outlay for the year

The two largest beneficiaries of United States economic aid were Israel and Egypt. Following the Camp David accords of 18 September 1978, the United States had a political interest in maintaining the economic stability of the two countries

Economic aid to Africa totalled $1,391 million, or nearly a quarter of the year's total

A further $431 million in U.S. economic aid went to Eastern Europe as a region. $12 million went to refugees from Iraq. $10 million went to the Israeli-occupied West Bank and Gaza Strip

Pacific Ocean

PHILIPPINES $225 million

INDONESIA $52 million

INDIA $815 million

AFGHANISTAN $81 million

SRI LANKA $65 million

Indian Ocean

OMAN $30 million

ISRAEL $1,200 million

SOMALIA $39 million

MALAWI $33 million

MADAGASCAR $43 million

MOZAMBIQUE $117 million

EASTERN EUROPE $431 million

EGYPT $892 million

MALI $34 million

ETHIOPIA $188 million

UGANDA $50 million

SOUTH AFRICA $76 million

MOROCCO $46 million

PORTUGAL $40 million

REPUBLIC OF IRELAND $40 million

SENEGAL $50 million

GUINEA $35 million

LIBERIA $53 million

GHANA $48 million

ANGOLA $34 million

ZAMBIA $78 million

Atlantic Ocean

HAITI $63 million

JAMAICA $41 million

COLOMBIA $74 million

BOLIVIA $176 million

UNITED STATES

GUATEMALA $43 million

El SALVADOR $252 million

HONDURAS $89 million

NICARAGUA $52 million

PERU $116 million

Pacific Ocean

0 kilometres 3,000
0 miles 2,000

134

DEFENCE PREPAREDNESS ON LAND, 1991

Legend:
- ⊙ Air Force Tactical Fighter Wings
- ◰ Strategic Offensive air bases
- ■ Strategic Offensive naval bases
- ▣ Strategic Offensive missile sites

From 1945 to 1990 the main thrust of United States defences was in the confrontation with the Soviet Union. With the collapse of Communist power from 1990, and the demise of the Warsaw Pact, defence priorities were under continuous scrutiny. This map shows the location of Air Force Tactical Fighter Wings, and of the Strategic Offensive Forces, in 1991. Further cuts in bases were made in 1992 and 1993

On 30 July 1991 the Department of Defence announced the shutting down of 72 United States military installations in Europe, and reduced operations at seven others

BASES TO BE CLOSED	
Germany	38
Britain	13
Italy	8
Turkey	7
Spain	5
Netherlands	1

© Martin Gilbert 1993

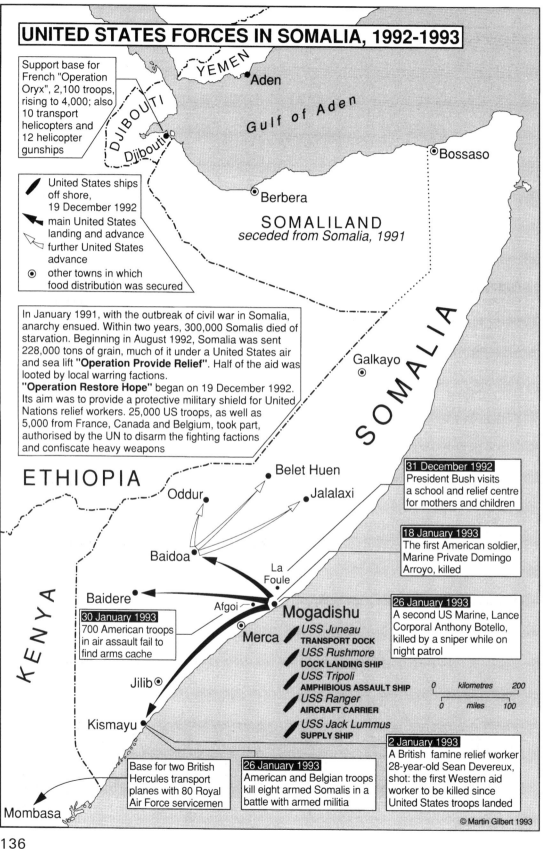

UNITED STATES FORCES IN SOMALIA, 1992-1993

Support base for French "Operation Oryx", 2,100 troops, rising to 4,000; also 10 transport helicopters and 12 helicopter gunships

United States ships off shore, 19 December 1992

main United States landing and advance

further United States advance

other towns in which food distribution was secured

YEMEN

Aden

Gulf of Aden

DJIBOUTI

Djibouti

Bossaso

Berbera

SOMALILAND
seceded from Somalia, 1991

In January 1991, with the outbreak of civil war in Somalia, anarchy ensued. Within two years, 300,000 Somalis died of starvation. Beginning in August 1992, Somalia was sent 228,000 tons of grain, much of it under a United States air and sea lift **"Operation Provide Relief"**. Half of the aid was looted by local warring factions.
"Operation Restore Hope" began on 19 December 1992. Its aim was to provide a protective military shield for United Nations relief workers. 25,000 US troops, as well as 5,000 from France, Canada and Belgium, took part, authorised by the UN to disarm the fighting factions and confiscate heavy weapons

Galkayo

SOMALIA

ETHIOPIA

Belet Huen

Oddur

Jalalaxi

Baidoa

La Foule

Baidere

Afgoi

Mogadishu

Merca

USS Juneau
TRANSPORT DOCK

USS Rushmore
DOCK LANDING SHIP

USS Tripoli
AMPHIBIOUS ASSAULT SHIP

USS Ranger
AIRCRAFT CARRIER

USS Jack Lummus
SUPPLY SHIP

Jilib

Kismayu

KENYA

Mombasa

31 December 1992
President Bush visits a school and relief centre for mothers and children

18 January 1993
The first American soldier, Marine Private Domingo Arroyo, killed

26 January 1993
A second US Marine, Lance Corporal Anthony Botello, killed by a sniper while on night patrol

30 January 1993
700 American troops in air assault fail to find arms cache

26 January 1993
American and Belgian troops kill eight armed Somalis in a battle with armed militia

2 January 1993
A British famine relief worker 28-year-old Sean Devereux, shot: the first Western aid worker to be killed since United States troops landed

Base for two British Hercules transport planes with 80 Royal Air Force servicemen

| 0 | kilometres | 200 |
| 0 | miles | 100 |

© Martin Gilbert 1993

136

EXPLORING THE SOLAR SYSTEM, 1962-1992

Beginning in 1962, the United States took the lead in exploring the solar system, starting with the launch of an unmanned *Mariner* spacecraft towards the planet Venus. On 3 March 1972 the unmanned, nuclear-powered spacecraft *Pioneer 10* was launched towards Jupiter: twenty years later it had travelled five billion miles from Earth

On 25 April 1990 the Hubble Space Telescope was launched, to study distant stars and galaxies, and to search for evidence of planets in other solar systems

26 January 1986
Voyager 2 passes, sends back details of planet's composition

● **URANUS**

2 March 1992
Pioneer 10 reaches five billion miles from Earth, the furthest distance travelled by any man-made object

3 December 1973
Pioneer 10 gives first close-up pictures
4 March 1979
Voyager 1 discovers rings and details of sixteen moons

3 February 1992
Ulysses flies to within 235,000 miles (and 416 million miles from Earth). Its signals take 37 minutes and 15 seconds to get back to Earth

1986
Pioneer 10 becomes the first man-made object to escape the solar system

29 March 1974
Mariner 10 takes 2,800 photographs

8 December 1992
Galileo, while bound for Jupiter (due 1995) passes within 200 miles of Earth. Its instruments detect signs of intelligent life on Earth!

PLUTO ●

●JUPITER

MERCURY

SUN ● **EARTH**
●**VENUS**

NEPTUNE ●

14 December 1962
Mariner 2 passes 21,648 miles from surface
5 January 1969
Soviet space craft lands on surface and returns

13 June 1983
Pioneer 10 crosses the orbit of Neptune

MARS ●

8 November 1968
Pioneer 9 achieves sun orbit

28 November 1964
Mariner 4 trajectory passes Mars and sends 22 pictures from 6,100 miles above the planet's surface
13 November 1971
Mariner 9 in orbit 862 miles above planet's surface

● **SATURN**

November 1980
Voyager 1 sends photographs, reveals winds of 1,100 miles an hour at Equator and a total of 17 moons

RELATIVE DISTANCE BETWEEN THE PLANETS

○ **Sun**
● Mercury
● Venus
● Earth
● Mars
● Jupiter
● Saturn
● Uranus
● Neptune
● Pluto

DEFENCE PREPAREDNESS IN SPACE, 1992-1993

On 31 December 1992 the United States Department of Defence awarded 6-year contracts to develop the "Brilliant Eyes" satellite. Each satellite was intended to carry sensors to monitor both space and Earth. Between 20 and 40 "Brilliant Eyes" would orbit at less than 1,000 miles above the Earth, in contrast to the 22,000-mile altitude of existing Early Warning satellites. This whole programme was cancelled by President Clinton on 13 May 1993 when he announced "the end of the Star Wars Era": a final affirmation of the end of the Cold War

In January 1992, Russian President Boris Yeltsin called for the United States and Russia to establish a Global Protection System. Following his call, talks began for the establishment of a Joint Missile Warning Centre that would receive data on missile launches

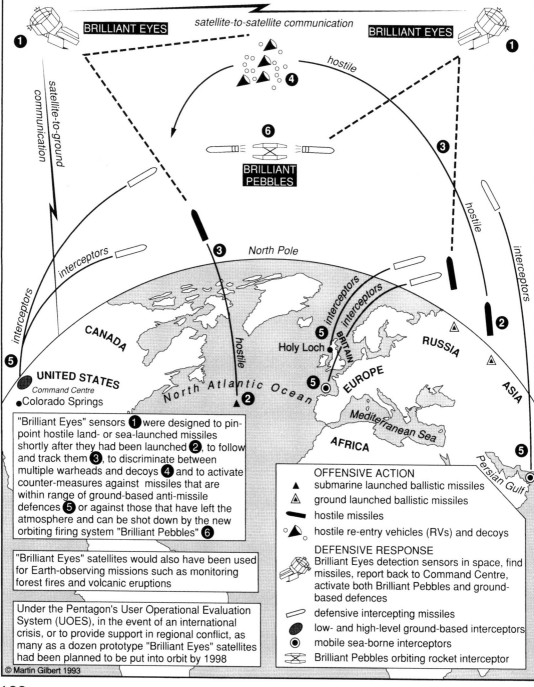

BRILLIANT EYES

satellite-to-satellite communication

BRILLIANT EYES

satellite-to-ground communication

hostile

BRILLIANT PEBBLES

hostile

interceptors

interceptors

interceptors

North Pole

hostile

CANADA

RUSSIA

Holy Loch

BRITAIN

EUROPE

ASIA

UNITED STATES
Command Centre
Colorado Springs

North Atlantic Ocean

Mediterranean Sea

AFRICA

Persian Gulf

"Brilliant Eyes" sensors ❶ were designed to pin-point hostile land- or sea-launched missiles shortly after they had been launched ❷, to follow and track them ❸, to discriminate between multiple warheads and decoys ❹ and to activate counter-measures against missiles that are within range of ground-based anti-missile defences ❺ or against those that have left the atmosphere and can be shot down by the new orbiting firing system "Brilliant Pebbles" ❻

"Brilliant Eyes" satellites would also have been used for Earth-observing missions such as monitoring forest fires and volcanic eruptions

Under the Pentagon's User Operational Evaluation System (UOES), in the event of an international crisis, or to provide support in regional conflict, as many as a dozen prototype "Brilliant Eyes" satellites had been planned to be put into orbit by 1998

OFFENSIVE ACTION
▲ submarine launched ballistic missiles
△ ground launched ballistic missiles
▬ hostile missiles
°▲° hostile re-entry vehicles (RVs) and decoys

DEFENSIVE RESPONSE
Brilliant Eyes detection sensors in space, find missiles, report back to Command Centre, activate both Brilliant Pebbles and ground-based defences
▱ defensive intercepting missiles
⬤ low- and high-level ground-based interceptors
◉ mobile sea-borne interceptors
⬡ Brilliant Pebbles orbiting rocket interceptor

138

The Twenty-first Century

FOREIGN BORN POPULATION OF THE UNITED STATES, 2000

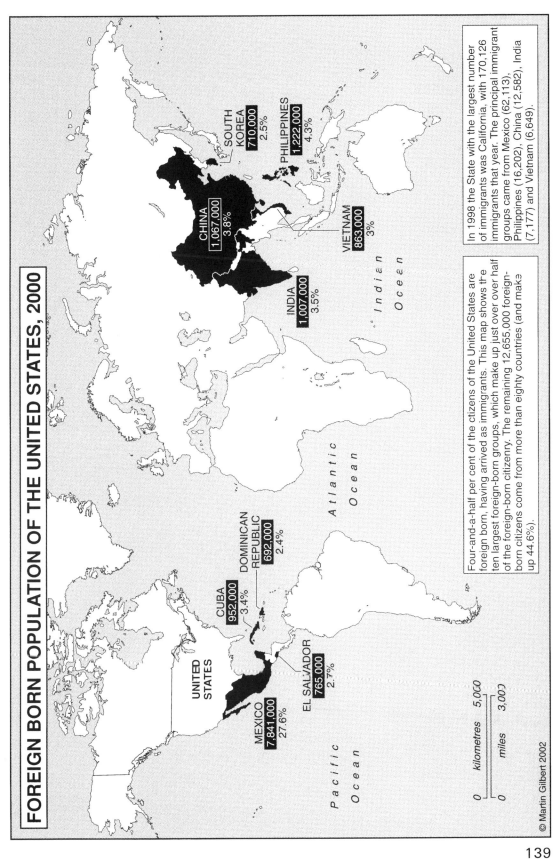

SOUTH KOREA 710,000 2.5%

PHILIPPINES 1,222,000 4.3%

CHINA 1,067,000 3.8%

VIETNAM 863,000 3%

INDIA 1,007,000 3.5%

DOMINICAN REPUBLIC 692,000 2.4%

CUBA 952,000 3.4%

UNITED STATES

EL SALVADOR 765,000 2.7%

MEXICO 7,841,000 27.6%

Indian Ocean

Atlantic Ocean

Pacific Ocean

In 1998 the State with the largest number of immigrants was California, with 170,126 immigrants that year. The principal immigrant groups came from Mexico (62,113), Philippines (16,202), China (12,582), India (7,177) and Vietnam (6,649).

Four-and-a-half per cent of the citizens of the United States are foreign born, having arrived as immigrants. This map shows the ten largest foreign-born groups, which make up just over over half of the foreign-born citizenry. The remaining 12,655,000 foreign-born citizens come from more than eighty countries (and make up 44.6%).

0 kilometres 5,000
0 miles 3,000

© Martin Gilbert 2002

139

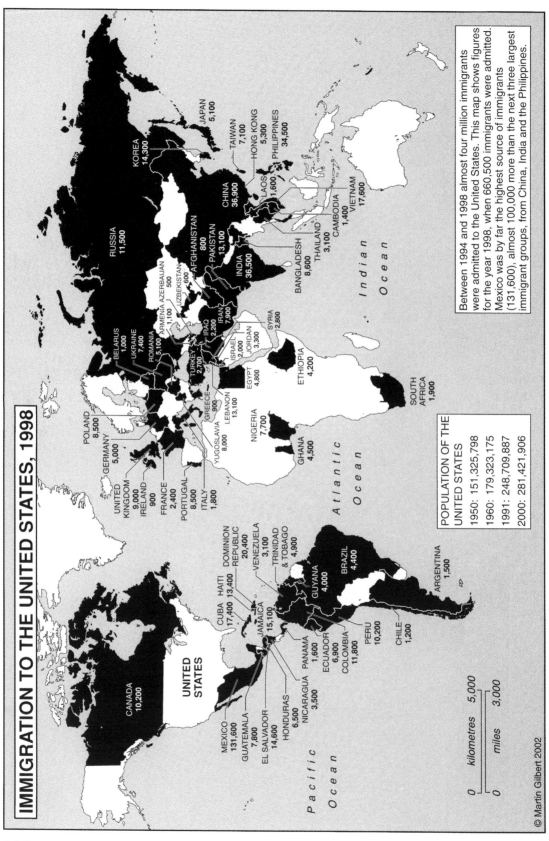

IMMIGRATION TO THE UNITED STATES, 1998

Between 1994 and 1998 almost four million immigrants were admitted to the United States. This map shows figures for the year 1998, when 660,500 immigrants were admitted. Mexico was by far the highest source of immigrants (131,600), almost 100,000 more than the next three largest immigrant groups, from China, India and the Philippines.

POPULATION OF THE UNITED STATES
1950: 151,325,798
1960: 179,323,175
1991: 248,709,887
2000: 281,421,906

JAPAN 5,100
TAIWAN 7,100
HONG KONG 5,300
PHILIPPINES 34,500
KOREA 14,300
LAOS 1,600
CHINA 36,900
VIETNAM 17,600
CAMBODIA 1,400
THAILAND 3,100
AFGHANISTAN 800
PAKISTAN 13,100
INDIA 36,500
BANGLADESH 8,600
ARMENIA 1,100
AZERBAIJAN 500
UZBEKISTAN 600
RUSSIA 11,500
IRAN 7,900
IRAQ 2,200
SYRIA 2,800
JORDAN 3,300
ISRAEL 2,000
ETHIOPIA 4,200
TURKEY 2,700
SOUTH AFRICA 1,900
BELARUS 1,000
UKRAINE 7,400
ROMANIA 5,100
GREECE 600
LEBANON 13,100
EGYPT 4,800
NIGERIA 7,700
GHANA 4,500
YUGOSLAVIA 8,000
POLAND 8,500
GERMANY 5,000
UNITED KINGDOM 9,000
IRELAND 900
FRANCE 2,400
PORTUGAL 8,500
ITALY 1,800

Indian Ocean

Atlantic Ocean

CANADA 10,200
UNITED STATES
MEXICO 131,600
GUATEMALA 7,800
EL SALVADOR 14,600
HONDURAS 6,500
NICARAGUA 3,500
PANAMA 1,600
CUBA 17,400
HAITI 13,400
JAMAICA 15,100
DOMINION REPUBLIC 20,400
VENEZUELA 3,100
TRINIDAD & TOBAGO 4,900
GUYANA 4,000
ECUADOR 6,900
COLOMBIA 11,800
PERU 10,200
BRAZIL 4,400
CHILE 1,200
ARGENTINA 1,500

Pacific Ocean

0   kilometres   5,000
0   miles   3,000

© Martin Gilbert 2002

140

UNITED STATES MILITARY PERSONNEL OVERSEAS, 2000: EUROPE

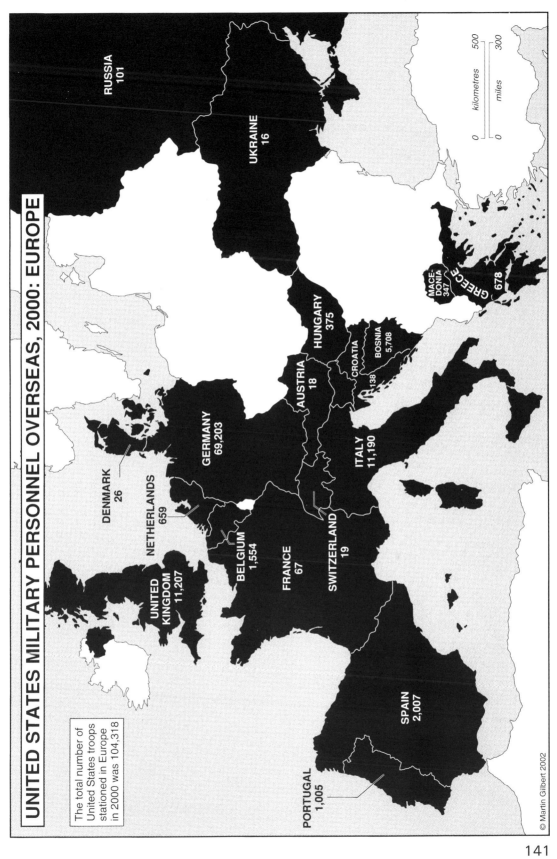

The total number of United States troops stationed in Europe in 2000 was 104,318

RUSSIA
101

UKRAINE
16

MACE-
DONIA
347

GREECE
678

HUNGARY
375

CROATIA
138

BOSNIA
5,708

AUSTRIA
18

GERMANY
69,203

ITALY
11,190

DENMARK
26

NETHERLANDS
659

UNITED
KINGDOM
11,207

BELGIUM
1,554

FRANCE
67

SWITZERLAND
19

SPAIN
2,007

PORTUGAL
1,005

0   500 kilometres

0   300 miles

© Martin Gilbert 2002

141

UNITED STATES MILITARY PERSONNEL OVERSEAS, 2000: GLOBAL

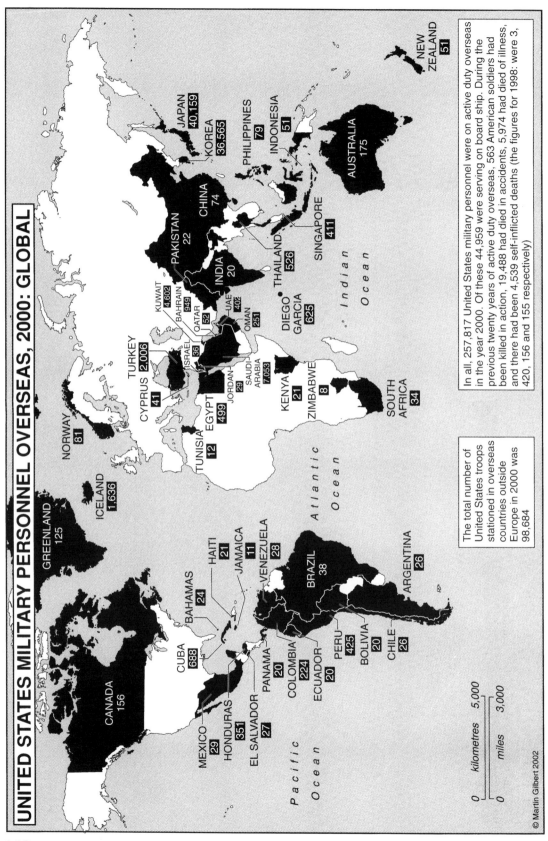

NEW ZEALAND 51

JAPAN 40,159

KOREA 36,565

PHILIPPINES 79

INDONESIA 51

AUSTRALIA 175

CHINA 74

PAKISTAN 22

SINGAPORE 411

THAILAND 526

INDIA 20

KUWAIT 4,602

BAHRAIN 949

QATAR 52

UAE 402

OMAN 251

DIEGO GARCIA 625

Indian Ocean

TURKEY 2,006

ISRAEL 36

SAUDI-ARABIA 7,053

JORDAN 29

KENYA 21

ZIMBABWE 8

SOUTH AFRICA 34

CYPRUS 41

EGYPT 499

TUNISIA 12

NORWAY 81

ICELAND 1,636

GREENLAND 125

Atlantic Ocean

HAITI 21

JAMAICA 11

VENEZUELA 28

BAHAMAS 24

BRAZIL 38

ARGENTINA 26

CUBA 688

PANAMA 20

COLOMBIA 224

ECUADOR 20

PERU 425

BOLIVIA 20

CHILE 26

CANADA 156

MEXICO 29

HONDURAS 351

EL SALVADOR 27

Pacific Ocean

In all, 257,817 United States military personnel were on active duty overseas in the year 2000. Of these 44,959 were serving on board ship. During the previous twenty years of active duty overseas, 563 American soldiers had been killed in action, 19,488 had died in accidents, 5,974 had died of illness, and there had been 4,539 self-inflicted deaths (the figures for 1998: were 3, 420, 156 and 155 respectively)

The total number of United States troops stationed in overseas countries outside Europe in 2000 was 98,684

0 kilometres 5,000

0 miles 3,000

© Martin Gilbert 2002

142

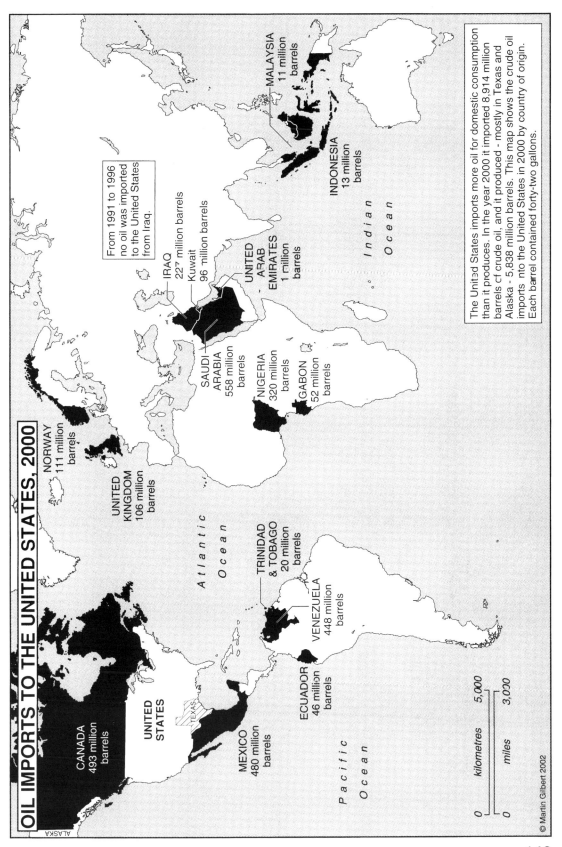

OIL IMPORTS TO THE UNITED STATES, 2000

ALASKA

NORWAY
111 million
barrels

UNITED KINGDOM
106 million
barrels

CANADA
493 million
barrels

UNITED
STATES

TEXAS

MEXICO
480 million
barrels

ECUADOR
46 million
barrels

TRINIDAD
& TOBAGO
20 million
barrels

VENEZUELA
448 million
barrels

Atlantic
Ocean

Pacific
Ocean

From 1991 to 1996
no oil was imported
to the United States
from Iraq.

IRAQ
227 million barrels

Kuwait
96 million barrels

UNITED
ARAB
EMIRATES
1 million
barrels

SAUDI
ARABIA
558 million
barrels

NIGERIA
320 million
barrels

GABON
52 million
barrels

MALAYSIA
11 million
barrels

INDONESIA
13 million
barrels

Indian
Ocean

The United States imports more oil for domestic consumption
than it produces. In the year 2000 it imported 8,914 million
barrels of crude oil, and it produced - mostly in Texas and
Alaska - 5,838 million barrels. This map shows the crude oil
imports into the United States in 2000 by country of origin.
Each barrel contained forty-two gallons.

0   5,000 kilometres
0   3,000 miles

© Martin Gilbert 2002

143

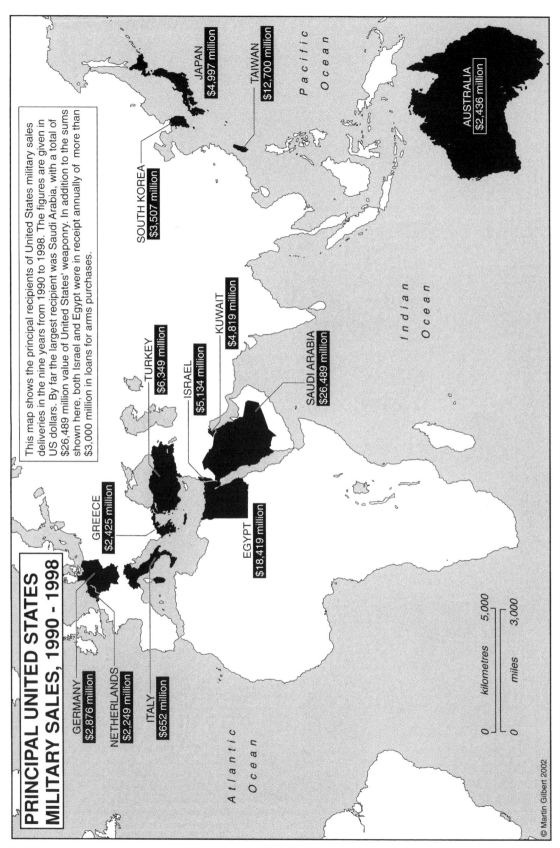

PRINCIPAL UNITED STATES
MILITARY SALES, 1990 - 1998

This map shows the principal recipients of United States military sales deliveries in the nine years from 1990 to 1998. The figures are given in US dollars. By far the largest recipient was Saudi Arabia, with a total of $26,489 million value of United States' weaponry. In addition to the sums shown here, both Israel and Egypt were in receipt annually of more than $3,000 million in loans for arms purchases.

JAPAN
$4.997 million

TAIWAN
$12,700 million

AUSTRALIA
$2,436 million

Pacific Ocean

SOUTH KOREA
$3,507 million

TURKEY
$6,349 million

ISRAEL
$5,134 million

KUWAIT
$4,819 million

SAUDI ARABIA
$26,489 million

GREECE
$2,425 million

EGYPT
$18,419 million

GERMANY
$2,876 million

NETHERLANDS
$2,249 million

ITALY
$652 million

Indian Ocean

Atlantic Ocean

kilometres
0   5,000

miles
0   3,000

© Martin Gilbert 2002

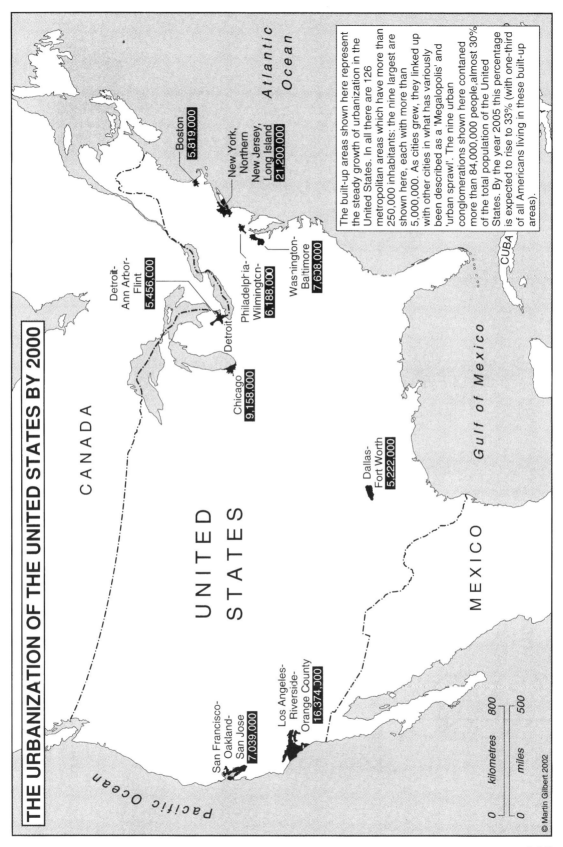

THE URBANIZATION OF THE UNITED STATES BY 2000

CANADA

UNITED
STATES

Atlantic
Ocean

Boston
5,819,000

New York,
Northern
New Jersey,
Long Island
21,200,000

Detroit-
Ann Arbor-
Flint
5,456,000

Philadelphia-
Wilmington
6,188,000

Washington-
Baltimore
7,608,000

Detroit

Chicago
9,158,000

San Francisco-
Oakland-
San Jose
7,039,000

Los Angeles-
Riverside-
Orange County
16,374,000

Dallas-
Fort Worth
5,222,000

Gulf of Mexico

MEXICO

CUBA

Pacific Ocean

The built-up areas shown here represent the steady growth of urbanization in the United States. In all there are 126 metropolitan areas which have more than 250,000 inhabitants: the nine largest are shown here, each with more than 5,000,000. As cities grew, they linked up with other cities in what has variously been described as a 'Megalopolis' and 'urban sprawl'. The nine urban conglomerations shown here contained more than 84,000,000 people, almost 30% of the total population of the United States. By the year 2005 this percentage is expected to rise to 33% (with one-third of all Americans living in these built-up areas).

0   800   kilometres
0   500   miles

© Martin Gilbert 2002

145

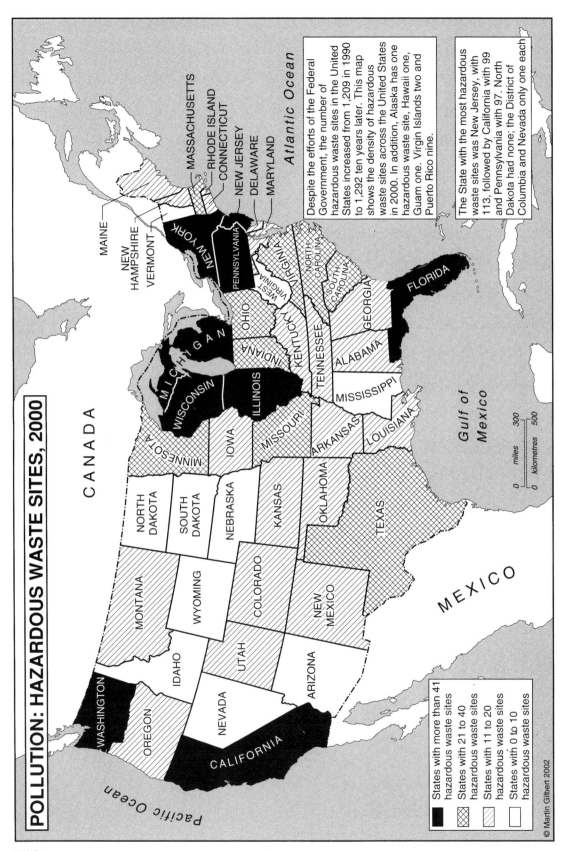

POLLUTION: HAZARDOUS WASTE SITES, 2000

Despite the efforts of the Federal Government, the number of hazardous waste sites in the United States increased from 1,209 in 1990 to 1,292 ten years later. This map shows the density of hazardous waste sites across the United States in 2000. In addition, Alaska has one hazardous waste site, Hawaii one, Guam one. Virgin Islands two and Puerto Rico nine.

The State with the most hazardous waste sites was New Jersey, with 113, followed by California with 99 and Pennsylvania with 97. North Dakota had none; the District of Columbia and Nevada only one each

States with more than 41 hazardous waste sites

States with 21 to 40 hazardous waste sites

States with 11 to 20 hazardous waste sites

States with 0 to 10 hazardous waste sites

Atlantic Ocean

Gulf of Mexico

Pacific Ocean

CANADA

MEXICO

© Martin Gilbert 2002

146

UNITED STATES CARIBBEAN AND PACIFIC TERRITORIES: 2000

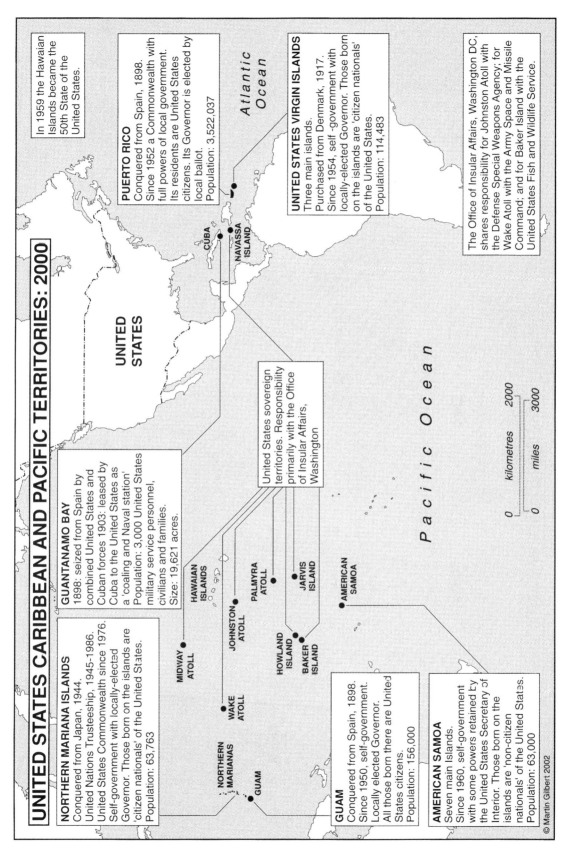

NORTHERN MARIANA ISLANDS
Conquered from Japan, 1944. United Nations Trusteeship, 1945-1986. United States Commonwealth since 1976. Self-government with locally-elected Governor. Those born on the islands are 'citizen nationals' of the United States. Population: 63,763

GUANTANAMO BAY
1898: seized from Spain by combined United States and Cuban forces 1903: leased by Cuba to the United States as a 'coaling and Naval station' Population: 3,000 United States military service personnel, civilians and families. Size: 19,621 acres.

PUERTO RICO
Conquered from Spain, 1898. Since 1952 a Commonwealth with full powers of local government. Its residents are United States citizens. Its Governor is elected by local ballot. Population: 3,522,037

UNITED STATES VIRGIN ISLANDS
Three main islands. Purchased from Denmark, 1917. Since 1954, self -government with locally-elected Governor. Those born on the islands are 'citizen nationals' of the United States. Population: 114,483

The Office of Insular Affairs, Washington DC, shares responsibility for Johnston Atoll with the Defense Special Weapons Agency; for Wake Atoll with the Army Space and Missile Command; and for Baker Island with the United States Fish and Wildlife Service.

United States sovereign territories. Responsibility primarily with the Office of Insular Affairs, Washington

GUAM
Conquered from Spain, 1898. Since 1950, self-government. Locally elected Governor. All those born there are United States citizens. Population: 156,000

AMERICAN SAMOA
Seven main Islands. Since 1960, self-government with some powers retained by the United States Secretary of Interior. Those born on the islands are 'non-citizen nationals' of the United States. Population: 63,000

In 1959 the Hawaian Islands became the 50th State of the United States.

Atlantic Ocean

Pacific Ocean

UNITED STATES

CUBA
NAVASSA ISLAND

NORTHERN MARIANAS
GUAM
WAKE ATOLL
MIDWAY ATOLL
JOHNSTON ATOLL
HAWAIAN ISLANDS
PALMYRA ATOLL
HOWLAND ISLAND
BAKER ISLAND
JARVIS ISLAND
AMERICAN SAMOA

0   kilometres   2000
0   miles   3000

© Martin Gilbert 2002

147

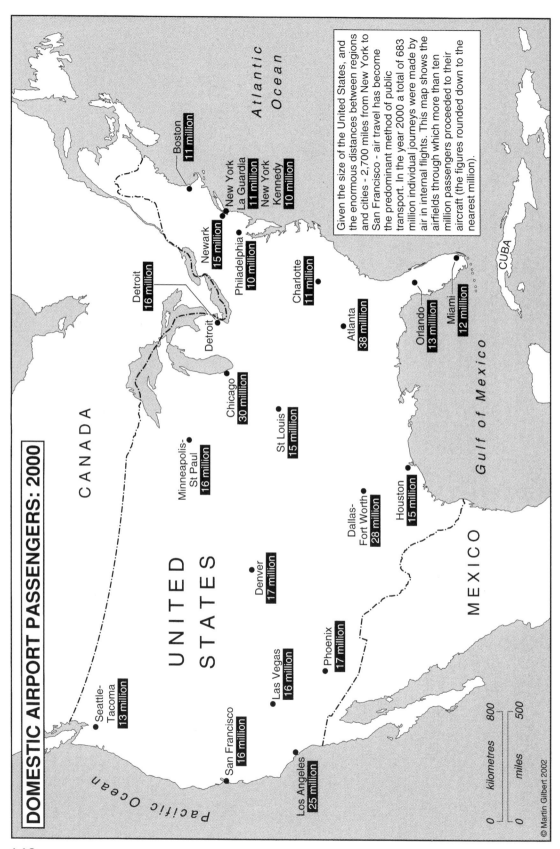

DOMESTIC AIRPORT PASSENGERS: 2000

CANADA

UNITED STATES

MEXICO

CUBA

Atlantic Ocean

Pacific Ocean

Gulf of Mexico

Boston
11 million

New York
La Guardia
11 million
New York
Kennedy
10 million

Newark
15 million

Philadelphia
10 million

Charlotte
11 million

Detroit
16 million

Detroit

Atlanta
38 million

Orlando
13 million

Miami
12 million

Chicago
30 million

St Louis
15 million

Minneapolis-
St Paul
16 million

Dallas-
Fort Worth
28 million

Houston
15 million

Denver
17 million

Phoenix
17 million

Las Vegas
16 million

Seattle-
Tacoma
13 million

San Francisco
16 million

Los Angeles
25 million

Given the size of the United States, and the enormous distances between regions and cities - 2,700 miles from New York to San Francisco - air travel has become the predominant method of public transport. In the year 2000 a total of 683 million individual journeys were made by air in internal flights. This map shows the airfields through which more than ten million passengers proceeded to their aircraft (the figures rounded down to the nearest million).

0   800
kilometres

0   500
miles

© Martin Gilbert 2002

148

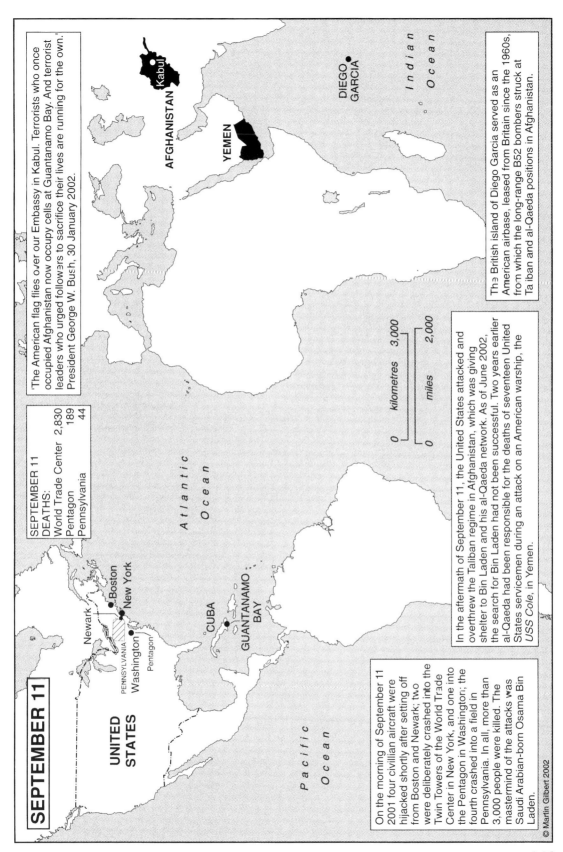

SEPTEMBER 11

'The American flag flies over our Embassy in Kabul. Terrorists who once occupied Afghanistan now occupy cells at Guantanamo Bay. And terrorist leaders who urged followers to sacrifice their lives are running for the own.' President George W. Bush, 30 January 2002.

SEPTEMBER 11
DEATHS:
World Trade Center 2,830
Pentagon 189
Pennsylvania 44

UNITED
STATES

Newark
Boston
New York

PENNSYLVANIA
Washington
Pentagon

CUBA

GUANTANAMO
BAY

Pacific Ocean

Atlantic Ocean

AFGHANISTAN
Kabul

YEMEN

DIEGO
GARCIA

Indian Ocean

On the morning of September 11 2001 four civilian aircraft were hijacked shortly after setting off from Boston and Newark; two were deliberately crashed into the Twin Towers of the World Trade Center in New York, and one into the Pentagon in Washington; the fourth crashed into a field in Pennsylvania. In all, more than 3,000 people were killed. The mastermind of the attacks was Saudi Arabian-born Osama Bin Laden.

In the aftermath of September 11, the United States attacked and overthrew the Taliban regime in Afghanistan, which was giving shelter to Bin Laden and his al-Qaeda network. As of June 2002, the search for Bin Laden had not been successful. Two years earlier al-Qaeda had been responsible for the deaths of seventeen United States servicemen during an attack on an American warship, the *USS Cole*, in Yemen.

The British island of Diego Garcia served as an American airbase, leased from Britain since the 1960s, from which the long-range B52 bombers struck at Taliban and al-Qaeda positions in Afghanistan.

0   kilometres   3,000

0   miles   2,000

© Martin Gilbert 2002

149

THE ELECTION OF PRESIDENT GEORGE W. BUSH, NOVEMBER 2000

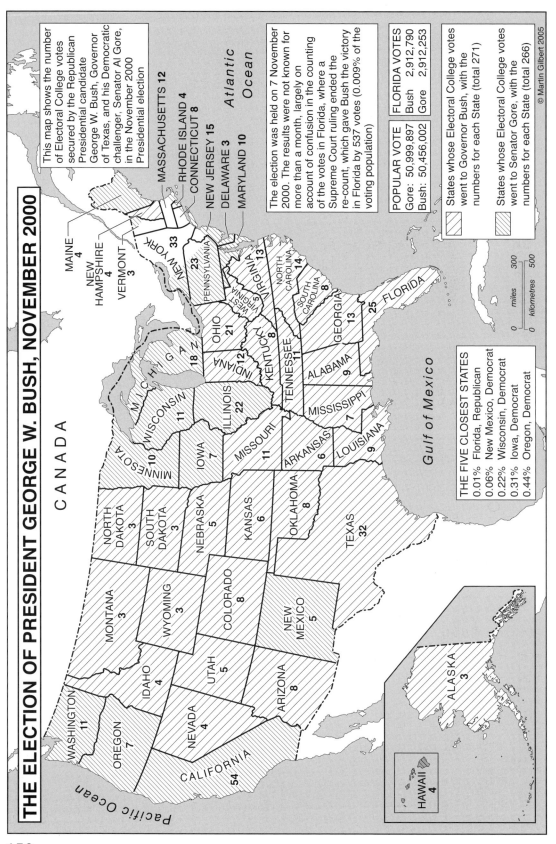

This map shows the number of Electoral College votes secured by the Republican Presidential candidate George W. Bush, Governor of Texas, and his Democratic challenger, Senator Al Gore, in the November 2000 Presidential election

The election was held on 7 November 2000. The results were not known for more than a month, largely on account of confusion in the counting of the votes in Florida, where a Supreme Court ruling ended the re-count, which gave Bush the victory in Florida by 537 votes (0.009% of the voting population)

POPULAR VOTE
Gore: 50,999,897
Bush: 50,456,002

FLORIDA VOTES
Bush 2,912,790
Gore 2,912,253

States whose Electoral College votes went to Governor Bush, with the numbers for each State (total 271)

States whose Electoral College votes went to Senator Gore, with the numbers for each State (total 266)

© Martin Gilbert 2005

MASSACHUSETTS 12
RHODE ISLAND 4
CONNECTICUT 8
NEW JERSEY 15
DELAWARE 3
MARYLAND 10

Atlantic Ocean

MAINE 4
NEW HAMPSHIRE 4
VERMONT 3
NEW YORK 33

CANADA

WASHINGTON 11
OREGON 7
IDAHO 4
MONTANA 3
WYOMING 3
NEVADA 4
UTAH 5
CALIFORNIA 54
ARIZONA 8
NEW MEXICO 5
COLORADO 8
NORTH DAKOTA 3
SOUTH DAKOTA 3
NEBRASKA 5
KANSAS 6
OKLAHOMA 8
TEXAS 32
MINNESOTA 10
IOWA 7
MISSOURI 11
ARKANSAS 6
LOUISIANA 9
WISCONSIN 11
ILLINOIS 22
MICHIGAN 18
INDIANA 12
OHIO 21
KENTUCKY 8
TENNESSEE 11
MISSISSIPPI 7
ALABAMA 9
GEORGIA 13
PENNSYLVANIA 23
WEST VIRGINIA 5
VIRGINIA 13
NORTH CAROLINA 14
SOUTH CAROLINA 8
FLORIDA 25

Pacific Ocean

Gulf of Mexico

THE FIVE CLOSEST STATES
0.01% Florida, Republican
0.06% New Mexico, Democrat
0.22% Wisconsin, Democrat
0.31% Iowa, Democrat
0.44% Oregon, Democrat

ALASKA 3

HAWAII 4

0   300   miles
0   500   kilometres

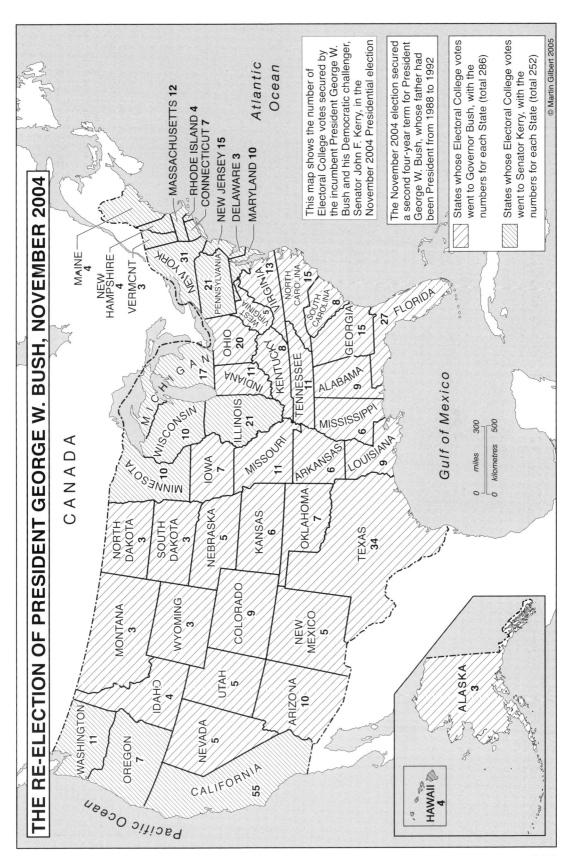

THE RE-ELECTION OF PRESIDENT GEORGE W. BUSH, NOVEMBER 2004

This map shows the number of Electoral College votes secured by the incumbent President George W. Bush and his Democratic challenger, Senator John F. Kerry, in the November 2004 Presidential election

The November 2004 election secured a second four-year term for President George W. Bush, whose father had been President from 1988 to 1992

States whose Electoral College votes went to Governor Bush, with the numbers for each State (total 286)

States whose Electoral College votes went to Senator Kerry, with the numbers for each State (total 252)

© Martin Gilbert 2005

CANADA

Atlantic Ocean

Pacific Ocean

Gulf of Mexico

MAINE 4
NEW HAMPSHIRE 4
VERMONT 3
MASSACHUSETTS 12
RHODE ISLAND 4
CONNECTICUT 7
NEW JERSEY 15
DELAWARE 3
MARYLAND 10

NEW YORK 31
PENNSYLVANIA 21
WEST VIRGINIA 5
VIRGINIA 13
NORTH CAROLINA 15
SOUTH CAROLINA 8
GEORGIA 15
FLORIDA 27

MICHIGAN 17
OHIO 20
INDIANA 11
KENTUCKY 8
TENNESSEE 11
ALABAMA 9

WISCONSIN 10
ILLINOIS 21
MISSISSIPPI 6

MINNESOTA 10
IOWA 7
MISSOURI 11
ARKANSAS 6
LOUISIANA 9

NORTH DAKOTA 3
SOUTH DAKOTA 3
NEBRASKA 5
KANSAS 6
OKLAHOMA 7
TEXAS 34

MONTANA 3
WYOMING 3
COLORADO 9
NEW MEXICO 5

WASHINGTON 11
OREGON 7
IDAHO 4
UTAH 5
NEVADA 5
ARIZONA 10
CALIFORNIA 55

HAWAII 4

ALASKA 3

0 miles 300
0 kilometres 500

151

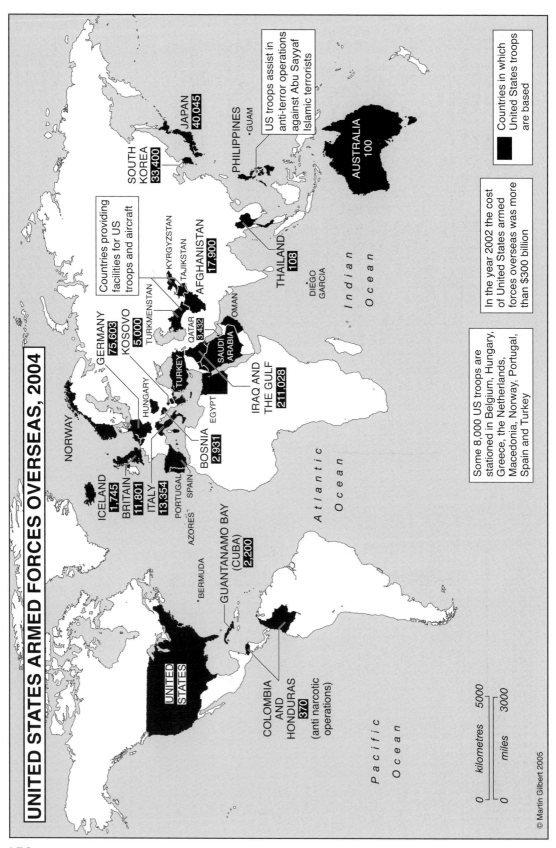

UNITED STATES ARMED FORCES OVERSEAS, 2004

JAPAN 40,045

SOUTH KOREA 33,400

PHILIPPINES
• GUAM

US troops assist in anti-terror operations against Abu Sayyaf Islamic terrorists

AUSTRALIA 100

Countries providing facilities for US troops and aircraft

KYRGYZSTAN

TAJIKSTAN

AFGHANISTAN 17,900

TURKMENSTAN

THAILAND 108

DIEGO GARCIA

Indian Ocean

GERMANY 75,603

KOSOVO 5,000

QATAR 3,432

OMAN

TURKEY

SAUDI ARABIA

IRAQ AND THE GULF 211,028

HUNGARY

NORWAY

EGYPT

BOSNIA 2,931

ICELAND 1,745

BRITAIN 11,801

ITALY 13,354

PORTUGAL SPAIN

AZORES'

Atlantic Ocean

GUANTANAMO BAY (CUBA) 2,200

• BERMUDA

UNITED STATES

COLOMBIA AND HONDURAS 370 (anti narcotic operations)

Pacific Ocean

Some 8,000 US troops are stationed in Belgium, Hungary, Greece, the Netherlands, Macedonia, Norway, Portugal, Spain and Turkey

In the year 2002 the cost of United States armed forces overseas was more than $300 billion

Countries in which United States troops are based

kilometres 0 — 5000

miles 0 — 3000

© Martin Gilbert 2005

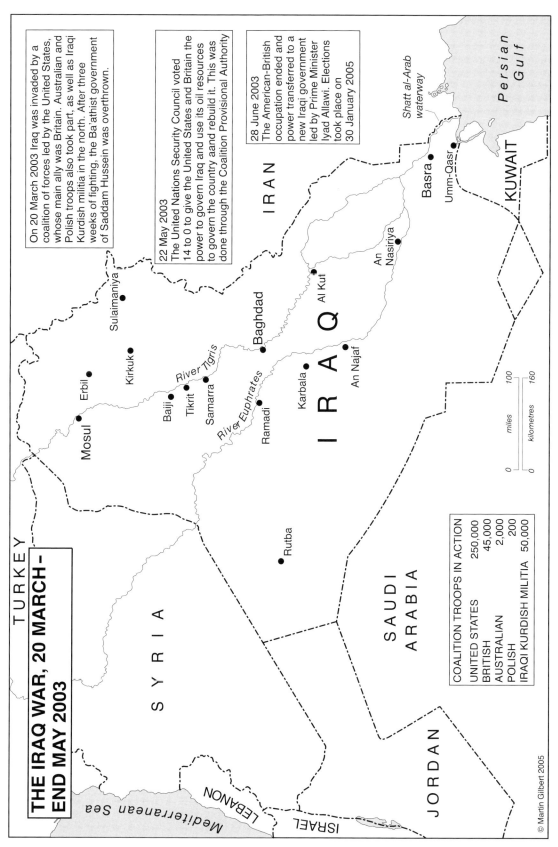

THE IRAQ WAR, 20 MARCH – END MAY 2003

On 20 March 2003 Iraq was invaded by a coalition of forces led by the United States, whose main ally was Britain. Australian and Polish troops also took part, as well as Iraqi Kurdish militia in the north. After three weeks of fighting, the Ba'athist government of Saddam Hussein was overthrown.

22 May 2003
The United Nations Security Council voted 14 to 0 to give the United States and Britain the power to govern Iraq and use its oil resources to govern the country aand rebuild it. This was done through the Coalition Provisional Authority

28 June 2003
The American-British occupation ended and power transferred to a new Iraqi government led by Prime Minister Iyad Allawi. Elections took place on 30 January 2005

Persian Gulf

KUWAIT

Umm-Qasr

Basra

Shatt al-Arab waterway

I R A N

An Nasiriya

Al Kut

Baghdad

Sulaimaniya

Erbil

Kirkuk

Mosul

Baiji

Tikrit

Samarra

River Tigris

River Euphrates

Ramadi

Karbala

An Najaf

I R A Q

Rutba

SAUDI ARABIA

JORDAN

ISRAEL

LEBANON

Mediterranean Sea

S Y R I A

T U R K E Y

COALITION TROOPS IN ACTION	
UNITED STATES	250,000
BRITISH	45,000
AUSTRALIAN	2,000
POLISH	200
IRAQI KURDISH MILITIA	50,000

miles 0 100
kilometres 0 160

© Martin Gilbert 2005

153

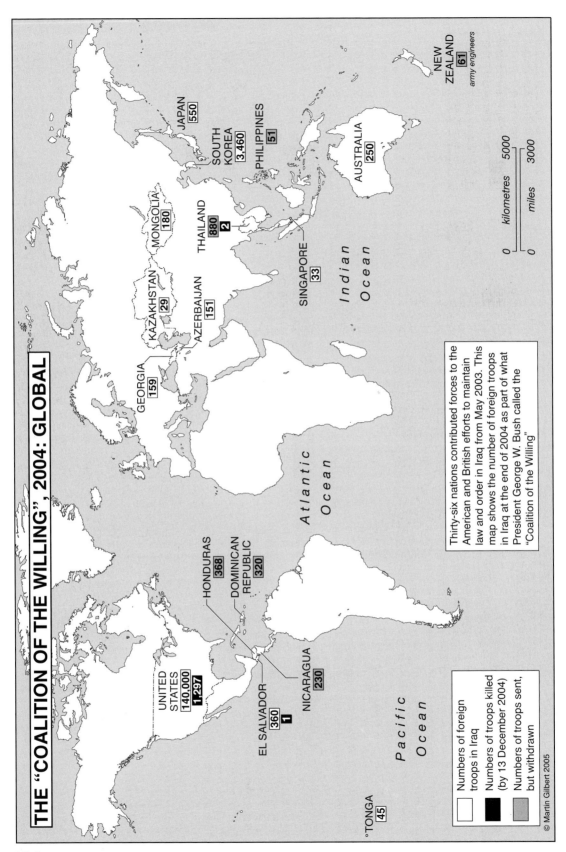

THE "COALITION OF THE WILLING", 2004: GLOBAL

TONGA 45

UNITED STATES 140,000 1,297

EL SALVADOR 360 1

NICARAGUA 230

HONDURAS 368

DOMINICAN REPUBLIC 320

GEORGIA 159

KAZAKHSTAN 29

AZERBAIJAN 151

MONGOLIA 180

THAILAND 880 2

JAPAN 550

SOUTH KOREA 3,460

PHILIPPINES 51

SINGAPORE 33

AUSTRALIA 250

NEW ZEALAND 61
army engineers

Atlantic Ocean

Pacific Ocean

Indian Ocean

Thirty-six nations contributed forces to the American and British efforts to maintain law and order in Iraq from May 2003. This map shows the number of foreign troops in Iraq at the end of 2004 as part of what President George W. Bush called the "Coalition of the Willing"

Numbers of foreign troops in Iraq

Numbers of troops killed (by 13 December 2004)

Numbers of troops sent, but withdrawn

0   3000   miles
0   5000   kilometres

© Martin Gilbert 2005

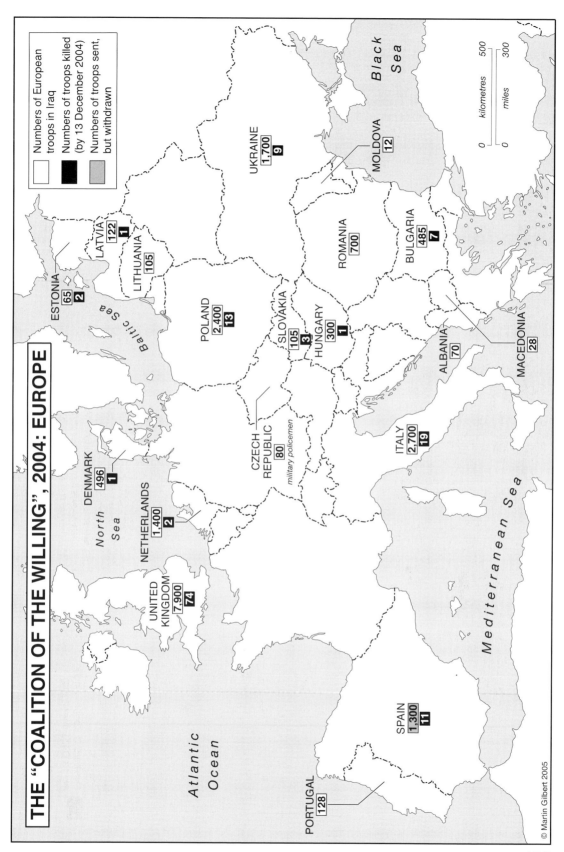

THE "COALITION OF THE WILLING", 2004: EUROPE

Numbers of European troops in Iraq

Numbers of troops killed (by 13 December 2004)

Numbers of troops sent, but withdrawn

Black Sea

Baltic Sea

North Sea

Atlantic Ocean

Mediterranean Sea

UKRAINE 1,700 **9**

MOLDOVA 12

LATVIA 122 **1**

LITHUANIA 105

ESTONIA 65 **2**

ROMANIA 700

BULGARIA 485 **7**

POLAND 2,400 **13**

SLOVAKIA 105 **3**

HUNGARY 300 **1**

ALBANIA 70

MACEDONIA 28

CZECH REPUBLIC 80 *military policemen*

ITALY 2,700 **19**

DENMARK 496 **1**

NETHERLANDS 1,400 **2**

UNITED KINGDOM 7,900 **74**

SPAIN 1,300 **11**

PORTUGAL 128

kilometres 0 — 500
miles 0 — 300

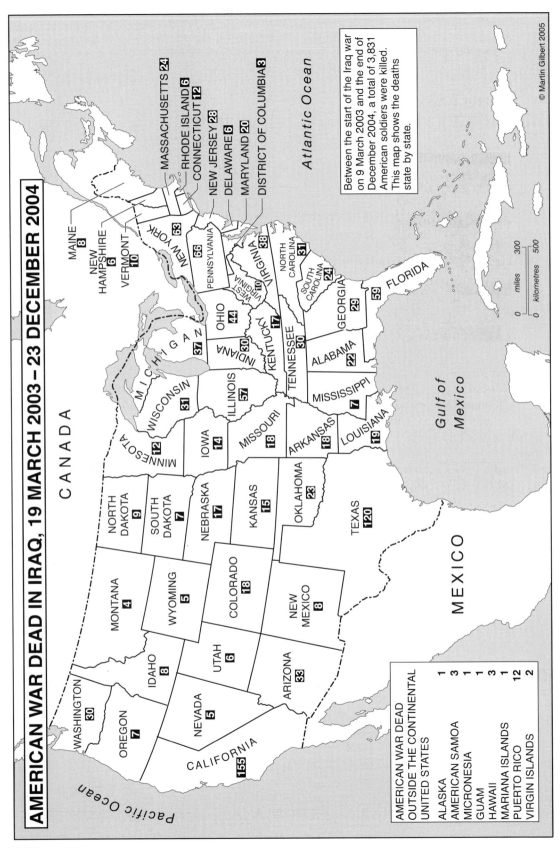

AMERICAN WAR DEAD IN IRAQ, 19 MARCH 2003 – 23 DECEMBER 2004

© Martin Gilbert 2005

Between the start of the Iraq war on 9 March 2003 and the end of December 2004, a total of 3,831 American soldiers were killed. This map shows the deaths state by state.

Atlantic Ocean

Pacific Ocean

CANADA

MEXICO

Gulf of Mexico

MASSACHUSETTS 24
RHODE ISLAND 6
CONNECTICUT 12
NEW JERSEY 28
DELAWARE 6
MARYLAND 20
DISTRICT OF COLUMBIA 3

MAINE 8
NEW HAMPSHIRE 6
VERMONT 10
NEW YORK 63
PENNSYLVANIA 66
WEST VIRGINIA 10
VIRGINIA 38
NORTH CAROLINA 31
SOUTH CAROLINA 24
GEORGIA 29
FLORIDA 59

OHIO 44
KENTUCKY 17
TENNESSEE 30
ALABAMA 22
MISSISSIPPI 7

MICHIGAN 37
INDIANA 30
WISCONSIN 31
ILLINOIS 57
IOWA 14
MISSOURI 18
ARKANSAS 18
LOUISIANA 19

MINNESOTA 12

NORTH DAKOTA 9
SOUTH DAKOTA 7
NEBRASKA 17
KANSAS 15
OKLAHOMA 23
TEXAS 120

MONTANA 4
WYOMING 5
COLORADO 18
NEW MEXICO 8

WASHINGTON 30
OREGON 7
IDAHO 8
UTAH 6
NEVADA 5
ARIZONA 33
CALIFORNIA 155

AMERICAN WAR DEAD OUTSIDE THE CONTINENTAL UNITED STATES	
ALASKA	1
AMERICAN SAMOA	3
MICRONESIA	1
GUAM	1
HAWAII	3
MARIANA ISLANDS	1
PUERTO RICO	12
VIRGIN ISLANDS	2

0   300 miles
0   500 kilometres

ROUTLEDGE HISTORY

Martin Luther King, Jr.
Peter J. Ling

Did Martin Luther King Jr. deserve the praise heaped upon him or was he a media creation, carried along by forces beyond his control? This new biography of the most celebrated African American in history provides a thorough re-examination of both the man and the Civil Rights Movement, showing how King grew into his leadership role and kept his faith when the movement weakened after 1965.

ISBN 0-415-21664-8 (hbk)
ISBN 0-415-21665-6 (pbk)

Available at all good bookshops.
For ordering and further information please visit:
www.routledge.com

ROUTLEDGE HISTORY

American Civilization: An Introduction – 4th Edition
David Mauk and John Oakland

'The best friend for American Studies students … '

Julio Canero Serrano, Alcala de Heneres University

'Every chapter states the major issues and offers clear synthesis of the main interpretations.'

Francesco Meli, IULM University

'Excellent for current information about the US … '

Felicity Hand, Universitat Autonoma

American Civilization is a comprehensive introduction to contemporary American life. It covers the key dimensions of American society including geography and the environment, immigration and minorities, government and politics, foreign policy, the legal system, the economy, social services, education, religion, the media and the arts.

This fourth edition has been thoroughly revised and includes many updated diagrams, tables, figures and illustrations, as well as coverage of the George W. Bush presidency, the 2004 election, the manifold effects of the 9/11 terrorist attacks, the Iraq Gulf War, and the war on terrorism. This new edition is accompanied by a companion website.

ISBN 0-415-35830-2 (hbk)
ISBN 0-415-35831-0 (pbk)

Available at all good bookshops.
For ordering and further information please visit:
www.routledge.com

ROUTLEDGE HISTORY

American Cultural Studies
Neil C. Campbell and Alasdair Kean

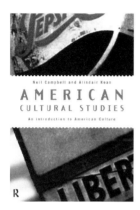

'Something of a godsend … as a teaching resource this book is second to none … achieves levels of multiplicity rarely, if ever, reached by others.'

Borderlines: Studies in American Culture

American Cultural Studies is an interdisciplinary introduction to American culture for those taking American Studies. This textbook:

- introduces the full range and variety of American culture including issues of race, gender and youth
- provides a truly interdisciplinary methodology
- suggests and discusses a variety of approaches to study
- highlights American distinctiveness
- draws on literature, art, film, theatre, architecture, music and more
- challenges orthodox paradigms of American Studies.

ISBN 0-415-12797-1 (hbk)
ISBN 0-415-12798-X (pbk)

Available at all good bookshops.
For ordering and further information please visit:
www.routledge.com

ROUTLEDGE HISTORY

The Routledge Companion to the American Civil War Era
Hugh Tulloch

The American Civil War era continues to fascinate and in this essential reference guide to the period, Hugh Tulloch examines the war itself, alongside political, constitutional, social, economic, literary and religious developments and trends that informed and were formed by the turbulent events that took place during American's nineteenth century. Including a compendium of information through timelines, chronologies, bibliographies, and guides to sources, key themes examined here are:

- Emancipation and the quest for racial justice
- Abolitionism and debates regarding freedom versus slavery
- The Confederacy and Reconstruction
- Industry and agriculture
- Presidential elections and party politics

Providing a complete guide to this vital period in US history this guide will be an essential purchase for students and scholars alike.

ISBN 0-415-22952-9 (hbk)
ISBN 0-415-22953-7 (pbk)

Available at all good bookshops.
For ordering and further information please visit:
www.routledge.com